Conversation: Striving, Surviving, and Thriving

Conversation: Striving, Surviving, and Thriving

◆

Searching for Messages and Relationships

Peter J. McCusker

Conversation: Striving, Surviving, and Thriving
Searching for Messages and Relationships

Contents

Introduction

You are alone and so am I. There is little separating the delicate membrane of our epidermis from the harsh void of nothingness. Our corporeal self could be snuffed out in an instant. This stark, existential reality lingers continuously in our unconscious minds and gnaws menacingly on our psyche. It is a primary reason why we have trouble sleeping in unfamiliar surroundings, and why we crave inter-personal contact.

The need for contact is a fundamental mammalian imperative, perhaps rooted in absolute, infantile dependence on our mothers. Some primate groups satisfy contact craving in part by reciprocal hugging, clinging, and grooming. Human society, by contrast, sanctions only brief, circumscribed displays of public affection among its citizens. There's work to be done. We've no time for hanging all over each other. So how do we satisfy our need for contact?

Conversation. It is our version of primate grooming (Dunbar, 1996). The overwhelming majority of what we say to each other has little, if anything, to do with transmitting cold, hard facts and everything to do with comfort-seeking and with securing and fortifying our inter-personal relationships. We want conversation to make us feel good. Sometimes reassurance is the issue, as when we mutter automatic acknowledgement or salutation to a passing stranger. Other times we crave intimacy, loving conversationally via prolonged, racy banter. In these, and in most cases, conversation provides a contact medium that is effective, safe, and comfortable.

We desire to speak casually with people primarily because of what we "get" from them and the way we feel in their presence, not because of their verbal eloquence. Conversation defines us and our relationships through what is expressed, not necessarily through what is said. When speaking together, we and our partner inadvertently communicate our relatively enduring moods, as well as changing, multifaceted emotions, and it is the quality of these affective communications that determines conversational success or failure. How often have you heard, "It wasn't what she said but the way she said it that made me angry," or "He didn't say much, but we had the nicest chat."

Communication is ubiquitous among living creatures; we even have compelling evidence that bacteria communicate with each another (Crenson, 2003).

More to the point, when we, humans, are together, it is impossible for us not to communicate (Watzlewick, Beavin, & Jackson, 1967). Anything that you say or do not say indicates something about you and about your view of the individual with whom you are interacting. Imagine a dentist's office in which all waiting room chairs are taken except one. If you enter the room, look at the chair, look at me sitting beside it, and then stand with your back against the wall, you have spoken loud and clear.

So, when it comes to conversation as rooted in social interaction, I agree with Dunbar that conversation-as-grooming is centrally important for inter-personal relationships, and even for one's very sense of self and personal security. However, conversation also is rooted in largely unconscious mental representation. Thought does not consist of single, clear visual or auditory images – not static, individual pictures or words. Rather, thought typically involves a dynamic assemblage of cryptic sensory, motor, and visceral mental representations linked associatively in our minds—aggregated bits and pieces of sights, sounds, smells, tactile sensations, movements, cardiovascular, respiratory, and gastrointestinal pulses, and other such elements abstracted from real physical experiences. Conversation results only after these vague, multi-sensory-motor-visceral mental representations first are distilled into a form that can be consciously apprehended by us and then encoded into verbal language coherent and rational enough to share with others.

Just as an unconscious sense of individual vulnerability and isolation drives conversation as rooted in social interaction, an even more fundamental process drives conversation as rooted in mental representation: It is the "life instinct." In the natural world, for a mobile organism, prolonged absence of movement usually means physical deterioration or death. All animals capable of movement confront one question above all else—where shall I go? Movement in one direction promotes health and life. Movement in another direction leads to deficit and death.

Any animal that can move, then, needs to make a primitive good-bad "judgment" that precedes movement toward a target (such as food or shelter) that it "expects" will influence survival. Action toward survival amounts to a relentless, expectant physical search for the resources necessary to promote health and life. For the most primitive moving organisms, such as insects, physical action, itself, is an enacted "decision." This physical action-toward-survival tendency, present in the earliest, "lower" organisms, evolved progressively with "higher and higher" organisms such that overt physical action gave rise to parallel, increasingly sophisticated internal mental action. Internal mental action, in turn, slowly evolved into a parallel, verbalizable symbolic action, or language, that made conversation possible.

Considered from the mental representation side of the equation, the evolution of conversation probably did not begin for the purpose of social interaction, since most lower organisms have no social organization that we can discern. It certainly was not for the purpose of grooming, which is observed only among relatively advanced animals. Rather, conversation as representation began as a means for ensuring individual, non-social survival. Mental representation likely started as a complement to rudimentary perceptual and memory capabilities. Even primitive mobile organisms need to be able to recognize and remember that which they can eat and that which can eat them.

Conversation as rooted in mental representation amounts to a relentless, expectant verbal search for the resources necessary to promote health and life. It facilitates survival by using language generally and communication specifically to obtain these necessities. It primarily is selfish; other people are means to self-serving ends. Conversation as rooted in mental representation seeks messages that an individual can use, even in complete solitude, to make herself more physically and/or mentally comfortable.

By contrast, conversation as rooted in social interaction is conversation acutely sensitive to the promises and perils of community. It seeks comforts resulting from relationship – grooming that counteracts the sense of individual vulnerability and isolation of which we spoke earlier. This is not to say that the message and relationship values of conversation are mutually exclusive. Far from it. Conversation's mental representation and social interaction/relationship roots intertwine inextricably. Typically, people seek and realize both message and relationship benefits from the same conversant partner at the same moment in time. Caroline Keating, Colgate University professor of psychology, endorses a total comfort-seeking view of conversation when, as quoted by Melissa Dribben (2002), she says, "Most communication is about getting your own way."

Our focus in this book is on casual conversation specifically rather than on communication in general. We concentrate on the verbal side of casual conversation, and drop the term "casual" to avoid excessive wordiness. The overwhelming majority of what is discussed draws heavily on research and theory in the fields of psychology, anthropology, and biology. Because research from diverse fields is being integrated and applied, terminology differences can cause confusion and obfuscation. Distinctions that are important for well-controlled experiments within a scientific subspecialty may not necessarily be so critical when applied to people in their daily lives. In fact, when phenomena are too narrowly and rigorously defined, scientists from related fields sometimes have trouble communicating with each other, or even have trouble being aware of the similarities that exist in studies across disciplines. Block (1995) and Kelley (1927) emphasize the detrimental effects of the "jangle fallacy" by which they mean the tendency to use different terms to describe the same phenomenon. An issue especially relevant for us is use of the concepts positive-negative, approach-avoid, good-bad, and pleasant-unpleasant. In everyday parlance, these four bipolar terms all indicate evaluation, but each connotes something significantly different. Strictly speaking, positive-negative is a global evaluation, approach-avoid is a behavioral or action evaluation, good-bad is a moral evaluation, and pleasant-unpleasant is a sensory evaluation. In scientific studies, however, differences among the terms blur and they are often used interchangeably to describe similar phenomena under similar conditions. Since the entire evaluative spectrum is critically important for understanding the whys, whats, and hows of conversation, I combine research and observations across scientific disciplines involving all four evaluation terms.

The information contained in this document is not intended to be the last word on the issues discussed. I am neither a theoretician nor a researcher. I am a clinician who, like many other lifetime clinicians, literally has evaluated and treated thousands of patients. This book represents my synthesis of scientific information for understanding and analyzing conversation as practiced by most people most of the time. Read mindfully it should empower you to better understand your conversing self and the conversing selves of those with whom you speak.

Conversation in Context

The Essential Continuity of Reality and Life

Reality is as it is. Features of reality are not neatly packaged to facilitate our comprehension. Science solves this problem by compartmentalizing. Nowhere is this more obvious than in disciplines that target living organisms where specialists from anthropology to zoology subdivide life into manageable chunks. Subspecialists then parcel life into smaller packages amenable to experimentation.

In truth, there is an irreducible unity to life. When we discuss people, it is not a matter of nature "or' nurture, mental "or" physical, rational "or" emotional, conscious "or" unconscious, but "and" in every case. The more natural the behavior studied and the more natural the environment in which it is studied, the tantalizingly closer we can come to sampling reality in all of its complexity, but, because of reality's complexity, the more elusive a comprehensive understanding becomes.

Since we have so much trouble wrapping our minds around the complexity of natural behavior in natural settings, we necessarily compartmentalize and artificialize life when attempting to comprehend the behaviors that we investigate. Despite my preference for unity and my best efforts to speak holistically in this book, I inevitably will do what all scientists must do: I at times will reach my conclusions based on studies of unnatural behavior expressed in artificial conditions, and I invariably will ignore, or even unwittingly distort, essential issues in order to present my beliefs. You, no doubt, will evaluate the information accordingly.

One other caution is necessary: At times I will speak in generalities that are only grossly true, as when stereotyping men and women based upon the research available to date. I will say, for instance, that, according to the scientific literature, women tend to be more sensitive to nuances of inter-personal relationships than men do. This clearly does not mean that all women behave that way all the time or that men are never more relationship-sensitive than women are. Obviously, there is a range of behavior in both genders, as well as in all people of all subgroups no matter what general trends are discovered by research.

An Holistic Approach to Conversation

While reality is a continuous, unified whole, our conscious awareness of reality is ephemeral and fragmentary, and our ability to verbalize our awareness is even less adequate. Of necessity, then, we speak about our experience of reality in a disjointed fashion.

The tendency to dichotomize is readily apparent in the centuries old tradition of separating mind and body. In our present age of genetics, biological explanations hold sway. The lay public has been virtually mesmerized by what we naively assume is the soon-to-be–realized scientific control of life itself. But eminent biologists know otherwise. Gibbs' August 2001 *Scientific American* article explains it well: " 'I could draw you a map of all the components in a cell and put all the proper arrows connecting them,' says Alfred G. Gilman, a Nobel Prize-winning biochemist at the University of Texas Southwestern Medical Center at Dallas. But for even the simplest single–celled microorganism, 'I or anybody else would look at that map and have absolutely no ability to predict anything.'" Rather than extolling the virtues of genetics as the lay public does, modern biological scientists describe the present era as one of "integrationism" that seeks to discover the many and complementary forces that make life possible (Gibbs, 2001). Body-mind integration, for instance, is emphasized by McKhann and Albert (2002) who explain that human beings must engage in a consistent regimen of physical activity in order to produce protein "trophic factors" that stimulate the development of new brain cells necessary for mental agility.

In the mid twentieth century, by contrast, psychological, rather than biological, explanations predominated. Their "truths" about malfunctioning psyches independently causing everything from high blood pressure (Alexander, 1939) to Schizophrenia (Tietze, 1949) now are derided as the height of psychological reductionism. Like biology's integrationists, leading psychologists of modern times, such as James Deese (1996), insist that psychological data is valid and useful only when viewed in context – physical, mental, social, and otherwise. Sternberg and Grigorenko (2001), for example, argue persuasively for a psychology that is integrated and multiparadigmatic.

During our current discussion, then, we assiduously must resist reverting to the false body versus mind dichotomy. Only by repeatedly referring to the essential indivisibility of body and mind can we ever hope to understand the underlying nature of conversation. While aware of the formidable obstacles to such an endeavor, I will do my best to emphasize the continuities between body and mind, conscious and unconscious, cognitive and affective, and intra-personal and inter-personal processes. Like that of all other creatures, each facet of man's being articulates with every other, literally, in a do or die attempt to promote life and health.

Conversation is volitional behavior and volitional behavior is never due to a single factor, but, rather, is multiply determined. If I were to ask you why you go to work, you might reply, "To make money." But there are many other reasons as well. You may go because it is expected of you, it would be boring to stay home, you enjoy your coworkers, you are fascinated by the tasks that you confront each day, and so forth. Thus, when we attempt to explain behavior we must be mindful that we are choosing to focus only on what we believe to be one or more primary causes; we are not exhaustively describing all the contributing causes and some of the non-primary factors may be important in their own rights. Our explanations for behavior also vary in level of precision, from very global to very specific. If I observe a person who shouts "Not again!" and who simultaneously slams his fist against the table, some of my explanations, ranging from global to specific, might be: He's in a negative emotional state, He's angry, He's angry because his current expectations have been thwarted, He's angry because he failed to perform in an area integral to his self esteem, and He's angry because he has not resolved his Oedipal complex. Global explanations of behavior are likely to be more accurate and more reliable in cross-situation or cross-person comparisons. The challenge for global explanations, however, is to show that they can offer insights that are more than obvious.

The most powerful global explanations are the ones with the broadest application. The principles of gravity enable us to understand not only falling apples but accelerating rockets, fluttering butterflies, and shaking buildings. While psychology has discovered very few broad-spectrum principles, it has made significant strides in that direction by attempting to demonstrate behavioral consistency across species, across the human life cycle, and across human groups.

In this book, our across-species explanation of the development of conversation is phylogenetic, meaning an explanation located within the context of Darwinian evolution. It posits that humans have inherited basic animal behaviors and have elaborated them to the point that the primitive origins may be obscure. I suggest that conversation is rooted in evolutionarily fundamental, primarily survival-oriented animal behavior.

Our across-life cycle explanation is ontogenetic, meaning an explanation located within the life cycle of an individual. It suggests that conversation is best understood by relating it to the unique physical and mental development of a person in her life space. The ontogenesis of conversation is to be found in basic biological, intra-psychic, inter-personal, and linguistic processes.

The explanation that we offer combines a perspective on a conversing individual having intrapsychic qualities with a perspective on a conversing group—in this book, the dyad—having inter-personal qualities. We must never lose sight of the fact that an individual's conversational behavior emanates from his own psychodynamics, the psychodynamics of his partner, and the reciprocal interaction of each with the other, all taking place within a biological-environmental context. Stephen M. Kosslyn and his associates (2002) endorse a similar holistic approach when they say:

> "We argue here that bridges between psychology and biology will be easier to forge if researchers treat each participant as an individual but conceive of individual differences within the framework of a general characterization of the population as a whole. The key to this orientation is to relate naturally occurring variation in a particular ability or characteristic to variation in the functioning of an underlying mechanism that characterizes the species in general. We note that although all members of the same species share the same fundamental mechanisms, biological systems are notoriously redundant and complex, affording many different ways to accomplish the same goal. Thus, people (or other animals) may differ not only in the efficacy of specific mechanisms but also in the frequency with which particular mechanisms are recruited (which in turn would make some more salient than others). If some people tend to rely on one "strategy" (i.e., combination of processes), whereas others habitually rely on alternative strategies, pooling data from both groups may be uninformative at best and outright misleading at worst. Appropriately collected, group data can provide a good starting point, but individual differences need to be respected if researchers are to understand the nature of the alternative mechanisms."

For our discussion of conversation, there is much interdisciplinary support for the centrality of certain key global explanations of volitional behavior that are worth knowing and using. Three converging lines of evidence are especially relevant. Evolutionary anthropology asserts a straightforward Darwinian fact: Whatever we do deliberately, we do in an attempt to enhance our comfort and survival. Psychology demonstrates the pleasure principle's power in determining our behavioral choices and shows it to be centrally important in the structure and use of language. Biology explains that living organisms act to maintain a satisfying, life-sustaining homeostatic balance. Let's briefly consider this evidence.

Evolutionary Roots of Conversation

Animal life primarily is defined in terms of sensing and moving. To sense without being able to move would be an evolutionary waste of precious life resources. To move without being able to sense would be equally maladaptive. All animal nervous systems are devoted principally to processing sensation and directing movement/action/behavior. Survival depends on interest in the environment and action in the environment. This is no less true for people than for animals. Thus, focusing specifically on humans, Piaget (1981) argued that an infant is so programmed toward encounters with the world that outward-directed interest constitutes its primary emotional experience.

An individual organism must survey the environmental field, integrate multiple sensory impressions, and then pass the gestalt impression through a serial processor which asks only one question, here anthropomorphized as: "Does the object of my sensory attention enhance or threaten my survival?" It implies a further question: "Should I approach it or avoid it?" The decision to approach certifies that, "In this context, at this time and place, this stimulus is good for me," or, in the case of a decision to avoid, the opposite. Newberg, D'Aquili, and Rause, (2001) believe that the amygdala, located in the middle of the brain's temporal lobe, is one of the structures involved in this process. They note that "When a stimulus requiring our attention is presented, the amygdala acts to analyze its significance in a very basic way, then directs that mind to pay attention to it by assigning emotional value." Gray (1982) also has addressed the issue, identifying the neurological bases of approach or avoidance inclinations. He refers to a behavioral activation system (BAS) with distinctive neurological circuits and neurotransmitters that are sensitive to cues that signal reward and to those that facilitate an active avoidance of threat, and to a behavioral inhibition system (BIS) with its own neurological circuits and neurotransmitters that facilitates a passive avoidance of threat.

The evaluation of good versus bad enacted by approach or avoidance, then, is primordial and automatic in the natural world. It is the most primitive mental module found in the animal kingdom – present even in non-mammalian creatures whose bodies are incapable of creating what most humans regard as thought or emotion. Animals' activities primarily consist of bodily actions that center on bodily survival – such as searching for food and protection. Because animals can influence their survival only through their overt behaviors, their evaluation of good versus bad amounts to an unconscious, virtually automatic "choice" made within a given self-environment context which must precede decisions to act and action itself. We presume that most animals' mental activities are minimal compared to ours. An animal's existence overwhelmingly involves overt physical actions in the physical environment – actions whose consequence is mostly direct and immediately felt in a bodily way. For instance, when a reptile is cold, it moves reflexedly toward the sun. Adaptive tendencies, by definition, naturally maximize physical approach to life-enhancing (good) stimuli and physical avoidance of life-threatening (bad) stimuli.

In contrast to those of animals, most contemporary human activities have relatively little to do with immediate action directed toward physical survival. Our focus tends to be on mental action – thoughts and feelings – and on enhancing comfort, physical and mental. However, most human evaluative action decisions are as unconscious, rapid, and automatic as those of other animals. Bargh and Ferguson (2000) explain:

> "Many studies have demonstrated that people automatically evaluate as either good or bad most if not all stimuli (objects and events, social and nonsocial alike) on encountering them (see, e.g., Bargh, Chaiken, Govender, & Pratto, 1992 ; Bargh, Chaiken, Raymond, & Hymes, 1996 ; Fazio, Sanbonmatsu, Powell, & Kardes, 1986 ; Glaser & Banaji, 1999). This classification of the stimulus as either good or bad occurs within a fraction of a second after its presentation (250 ms or less) and does not depend on the individual having the intention to evaluate or the awareness that he or she is doing so (see, e.g., Bargh, Chaiken, et al., 1996). Research on evaluative priming has suggested that people tend to automatically evaluate visually presented words (see, e.g., Bargh et al., 1992 ; Bargh, Chaiken, et al., 1996 ; Fazio et al., 1986 ; Glaser & Banaji, 1999), faces (see, e.g., Baldwin, Carrell, & Lopez, 1990 ; Murphy & Zajonc, 1993 ; Niedenthal, 1990 ; Niedenthal & Cantor, 1986), pictures (Giner-Sorolla, Garcia, & Bargh, 1999), and odors (Hermans, Baeyens, & Eelen, 1998)."

Bargh and Chartrand (1999) underscore the automaticity of the good-bad evaluation process by suggesting that people often know their preference among items before they can give a reason for it. They state that "…a separate mental system was not necessary – one could consider an evaluation as a node in an associative representation of the environmental object. Moreover, this evaluative 'tag' (good vs. bad) to the object representation could become activated immediately on perception of the object, following the principle that all elements of integrated, schematic representations become active in an all-or none fashion." In other words, the good-bad evaluation tag is an integral part of an associative network and integrally connected to the "idea" in the mind that matches the item in the environment.

While people obviously can and do make some reasoned, deliberated good-bad choices, these clearly are the exceptions. Typically, we automatically assign a good-bad tag and we automatically, relentlessly search for and move toward the good. As quoted by Steven Pinker (1999), William James, the early 19th century psychologist and philosopher, recognized this when he explained:

> "Why do men always lie down, when they can, on soft beds rather than on hard floors? Why do they sit round the stove on a cold day? Why, in a room, do they place themselves, ninety-nine times out of a hundred, with their faces towards its middle rather than to the wall? Why do they prefer saddle of mutton and champagne to hard-tack and pond-water? Why does the maiden interest the youth so that everything about her seems more important and significant than anything else in the world? Nothing more can be said than that these are human ways, and that every creature likes its own ways, and takes to the following them as a matter of course. Science may come and consider these ways, and find that most of them are useful. But it is not for the sake of their utility that they are followed, but because at the moment of following them we feel that that is the only appropriate and natural thing to do. Not one man in a billion, when taking his dinner, ever thinks of utility. He eats because the food tastes good and makes him want more. If you ask him why he should want to eat more of what tastes like that, instead of revering you as a philosopher we will probably laugh at you for a fool... And so, probably, does each animal feel about the particular things it tends to do in presence of particular objects."

Volitional behavior can only be directed toward or away from the environmental target of attention, because ignoring the target is, by default, directing behavior away from the target and toward something else. If the "something else" has survival implications, it too will be evaluated either as good or bad and, therefore, as life enhancing or life threatening.

Action instinctually oriented toward the "good" and away from the "bad" is every species' most essential, unconsciously programmed survival mechanism. Species endure only because they have had this inborn, automatic, good/bad evaluation and response tendency operating adequately for eons.

Overt sensory reception and goal-directed action comprise an animal's primary repertoire for perceiving and behaving in the natural world. Humans are more fortunate. We have language, a secondary level mechanism for indirect, non-overt sensing and acting. At the **representational** level, language enhances sensation by taking sensory impressions and transforming them into a mental form that is especially amenable to extensive additional processing, such as further analysis of a particular sensory impression or synthesis of multiple ones. At the **communicational** level, language constitutes a special form of purposeful action not only because speaking is a motor act, but because language, in a sense, permits us to act upon ourselves through self-vocalization or upon other persons through dialogue without requiring any movement through actual space. Imagine a chimpanzee who has discovered a berry-rich cluster of bushes and who wants to share his knowledge with a troop member. Imagine further that he knows that the berry-rich area is frequented by a leopard every day at noon, and, therefore, should be avoided at that time. Only by overt action, taking his troop member to the area at a noon and non-noon time, could he even hope to communicate these simple ideas. With human language, he could have transmitted the information to his partner in less than one minute, without ever having to return to the berry area at all; the only movement required would have been the movement coincident with speaking. We intuitively equate conversation with motor action when we say such things as: You lost me. Where is this discussion going? Let me run this past you, I'm not following you, and You're talking in circles.

Developmental Progression

As one of the most uniquely human, most complex capacities, conversation becomes possible only when multiple physical and mental language-oriented skills mature and their lines of development converge. Hearing and listening are primary receptive language capabilities and speaking is a primary expressive skill in that they emerge early in development and without need for formal instruction. Reading is a secondary receptive capability and writing is a secondary expressive capability. Both of these literacies are secondary because they depend on primary language skills and on explicit schooling, and both capabilities enrich conversational competence.

Conventional conversation requires that persons hear each other. This usually is a minimal challenge. Neonates orient toward sound within the first hours of life. Hearing is an involuntary, automatic process that requires no more than an intact acoustic nervous system, internal and external organs of auditory reception, and the vibration of air molecules. Listening, however, is more demanding. It presumes hearing along with a deliberate focusing of attention and an active attempt to understand. When attention wanes, so does listening. Listening also requires at least some modicum of knowledge within which to fit what is heard and some motivation to do so. Children, and adults as well, need a reason to listen.

To say that listening requires attention and motivation is to say that the individual decides what he will listen to and what he will resist. Listening is directed toward items that we anticipate can give us some satisfaction. Listening, then, depends on our sense of self and on our personality. Some personalities are more listening-friendly than others. The reflection-impulsivity dimension of temperament is an especially important dimension. A reflective person is more thoughtful and, therefore, more listening dependable; an impulsive one is more action-oriented and less listening dependable. Other personality patterns also are relevant. Measuring personality by questionnaire, Weaver and associates (1996) found that listening styles differed according to three personality dimensions: The psychoticism personality type, characterized by coldness and unfriendliness, had a socially callous listening style. The extraversion personality type, characterized by enthusiasm and outgoingness, listened in a manner that was friendly, supportive, and people- oriented. The neuroticism personality type, characterized by anxiety and fearfulness, evidenced a listening style that minimized the time spent in interaction.

Reading is another volitional receptive language skill that demands attention and motivation and that shares essential features with conversation. Foremost is that we read to achieve language-instigated satisfactions. In the words of Bloom (2000), "Ultimately we read-as Bacon, Johnson, and Emerson agree-in order to strengthen the self, and to learn its authentic interests. We experience such augmentations as pleasure, pleasures of reading indeed are selfish…"

Conversationalists must be proficient not only in language reception but also in language expression. Most laypersons accept this notion and equate conversational prowess with speaking prowess. Writing, of course, is not conversation, but it is instructive to briefly juxtapose speaking and writing because, like speaking, writing is an expressive language skill that reveals much of the verbal thought processes and communication competencies that make conversation possible.

Chafe and Danielewicz (1987) conducted an investigation that compared four types of expressive language—casual conversation, informal lecture, informal written letters, and formal academic journal or book writing. A total of twenty either professors or graduate students from the University of California, Berkley or University of New York, Albany were subjects and all twenty were assessed on all four expressive language types. The authors concluded that conversations and informal lectures were similar in that they were characterized by limited vocabulary, inexplicit references, and hedging. Intonation units (defined as "stretches of language between punctuation marks," generally a single clause) were only slightly longer and vocabulary was only slightly more literate during informal lectures. As one would expect, more speaker-listener interaction occurred during conversations. On the other hand, informal letters and formal academic writing were very dissimilar. In fact, the language of informal letters was much closer in word use and content to conversation than to academic writing whose vocabulary was emotionally detached, maximally varied, explicitly referenced, and absent hedging with long intonation units having maximal coherence.

The significance of the study for us is that the expressive language of conversation, informal lecture, and informal letter writing are similar both for representational and communicational reasons. All three modes of expression represent ideas that primarily are being developed immediately before they are delivered; as such, the actor is less able to censor his thoughts consciously. At the same time, in all three modes, during communication, the actor is acutely aware of the personalities of his communication partners, either due to their physical presence or because of the clarity with which they are present in his mind's eye. The actor is inclined to alter his remarks to suit his well-known communication partners, and it is through this real-time compromise process that he derives pleasure. By contrast, the formal academic writer takes his mental representations as objects that must be honed to perfection. He principally is engaged with his own thoughts and himself, rather than with particular communication partners. Because he only has a general sense of his audience, the formal writer is much less inclined to "compromise" his beliefs. His pleasure consists mostly of self-dispensed satisfactions, independent of any single communication partner. Levy (2000), who recognizes the essential link between conversing and writing, suggests combining both expressive modalities by advising that an individual hold a written, make-believe "paper conversation" with a particular person as rehearsal for an anticipated demanding oral conversation with him. To do so effectively would be to maximize chances of deriving pleasure from others by satisfying the demands of communication with them and self-centered pleasure by satisfying one's own internal standards.

In all communication then, speaking presumes an individual who has a need to say something that will move her in a good, survival-oriented, direction. This tendency begins very early in life. Think about the infant. What does she "talk" about? : Only herself and her needs. Her conversation-like babblings are strident demands to feel good: shrieks, coos, and cries that insist – "Hold me; feed me; change me; comfort me; close that window I'm cold, and while you're up grab my pacifier, I have sore gums" – that she expects the listener to satisfy. With age and socialization, our reasons for conversing are less transparent, but no less egoistic. Now we are willing to listen to others' remarks, but only if they, in turn, will listen to and satisfy us.

Herein is the conversational rub—we need people to do it. And they need us. We also need social conventions that have evolved to facilitate verbal interaction. Conversation is an intra-personal, inter-personal, and social transaction. Unlike an infant, we rarely are blunt and uncompromising in our conversational quest for satisfaction. We know how to play the conversational game, and, most important, we know that we can only diverge so far from conventions if we are to keep our conversational partner sufficiently engaged so that we can achieve our own goals. The speaker is no less influenced by the listener than vice versa.

What is Casual Conversation?

Virtually all animals communicate with their own kind, with communication ranging from the elementary body language of the most primitive insects to the intricate "songs" of the most intelligent whales and dolphins. This animal communication, as far as we can determine, is for immediate, pragmatic purposes such as to summon, to warn, to locate one another, or to invite mating. Human communication surely first evolved for similar purposes. Like other animals, our ancestors recruited vocalization and auditory reception to augment their abilities to satisfy primary drives like hunger, thirst, safety, and sex: there was little time or energy back then for applying personal capabilities to anything other than the basics requirements of life. Language was inextricably linked to basic need satisfaction and, therefore, to basic survival.

The aspect of language that we call casual conversation, however, is uniquely human, one of the few qualities that unequivocally separates us from all other creatures on this planet. By definition, casual conversation is not necessary in a physical sense. Neither is it limited to the here and now, or even to reality. For purposes of this book, let's consider casual conversation to involve any more or less rational connected discourse wherein two or more persons voluntarily initiate comments to each other and voluntarily respond to each other verbally at least twice in a single meeting. Accordingly, if two persons are passing by and each says, "Hi," no conversation has occurred. But an exchange as perfunctory and brief as, "How are you? Oh, pretty good. How are you? I'm fine. What've you been doing? Not much. How about you? Not much either." does.

The aforementioned casual conversation obviously is as much ritual as discussion. No significant new information was exchanged between the two conversants. So, why bother?

Social scientists have devoted decades to answering this question and filled volumes trying to explicate it. And while there is far from unanimity on the details of the answer, the strong general consensus is that casual conversation evolved to facilitate the actual physical and mental survival of individual primates and their groups.

Survival and Reproduction: First Things First

Genes and Individuals

Survival is life's first and foremost imperative. Prolongation of survival is its second. Species whose members do not survive at least long enough to reproduce in sufficient quantity pass like dust in the wind, replaced by other, better-adapted species. In the natural environment, entropy is king; most external forces operate to tear down the life of an organism (Ball, 2001). A living creature can depend only on itself and its innate self-sustaining propensities to oppose entropy's destructive assault. Richard Dawkins (1976) asserts that each individual animal engages in "ruthlessly selfish" behavior whose goal is to ensure the continuation of his own genes rather than of the species per se. Dawkins emphasizes the ruthlessness of genes in this equation. But when he speaks of a gene as an independent, self-replicating entity, by default he is saying that the rest of the body (cells, organs, systems) is the gene's environment. Since an organism's survival is contingent on its relationship to its environment and because all evolution occurs relative to a specific environment, the gene needs all the rest of the body no less than each body organ needs each other. No organ can exist without nutrition from the stomach, blood from the heart, purification by the liver and kidneys, and so forth. An individual is the "package" of cooperating, systemically interlinked and organized, interdependent cells, organs, and systems. The fate of the package is the fate of its constituents. Unchecked, a small patch of necrotic skin eventually will stop the most robust heart and silence the most insightful brain. A gene without a body is an inert assemblage of chemicals, nothing more.

I contend that the struggle for survival is the struggle of a fully integrated, total organism. My view is that a species can endure even if it transmits sub-optimal genetic material provided an adequate number of its members survive long enough to procreate. Moreover, the species is more adaptable when it is diverse. This is why zoologists are so concerned about maintaining an adequate gene pool that they sometimes literally transport breeding animals around the world. Conditions may change such that the gene that appears so optimal today becomes deadly in a future environment. Most significant is the fact each individual animal's success in his own selfish survival and heartiness strivings inadvertently contributes to establishing a higher survival standard for the breed as a whole.

Survival is more than just having the best genes. Even the most genetically fit animal can fall prey to accidents and other acts of fate, rendering it incapable of reproducing. Animals first need genes that maximize the survival chances of individuals. An individual member of the species obviously needs to survive long enough to reproduce and the mothering organism must survive at least long enough to succor her offspring to the point that it has a fighting chance to survive **as an independent individual**. The selfish individual makes the selfish gene possible more so than the converse.

Reproduction ideally occurs when animals have reached the point in the life cycle when they are hardiest. Genetic endowment, therefore, confers its greatest advantage by promoting development/survival of individuals at least to that hardiest point. But in order to do so, it must have maximized the survival inclinations of the immature individual as well, since this best facilitates its achieving maturity. The young and the old are not programmed to reproduce because their organismic survival "equipment" is not robust enough to enable them to perform all life requisite functions for successful pre- and post-coital reproductive success.

Everywhere in the natural world we see that the survival instinct is more fundamental than the reproductive instinct. Phillip Ball (2001) agrees, saying "...we are not, even the most amorous of us, trying to reproduce all the time. Yet, if we stop metabolizing, even for a minute or two, we are done for."

Animals too aged ever again to reproduce use whatever feeble resources they can muster to resist dying. Despite our moralistic tendency to trumpet how a mother animal will fight to defend its young, if in the process her life too becomes gravely threatened, she almost always will flee selfishly. The power of survival over reproduction explains also that when two males compete for reproductive rights to a female, the weaker invariably chooses to escape rather than to continue combat until his last breath. Finally, basic individual survival must take precedence over optimal genetic transmission because environmental contingencies and acts of fate can prevent even the best genetically equipped member from performing procreative or gestational activities. The primacy of individual survival, then, ensures that an adequate number of genetically acceptable, albeit genetically suboptimal, individuals are available, healthy, and active enough to fill the reproductive void. A species simply cannot survive without the automatic, ruthlessly selfish behavior of its individual members. This single-minded selfishness explains why a robust male lion will chase his terminally malnourished mate from her kill so that he can gorge himself first. He cares more for personal survival and comfort than for reproductive success.

Memes and Individuals

At the conclusion of *The Selfish Gene*, Richard Dawkins (1976) moves beyond the physical dimension, introducing the concept "meme" to describe a gene-like unit of cultural transmission. Like genes, memes replicate in a single-mindedly selfish manner and, like genes, they do so with fidelity, fecundity, and longevity. By this we mean that behaviors or ideas qualify as memes when they faithfully, widely, and lastingly spread through a culture or subculture. They include phenomena as diverse as individual words, the handshake, the "Happy Birthday" song, and the notion of god.

The meme, itself, achieved meme status in some scientific subcultures, spreading due to the efforts of several champions. Foremost among them is Susan Blackmore (1999) who uses it to explain the development of language and even consciousness. Her central assertion is that human nature itself can be described in large part as the result of genetic and memetic influences – genes and memes, each by selfishly reproducing, inadvertently shaped human evolution.

In the Dawkins-Blackmore scheme, genes and memes transmit themselves mindlessly from one organism to the next with no regard for anything other than their own replication. That premise, however, fails to consider the fact that organisms who are the targets of transmission are not inert receptacles. Gene deposited is not necessarily gene received. For instance, at least 20 percent of human zygotes (Klug & Cummings, 2000; Geyman, et. al., 1999), with estimates up to 75 percent (encyclopedia.com, 2001), are spontaneously aborted, taking their selfish genes with them. Some women even are believed to be "allergic" to their mate's semen (Ludman,1999). Similarly, meme offered is not always meme accepted. Not everyone dances the Macarena or talks about Seinfeld, and those who dance the dance or talk the talk may do so in ways that differ significantly from their peers.

An integrated, selective, individual organism is at the center of both physical and mental evolution. Massimini and Delle Fave (2000) endorse this position when they say,

> "Being both reproducer and transmitter of bio-cultural information units, each human being actively influences the survival and replication of biological

and cultural pools. This influence is again based on a selective process, which has been defined as psychological selection of bio-cultural information (Csikszentmihalyi & Massimini, 1985). The process is shaped by two specific human features: the subjective-objective awareness and the limited amount of attentional resources (Csikszentmihalyi, 1978). Individuals cannot pay attention to all occurring environmental stimuli at the same time. Thus, they have to select a subset of this information – daily activities, situations, and social contexts – to be involved in. As a wide range of studies have pointed out, the main factor directing psychological selection is the quality of experience. Individuals preferentially invest their attention in environmental opportunities associated with positive and rewarding states of consciousness(Csikszentmihalyi, 1975, 1978; Csikszentmihalyi & Csikszentmihalyi, 1988)"

Indivemes

The genetic code that is passed from parent to offspring is the genotype. The actual physical characteristic that the genotype delivers is the genetic phenotype. For example, a male with blood type A and genotype AI i can father a child with any blood type—A, B, AB, or O—depending on the genotype of the female with whom he mates. The nature of the receiving individual organism is critical in deciding the phenotypic expression of the genotype offered.

Analogously, we can think of the memetic code that is transmitted from one individual to the next as the memotype and the information that endures in the receiving individual as the memetic phenotype. The physiologic information encoded in a gene or the mental information encoded in a meme is processed by a whole, finely-articulated individual organism that has its own preexisting physiology and mind. It is this preexisting complex that determines whether the gene or meme can be incorporated at all and the extent and quality of the incorporation. In short, the fidelity of a gene or meme requires communion of sender and receiver. Fidelity presumes an intra-individual readiness and inter-individual match if the phenoype is to be a faithful copy of the original.

Like genes, memes cannot exist in isolation. Just as every gene must be embedded in a matrix of cells, tissues, and systems, memes must be incorporated into a network of preexisting thoughts and feelings. In the real world then, every gene and every meme is a unique phenotypic element, expressed in the context of an individual, integrated organism.

The unique organism-consistent phenotypic expression of a gene or meme is, to coin a term, an "indiveme," an individual-specific phenotype that differs in some significant, functional, or even structural, ways from the genotype or memotype that existed in the offering organism and whose precise character is determined by the totality of the receiving organism. The indiveme is the physical-mental element that makes individuals individuals, that gives each organism its unique enduring characteristics through which it acts upon the world and is acted upon by the world.

Memes are never discussed in conversation. Only indivemes are discussed because what we say is not a static, socially-prescribed, cookie-cutter meme of an idea that has an objective connection to any given situation. What we say has our unique mark all over it. The content of our conversations is characterized by an idiosyncratic, personal, cognitive-affective tone uttered at a time and place in the flow of discourse that reflects our unique self and its strivings at that moment. Our indivemes are located in our own unique associative web of ideas that hang together because of who we are. The indivemes come to mind at a given time with a particular cognitive-affective significance because they literally are organically related to our physical-mental experience of the moment. The indivemes are introduced by us when they are because at that time and with that person they offer the possibility of physical and/or mental satisfaction.

An Irreducible Unity: Organism in Environment

The selfish gene and selfish meme never will provide a sufficient explanation for a living being of any kind. Genes and memes cannot be meaningfully understood in isolation from the totality of the individual organism. But, there is another ingredient, as essential as the integrated body and mind—it is environment. The human body and mind evolved in an environment that literally shaped them, an environment of evolutionary adaptation (EEA), that was absolutely necessary in order for our species to have endured (Reis, et al., 2000). According to Fenichle (1945), every physical and mental need has an aim (satisfaction), source (bodily and mental substrate), and object (an outside-the-self target). The object is essential to the need. Without the object, which always has a significant environmental aspect, there can be no satisfaction; organisms only exist because they evolved together with their objects.

Individual plus environment, then, comprise an irreducible unity, because an individual always is in an environment where he is both acting and being acted upon, and where he attempts to satisfy his needs. To be is to be somewhere, and the place powerfully determines specific qualities of an individual organism's body, mind, and action. An individual in a stimulating environment is different from that same individual in a monotonous one. An individual in a safe environment is different from that same individual in a perilous one: Its body is different; its mind is different; its action is different.

Elizabeth Susman (2001) distills the essence of my argument when she refers to the "field of developmental science," especially as espoused by Magnusson, and says that:

> "A basic proposition of developmental science is that the individual is viewed as an active, intentional part of an integrated complex, dynamic, and adaptive person-environment system, and that individuals develop in that context from the fetal period until death (Magnusson, 1999). This model of development can be summarized in a set of fundamental principles (Magnusson & Cairns, 2001): An individual :
>
> - develops as an integrated organism,
>
> - in a dynamic, continuous, and reciprocal process of interaction with the environment. This functioning
>
> - depends upon and influences the reciprocal interaction among sub-systems within the individual (perceptual, cognitive, emotional, physiological, morphological, and neurobiological).
>
> - Novel patterns of functioning arise during ontogeny and
>
> - differences in the rates of development may produce differences in the organization and configuration of psychological functions that are
>
> - extremely sensitive to the environmental circumstances in which they are formed, particularly the environment as it is perceived and interpreted by the individual. It follows that an individual is viewed as an active, intentional part of an integrated complex, dynamic and adaptive person-environment system.

Within this person-environment system, the individual is viewed as functioning and developing as an integrated organism in which biological, psychological, and behavioral factors operate in reciprocal interaction and dependency (Lerner, 1998 ; Magnusson, 1999). Each aspect of the structures and processes that operate within the individual (perceptions, plans, values, goals, motives, biological factors, and conduct), as well as each aspect of the environment, takes on meaning from its role in the total functioning of the individual. Magnusson's (1999) innovative approach also posits that the holistic nature of the functioning of the integrated organism lies in a psychological-biological process not being determined by a single factor. As a consequence of the holistic nature of humans, the processes cannot be subdivided into independent parts in the analysis of the integrated organism's way of functioning. To understand and explain the role of a specific element in the functioning and development of an individual, it has to be analyzed in the context of the relevant system to which it belongs. This notion applies to a range of phenomena that encompass the molecular and cellular level to the level of the individual as an active, intentional part of an integrated sociocultural person-environment system."

Shu-Chen Li (2003) adds that our understanding of human development is truly holistic only when we recognize that people **simultaneously** are influenced by phylogenetic, ontogenetic, and moment to moment neurobiological, cognitive, behavioral, and sociocultural forces. Specifically rebutting the current popular tendency to reduce humanity to genes and neurotransmitters, she emphasizes that a nervous system can not be viewed as an isolated entity, asserting that

"Genetic activities and neuronal mechanisms themselves possess remarkable plasticity awaiting environment and culture to exert selective development- and experience-based reciprocal influences (cf. Edelman, 1987) on them and to be the "coauthors" of mind and behavior. People are more than mere biological organisms; human mind and behavior need to be understood by situating them properly within a brain in a body that lives in an eventful world abounding with objects and people. Indeed, the brain offers the necessary biophysical reality for individual cognition and action; it alone, however, is not sufficient to engender the mind or behavior. On the mind-brain continuum, the individual mind is the expression emerging from the personalized brain (Greenfield, 2000; Llinas & Churchland, 1996). The very processes for personalizing the biological faculty of the mind take place throughout life span development in environmental and sociocultural contexts, which entail intimate dynamical exchanges between nature and nurture."

So the individual – with its body and mind—must be seen in environmental context. And, for our purposes, there are two classes of environments. Veridical environments are objectively and irrefutably present. They define us at any given point in time, such as, "I am a runner, running through the countryside." Veridical environments must exist because we must be somewhere at all times, and they exert a significant influence on us that occurs independent of our interpretation of them. A thunderstorm is this. However, veridical environments are not limited to the natural world. If I am driving a car, the car – a man-made object—is part of my veridical environment.

In contrast, presumed environments exert a significant influence on us only due to our interpretation of them (Kelly, 1955), although the effect can be as powerful as that of a veridical environment. A presumed environment could be a "boring party" that I am attending. While the physical space, the house, is part of the veridical environment and is objectively present, my presumed environment characterization of the space as boring, or even as being a party, is open to debate. Veridical environments influence us naturally; presumed environments may or may not. The individual must impose an interpretation plus a value on the latter for it to have significance. A thunderstorm is always a thunderstorm; a party is not always a party.

Conversation is special in that it has both veridical and presumed environment characteristics – veridical because conversations require each person simultaneously to be part of the objectively-present physical environment of each conversational partner and presumed because all the contents and processes of conversation are subject to interpretation by the participants.

If you are beginning to feel that the self-environment distinction sometimes can be fluid, you are right. When I pluck an apple from a tree, the apple and I are two distinct entities. But after I have swallowed a piece of apple there is a point at which the apple's constituents and my digestive constituents are so intermingled chemically that neither I nor the apple are totally separate from one another and, at that point, neither of us has a separate identity. The point of I-apple merger is analogous to the point at which information ceases to be an element in the environment and becomes part of me—an indiveme – information that has become uniquely mine to be used for satisfying my own unique needs. For instance, if you tell me and another listener that your boss cut his tongue when licking an envelope, the mental associations triggered by that statement and the relevance of them will be vastly different for each of us.

An idea/meme is like environmentally-available food that becomes organismically useful in terms of its match to the individual's state at the moment of reception. As information is presented to me, I can assimilate it with minimal modification or I can radically modify it. In either case—and this is the essence of an indiveme—the information is filtered through my mind every time that it is received, recorded, and utilized. Filtering occurs whether the information presented is an idiosyncratic, highly unusual idea, or whether it is a common, widely held meme, and it is only the filtered information that remains and that has the potential to influence my behavior.

Continuing the apple analogy, think of information, including memes, as environmentally available food that must be chewed into manageable chunks. Some chunks are digestible; some are not. Digestibility is individually determined. Some chunks of the information pass right through us with no significant absorption; others are broken down into constituent nutrients depending on what we are able to assimilate at the time. If you tell me that Harry Jones just has been inaugurated as President of the United States, we share that fact only in the narrowest, most denotative sense, because at the very moment you tell me, that fact it is inserted into a complex cognitive-affective associative web in my mind. The information will be understood and used only in cognitive-affective contexts and for cognitive-affective purposes unique to me and to my attempts to satisfy my needs. The fact that you presented is different for me than it is for you, and the way that I apply the fact will be different too.

Many people readily acknowledge that the body and its environment interact. They might know, for instance, that sightless moles lost their vision over evolutionary time due to having adapted to their lightless environment. That there is a special relationship of the mind and environment is less well known, but no less true. John Pearce and his associates (2001), for instance, suggest that the ability of an animal to know the shape of its environment is a special skill not explainable by the usual laws of learning. Special mind-environment mechanisms extend to the animate environment as well. The habits of prey are influenced by the habits of the predators that make up the local community and vice versa. The smiling response of human infants is shaped by the responses that it elicits in the interpersonal environment that, in turn, is shaped by the infant's smiling response.

Since environment includes all elements of the natural and man-made world, people are part of our environment. Some psychologists, myself included, would say that, emotionally speaking, people are the most essential element of our environment. Why?

For one thing, in contemporary society, people control access to most of what we need physically and emotionally. Few of us independently could produce the food, shelter, and clothing necessary for survival. Equally important, people almost always control access to essential non-physical or mental resources. We, for instance, get succor from our loved ones and affiliation from our friends, and these resources are dispensed via language, and conversation, its handmaiden.

In addition to dispensing such emotional resources as succor and affiliation, the people of our environment, in and of themselves, constitute a major component of our emotional environment. People influence our emotional environment because we are emotionally impacted by their traits, moods, and emotions – traits meaning their enduring personality-based emotional response predispositions, moods meaning their background emotional tone that persists from hours to days, weeks, or months, and emotions meaning brief, intense, episodes of feeling accompanied by emotion-specific physical changes such as the flush of embarrassment or the pallor of fear (Buck, 1999).

To have our environment populated by persons with predominantly positive traits, moods, and emotions is to have an environment that facilitates our efforts to attain satisfaction, because such persons are better willing and able to dispense the physical and emotional resources that we seek. Since non-physiologically-oriented targets for our satisfaction require us to make a subjective judgment as to their value, an environmentally positive inter-personal environment also models the behaviors that help us to interpret ambiguous targets and situations in a positive light. We make our value judgments in part by observing the value judgments that others make; the more positivity that we detect from others, the more inclined we are toward positive evaluations of our own.

For all the reasons that we have just discussed, the people who comprise our environment are critical to our physical and mental survival, and, therefore, to our achieving satisfaction during conversation. Not surprisingly, then, psychologists carefully investigate relationships in order to determine their effects. Bugental (2000), for instance, sees the inter-personal environment component of the presumed environment as comprised of five central social domains: attachment, hierarchical power, coalition, reciprocity, and mating. She notes that Wish, Deutsch, and Kaplan identify four domains: cooperative-competitive, equal-unequal, intense-superficial, and formal-informal. But regardless of how the inter-personal world is parsed, all else being equal, we fare best physically and mentally when we spend the majority of our time conversing with persons most inclined toward positive traits, moods, and emotions. These inter-personal-conversational issues will be addressed comprehensively when we consider the dangers of conversation.

It is obvious that individual organisms cannot be understood without reference to their veridical and presumed environments. The notion of organism-in-environment needs to be applied not only to global inter-personal relations, but also to basic human capacities. John Sutton (1998), for example, believes that scientists never will understand human memory until they investigate it in terms of its "exograms," or environmental memory supports. Exograms, including pictures, photographs, and computers, among other things, are external systems that "…in various ways complement, rather than replicate, quite different operations within the head." In other words, human memory exists as it does today because inside-the-head memory processes have developed in association with environmental exograms. Wegner, Erber, and Raymond (1991) emphasize that the memory environment includes people. According to their concept of "transactive memory," persons in familiar, close relationships at times automatically depend on each other to remember certain aspects of situations conjointly experienced.

Each member consciously or unconsciously takes responsibility for recalling some element of a shared experience and for retrieving and producing the information as needed.

Every gene and every meme, then, requires an environment in which to exert an effect. Genes and memes need an integrated, functioning body and mind to house and nurture them. In addition, memes need an individual or group to introduce and advocate for them. Sometimes the advocacy is the raison d'ete for an individual's or for a group's existence, as is true for evangelists, lobbyists, and advertisers. Sometimes the advocacy is inadvertent, as when a meme is promulgated because it has been endorsed by a high status person, or because the meme, itself, has some inherent quality, such sensory salience (e.g., a melodic tone), that makes its especially "catchy" and repeatable (Blackmore, 1999). In all cases, however, an environmentally-situated gene or meme exists within a unique individual as a one-of-a kind indiveme.

Reasons for Living

GBH

Individual organisms with their integrated bodies and minds pursue integrated lives in their veridical and presumed environments. More than anything else, they selfishly direct their energies toward survival. But how does an individual animal "know" how to act to promote survival? If you answered "instinct," this does provide a reasonable explanation for the broadest, most species-specific, most fixed, repetitive behaviors such as a lion's tendency to lower his head, fix his gaze on the prey, and stealthily move within striking range before exploding into a headlong dash to the victim. But what about the specifics of this behavioral sequence? What makes a lion pursue his wildebeest at 10:02 A.M. rather 09:47 A.M.? Why does the lion pick one member of the herd over another? What determines when the lion will freeze and when he will dash? These are intra-individual, volitional "choices" that the lion makes in real time from moment to moment. In each case, overwhelmingly, the lion makes his selfish choices due to his innate drive, the innate drive of all animals, to behave in ways that will enable him to feel good, better, or, at least, homeostatic (GBH).

For our purposes, "good" (G/GBH) means a pleasant/comfortable physical and/or mental state. "Better" (B/GBH) means an improvement in pleasantness regardless of the level of pleasantness of the preceding state. And "homeostatic" (H/GBH) means a state of internal balance and/or relatively adaptive level of tension.

Among other things, physical homeostasis involves processes as basic as maintaining blood pressure, breathing, and heart rate within normal limits. Physical homeostasis is an absolutely essential ingredient for life. Ackerman (2001) exquisitely describes the critical nature of water homeostasis when she says, "For humans, at least, lack of water is the taste of death. A drop of 2 percent in our body fluid immediately manifests itself as thirst; a 5 percent loss induces hallucinations; and a loss of 12 percent will kill us. Water is the medium of all our chemistry. Neither root nor flesh can absorb nutrients unless they are dissolved in

24

water. Only by water squeezing through the wall of the kidneys, the sweat glands, and the lungs can we excrete our own poisons."

Mental homeostasis will be fleshed-out later when we speak about baseline consciousness. For now, think of mental homeostasis as being the state opposite to a state of emotional arousal. In emotion, our mental self is being precipitously "moved" toward some change. We seek immediate change from the preexisting condition to some other condition, such as to greater security or assertion. In mental homeostasis, we, in a sense, are at mental rest, not compelled toward immediate change. Mental homeostasis is comprised of two major parts: Cognitive homeostasis refers to an intellectual state of an individual in which information presented is readily assimilated into his preexisting knowledge structure, as when he sees a new breed of cat and readily accepts it as such. Emotional homeostasis is similar to cognitive homeostasis, except that the information presented has a significant affective valence. Thus, if the individual is predisposed to thinking of dogs as vicious and he sees a snarling, snapping dog, he readily regards this as status quo. Both cognitive and emotional homeostasis is a matter of congruence between information presented and expectations affirmed. The fact of mental homeostasis is apparent in mundane features of daily life such as when advertisers want us to associate their product with getting back into balance, to getting to the preferred resting state.

My physical versus mental homeostasis distinction is useful for our discussion, but, strictly speaking, the distinction is an illusion. Loss of mental homeostasis and its subsequent reestablishment are accompanied by changes in physiology. To cite but one example, Pavlidis and colleagues (2002) demonstrated that lying during conversation, a state of disrupted mental homeostasis, is accompanied by increased blood flow around the eyes that dissipates as the lie becomes more remote in time.

Biologists and psychologists agree that physical and mental states always coexist and that they are inextricably linked. Natsoulas (1998) asserts this position when he says that "…every basic durational component of the stream (of consciousness), each successive state of consciousness, is an integral pulse of mentality possessing a feeling aspect and a cognitive aspect." In this context, the term "feeling" refers to a constellation of combined physical and mental experiences. Tension in the body produces tension in the mind and vice versa, and either or both motivate us to act. Tension signals us that quick, decisive action is necessary. A special branch of the nervous system—the autonomic nervous system—in fact, operates specifically to facilitate such action, not merely to regulate "fight or flight" as it colloquially is said to do (Pinker, 1999).

Constituents of Human GBH

What is the nature of the GBH that people seek? Abraham Maslow (1970) portrays it according to a hierarchy of bodily and mental needs, with those most essential to life at the bottom and higher level, "luxury," needs at the top, as follows: Physiological needs (such as for food and water), Safety Needs (such as for freedom from fear), Belongingness (such as acceptance by primary groups), Esteem (such as positive self identity), and Self Actualization (such as reaching one's full potential). According to him, an individual first must achieve satisfaction of lower level needs before he can achieve higher-level ones. Reiss (2000) speaks in terms of 16 basic human desires, many of which overlap with Maslow's needs. These include eating, physical activity, tranquility, order, saving, power, independence, acceptance, social contact, family, status, romance, curiosity, vengeance, honor, and idealism. Sheldon Elliot, Kim, and Kasser (2001) approach GBH empirically, testing 10 candidate psychological needs that appear most frequently in professional research and theory. They conclude that people most desire autonomy, competence, and relatedness. They also consider self-esteem to be important. Such needs as for popularity and money are described as "less important."

As the lists above suggest, GBH targets of human beings involve both physical and mental needs. I provide the lists to show that animals share some physical and mental needs with us, such as physiological and safety needs, and probably not others, such as esteem and self actualization needs. In this way I emphasize again that there is significant GBH continuity from animals to people. I also include the list to assert again the arbitrary nature of dichotomizing the human body and mind—of considering needs to be either physical or mental, rather than both physical and mental. For instance, could you with confidence decide that tranquility, power, romance, or curiosity belong only in the physical category rather than in the mental category, or vice versa?

That having been said, physical and mental GBH are significantly different in some respects. With the body at its center, physical GBH proceeds from a fundamental homeostasis that sets objective limits on the amount of bodily satisfaction or deprivation that is compatible with life for any given organism. With the psychological self at its center, mental GBH literally is subjective. Mental GBH has no objective limits, because mental GBH proceeds from one's beliefs about what is desirable, from what one values at a given moment and place. Mental GBH, therefore, can be capricious and insatiable.

Viewed from outside, the GBH-seeking individual sometimes might appear to be passive and content. But within there is a never-ending torrent of physical and mental activities – circulation, respiration, digestion, thoughts, and feelings, to name a few—that impel the individual to go places and do things that maintain and enhance well-being. There is no static life. There is only static death.

An Expectant, Relentless Search

Thus, we have more than a "need" for a GBH targets; we have a need to engage in an **expectant, relentless search** for them. Survival is not a place. It is a journey. Not an objective, but a process. The GBH search is relentless because the demands of life are unceasing. At the physical level, mobile animals deplete their resources by sensing, moving – even merely by lying quietly. They must replenish themselves by securing the raw materials necessary to maintain their bodies and minds, and the only way to maintain the critical life balance is to decide where the "good" raw materials are and to seek them out. Peter Marchand (2000), for example, opines that mammals do not hibernate primarily to escape the cold.; they hibernate when resources to sustain life are low. In effect, the hibernating mammal suspends its relentless search because it "expects" that the chances of obtaining GBH targets are severely reduced.

This kind of search for and evaluation of the good is outer-directed, toward an external environmental target as it impacts an animal. At this point, I am not commenting on an animal's inner-directed evaluation of its own internal, "mental" state. I am saying that all living things engage in an expectant search that drives behavior, not necessarily thought, toward a hoped-to-be-good external, environmental target. Elsner and Hommel (2001) emphasize the goal-directed basis of behavior saying "Actions are performed to attain desired goals, hence, to intentionally produce particular events…According to this logic, intentional action requires, and is actually controlled by, some anticipatory representation of the intended and expected action effects." Maria Miceli and Cristiano Castelfranchi (2000) explain that

> "Expectations are complex mental attitudes consisting of both goals and predictions (i.e., beliefs about the future). In fact, whereas a pure prediction of p is simply the belief that p is (more or less) likely to occur (within a certain time), an expectation of p is a prediction of p combined with the goal p (positive expectation) or not p (negative expectation): I foresee a certain event and I have the goal that it occurs or does not occur.…Expectations play a crucial role in the decisional phase, in that they influence intention formation and

maintenance. Broadly speaking, to become (or remain) an intention, a goal should be viewed as (a) attainable and (b) convenient; that is, the benefits gained through its satisfaction (realization of some superordinate goal, as well as positive side effects of p 's realization) should be viewed as greater than the costs of its choice (including renunciation of other possible goals) and pursuit (both resources to be spent and negative side effects of p 's realization)."

Human infants young as 6-months-old demonstrate differentiated expectations as sophisticated as expecting that when people talk they are talking to someone, but when they reach for and swipe they are reaching for or swiping at an object (Legerstee, Barna, and DiAdamo, 2000). Current research also has reaffirmed decades old research indicating that even animals form expectations. Forester, Higgins, and Idson (1998) remind us that, when stopped by an experimenter, harnessed rats moving toward food pull harder on their restraints the closer they get to the meal. Shidara and Richmond (2002) find an anatomical site, located in the anterior cingulated cortex, that fires with progressive frequency as monkeys get closer to completing an activity that they have learned will end in their being rewarded with a drink of juice.

Yet, the fact of a relentless, expectant search for GBH does not even require conscious awareness or consciously-directed behavior. At base, it is an intuitive, automatic, evaluative process. The search occurs regardless of the animal's current "mental" state." For example, a starving animal, searching for food does not feel good at the time of the search, but it is searching in the *expectation* of finding something to make it feel good, better, or at least homeostatic. Dragoi and Staddon (1999) state that animals are capable of being conditioned precisely because they develop both short term and long term expectations of reward. As Elsner and Hommel (2001) suggest above, organisms engaged in volitional activity have an anticipatory mental representation of their "intended and expected action effects."

The outer-directed, animal-based relentless search and evaluation system, in humans at least, has a parallel inner-directed, search and evaluation system in which a person consciously or unconsciously asks herself whether she is feeling good or bad. This is an example of the evolutionary tendency for living things to take a preexisting capability, in this case the primitive ability to search for and evaluate objects in the environment, and adaptively use it for another purpose, in this case apprehending the self, or some aspect of it, as something to be searched for and evaluated. The adaptive benefit is that the individual, herself, is the most constant feature of her own, personal experience and, therefore, the most available and dependable instrument by which to judge the adaptive or maladaptive nature of any given experience. Looking at herself in a situation and deciding that she feels "good" causes the individual to tag the self-situation as good, to be sought and repeated, and looking at herself in a situation and deciding that she feels "bad" causes the individual to tag the self-situation as bad, to be eschewed and avoided.

The relentless, expectant search for mental GBH is necessary because we crave mental comfort, just as we crave physical comfort. Like physical comfort, once achieved, mental comfort wanes and must be renewed. The reduction in mental comfort over time can be explained in many ways. Consider three: First, according to the opponent process theory (Solomon, 1980), emotions occur as pairs of opposites such that every experience of an emotion triggers a weak version of its opposite. With each repetition of the experience that caused the original emotion, the opposing one is strengthened while the original one is weakened. The classic example of this theory describes a person walking along a trail who sees a bear and has a strong fear response along with a weak curiosity response. With repeated encounters, involving no untoward consequences, the individual becomes less and less fearful and more and more curious of the bear. In ordinary circumstances, too, repeated pleasure of one type often is replaced by non-pleasure, a process called "habituation," which prompts us to direct our attention toward more inviting prospects. This find-the-good, savor it, abandon it, and look for the next good strategy is common to our daily experience. For one thing, the strategy characterizes our eating habits. You might love ice cream, but not for every meal. As demonstrated by Raynor and Epstein (2001), given multicourse meals, each with a different variety of foods, people consume 44 percent more than they do when the multicourses each contain the same foods.

Second, and similarly, mental comfort may decrease over time due to the "hedonic treadmill" effect (Brickman & Campbell, 1971) by which an experience initially enjoyed becomes taken-for-granted, depreciated, and replaced by another coveted experience. We all have had the experience of wanting something, such as car, so desperately that we are convinced that once it is obtained all will be well with the world only to find that a few weeks after securing the coveted item we become oblivious to it and lust after something entirely different.

Third, the pleasure of an experience can extinguish quickly because animate beings survive in large part due to the motivational affects of "interest," an inherent drive to encounter the world (Piaget, 1981), which causes them to "want" more and different life-enhancing opportunities. Interest/desire is a necessary mental component in the lives of human beings. Without such a drive, we would have a much diminished capacity to perform such routine tasks as finding foods, shelters, and mates. The centrality of interest for human existence is underscored when we consider conditions of impaired adaptive functioning such as Alzheimer's Disease and Clinical Depression in which life literally is threatened due to the profound absence of interest, or apathy, of its victims.

The desire to relentlessly search for GBH targets explains why leashed dogs drag us through the neighborhood, why cats scratch to get out of the house at night, why thrill-seekers dive off cliffs, why shoppers shop, and why people converse. Advertisers know this. They don't say, "buy our product," but instead, propagandize it as "good" and then wait for our natural approach toward the good "instinct" to consummate the sale. I am being only half facetious when I mention that even Thomas Jefferson acknowledged the prominence and power of the GBH search drive when he wrote, "We hold these **truths to be self evident** that all men are created equal that they are endowed by their creator with certain inalienable rights. Among these are life, liberty, and the **pursuit of happiness.**"

The GBH action tendency is more physiologically primitive and necessary than is emotion. It is programmed into every living cell, organ, system, and organism and primarily is an unconsciously operating force that makes life possible. While there are exceptions, in general, at each level, conditions favoring growth and health "feel right" in a physical, bodily sense and each living unit or subunit strives toward such conditions. Degeneration and disease "feel bad" in a bodily sense and each living unit or subunit moves away from conditions coincident with them. This, obviously, is not a perfect system. For instance, animals sometimes seek out and consume a substance that ultimately causes their demise, but the strategy works for most creatures most of the time.

To a considerable extent, the survival instinct really is the GBH instinct. To paraphrase an old song, animals want to live, not merely survive. Life is not programmed to frantically lurch from one feverish gulp of breath to the next. Animals do not seek just enough food to prevent utter starvation or just enough warmth to avoid death-dealing hypothermia. Life is oriented toward behaviors that promote comfort – behaviors that promote physical and/or mental states that are good, better, or at least homeostatic. GBH also is the feature that makes the survival instinct primary over the reproductive instinct because it gives reproduction the behavior-influencing power of sexual desire on which reproduction depends and because GBH is coveted by individuals too old or too young to have sex.

At first, actions that result in bodily satisfaction promote an internal, physical GBH condition within an individual animal. Over time, the individual animal's satisfactions coincident with repeated successful selfish choices become associatively attached to external stimuli present at the time of a GBH episode. At that point, those external stimuli can become capable of instigating internal GBH feelings themselves. Now, the animal might feel GBH either due to actual physical satisfactions within his internal world or in response to cues in the external world that mentally remind him of past personally experienced physical satisfactions. The process is essentially conditioning, the primary mode of animal learning.

A behavioral "decision" made in an expectant search for GBH need not be a decision in the traditional sense of a consciously deliberated conclusion. Rather, it can occur as a result of phylogenetically-inherited action proclivities such as explain why a lion decides to seek meat rather than grain. Other animal decisions might involve making a choice based upon bodily feedback, as when a monkey with a relatively full stomach selects a small fruit over a large one. Finally, I agree with some biologists, such as Lee Alan Dugatkin (2001), that at least some of the "higher" animals are not limited to behavioral decisions exclusively due to instinct or to conditioning, but are capable of "imitating" the decisions of their peers, making GBH choices due to having observed others' successful choices.

GBH, Imitation, and Culture

In the recent past it had been assumed that animals need direct personal experience – conditioning experience – in order to learn. Blackmore (1999), for instance, asserts that imitation is uniquely human and responsible for uniquely human social evolution. However, some scientists strongly disagree, suggesting that even "lowly" fish are able to learn merely by observing other fish of the same type. Dugatkin (2001) refers to this as *The Imitation Factor* or "culture," defined as behaviors or ideas acquired from and shared with others of one's reference group that differs from behaviors or ideas held by others in other groups (Newsweek, March 26, 2001). He asserts that imitation can propel animals to higher levels of adaptation. He cites research purporting to show, for instance, that guppies in his and his colleagues' experiments chose to copy the successful, but not the unsuccessful, mate selection and fight strategies of others whom they had watched. For those unwilling to ascribe culture to fish, consider recent findings regarding mammals. Rendell and Whitehead (2001) describe discrete pods of killer whales who seem to have developed the ritual of lining up and facing off prior to approaching each other informally, and other discrete pods whose members have vocalizations that are distinctively different from the usual killer whale vocalizations. Whiten and Boesch (2001) explore chimpanzee culture by surveying field primatologists and discovering 39 examples of chimpanzee subgroup-specific behaviors including ones involving characteristic styles of tool use, grooming, and courtship. Van Schaik and associates (2003) even find that some orangutan verbal signals (e.g., "kiss squeak" signal) vary from group to group.

These findings supporting animal culture, though not essential to my argument, are easily incorporated into it. In all cases, imitated behaviors are ones that offer the imitator a chance to achieve GBH. An animal species that evidenced imitation or culture would demonstrate an essential continuity between itself and humans as cultured animals, implying that the expectant search for GBH satisfaction began phylogenetically in the actions of animals, was handed-down to humans who also initially sought GBH in direct action, and who then developed language and conversation as further GBH vehicles.

To accept that at least some animals imitate is to acknowledge their intellectual prowess and continuity with us. The eminent cognitive psychologist, Jean Piaget (1962) emphasized imitation as an aspect of thought. He considered imitation to be an accommodative process in that the observer **changes** its behavior to match the object of imitation. To imitate, the observer must fix attention on the object, value its action, and "understand" the action sufficiently to reproduce it. When the observer does not perform the imitation while immediately in the presence of the object but only later, it demonstrates "deferred imitation" and, in the Piagetian model, deferred imitation is felt to signify the presence of a mental image held in memory. Piaget would have been impressed by any animal capable of deferred imitation, since he theorized that the capability is not present in humans until about 18 months of age.

Regardless of the outcome of the animal imitation/culture debate, no one can deny that imitation and culture mightily contribute to the human quest for GBH. Cultural forces help us to identify what we need to survive and thrive, and cultural forces help us to get it. Like Blackmore, Tomasello (2000) believes that cultural transmission is the central factor responsible for human intelligence and achievement. He asserts, "I'm maintaining that without all of the cultural things that children inherit, it would pretty much be ape cognition…the nature of human cognition is cultural to its core."

If culture is the keystone of human thought, then language is the keystone of culture, and conversation is the keystone of language. More than anything else, culture depends on the communicative function of language for disseminating ideas from one cultural member to another. And, as we shall see in the next section, language in general and conversation in specific not only are special instruments used to achieve non-language GBH, but also are themselves instruments that deliver verbal GBH.

The Body and Mind as Reciprocal Vehicles for GBH

Conversation requires a body in a mind, body/mind, and a mind in a body, mind/body, both of which naturally work to increase chances of survival by continually striving toward GBH. The body/mind relentlessly seeks GBH in the world of the flesh. And the mind/body is no less driven to GBH in the world of the abstract. Most often, satisfaction of the body/mind promotes satisfaction of the mind/body and vice versa. This is true in large part because of the interrelatedness of physical and mental satisfaction. Many psychologists believe that in both a phylogenetic and an ontogenetic sense, mental satisfactions have developed as elaborations of physical satisfactions. They reason, that, as we discussed earlier, to survive, all animals, including humans, instinctively must act to reduce such physical needs as hunger and thirst and that reduction of these primary tensions constitutes pleasure in its rawest form. Food, drink, and all physically-based satisfiers that are inherently valued, are called "primary reinforcers." Both animals and humans relentlessly pursue primary reinforcers automatically, in part because nervous systems are hard-wired to drive attention toward primary reinforcers. According to Lang et al. (1998),

> "To the extent that primary reinforcement systems (with their associated pleasant and aversive affects) are engaged, the phenomenon of attention in humans involves response patterns and supporting neural pathways that are, in broad outline, consistent with those of many less complex organisms...Human attention is therefore viewed here as information processing that involves procedures of selection and evaluation of motivationally relevant input, similar to that occurring in an animal as it forages in a field, encounters others, pursues prey or sexual partners, and tries to avoid predators and comparable dangers...It is proposed that the motivational states elicited by these affective cues (and the reflexive, somatic, cortical, and autonomic substrates of their perception) are fundamentally similar to those occurring when more primitive mammals stop, look, and listen, sifting through the environmental buzz for cues of danger, social meaning, and incentives to appetite."

By definition, we must learn to value all other reinforcers, called "secondary reinforcers," and all of them derive their reinforcing power by their association with primary reinforcers. Money, being a secondary reinforcer, has no inherent value. It is worthless unless it is exchanged for some item or experience of physical and/or mental pleasure. Even someone who collects money as an item in its own right, without ever spending it, will find pleasure only if he perceives the money as something that makes him attractive to others, is a badge of his importance, and so forth. And, in these cases, it is the physical and mental satisfaction of contact by adoring others, personal tension reduction, and other carnal pleasures that constitute primary reinforcement underlying money's secondary reinforcing value.

Despite our culture's preoccupation with money as the ultimate secondary reinforcer, the secondary reinforcing power of language is infinitely greater. Persons skilled in the use of language literally can get anything that money can buy and more. This is true both of language as representation and as communication; both facilitate physical and mental GBH. As representation, language enables us to mentally anticipate and explore the veridical environment and the presumed environment so that we can find resources necessary to maintain our bodies and minds. As communication, language links us to others who possess resources and skills that they can share overtly or inadvertently to make our expectant, relentless search for GBH more successful. In fact, communication with people is, itself, a source of GBH and, therefore, a goal of our relentless search. Among other things, verbal communication is a source of GBH because conversation enables us to mentally re-experience past physical and mental pleasures. By conversing with you, I can relive the moment when I caught the game-saving pass as the clock ran down. Moreover, unlike simple material objects, considered as stimuli, people are naturally interesting and rewarding to us, since long-term interest is most captivated by a stimulus about which we have abundant, elaborated knowledge and which incite conflict in us (Silvia, 2001). Conversation with people, then, at least with some people, tends to be a major route that we follow in our relentless, expectant search for GBH.

The Good and the Bad

The Dialectics of Life

Experience sometimes is described in terms of polarities between extremes. Black is defined as the absence of color. Cold is the absence of heat. An ancient Chinese philosophy regards the world as operating according to an organizing principle, the Tao, which is divided into two subprinciples, opposing forces that produce each other. For instance, the yin of femaleness and the yang of maleness are reciprocally defined. Western folk wisdom invokes the interconnectedness of polar opposites by suggesting that one cannot know great joy without having known great pain. George Kelly (1955) describes human experience similarly, as a matter of an individual's creating "personal constructs" which guide their perceptions and behaviors. The constructs are bipolar with each pole being the opposite of the other. He suggests that you decide that someone is "happy" by contrasting him with someone that you regard as "sad" and vice versa.

As we saw earlier, Solomon (1980) proposes an "opponent process theory" in which emotions are considered bipolar, every emotion triggering an opposing emotion in a way that causes emotions to tend toward balance. Each repetition of an event that arouses an initial emotion strengthens the opposing emotion and weakens the initial emotion, explaining why with repetition the opposing emotion becomes stronger – a phenomenon that Solomon believes is at the root of the pain of heroin withdrawal that follows the pleasure of heroin use.

So What's So Good About That?

Anything that satisfies physiological and safety needs is objectively good in that it promotes an organism's survival. On the other hand, one encounters difficulties in determining what is good relative to satisfying primarily mental needs, such as those above Maslow's safety level. For them, there is no obvious, nonambiguous, objective standard that defines the good. The decisions become murky and subjective when we confront questions as to whether the target item is **inherently** good, versus whether we "**believe**" that it is good, versus whether we, **ourselves**, feel good because of it.

To discuss conversation, then, we need to establish criteria that define what is good. I propose two standards – overt, behavioral effects and personal, subjective interpretations. By overt behavioral effects, I mean objectively defined, good-bad situations occurring with or shortly after the conversants' statements; for instance, a good situation would obtain when conversants use many positively-valanced words during their talk. By personal, subjective interpretations I mean the conversants' good-bad opinions about themselves, their conversant partners, and the content of their conversation; for instance, when conversants mention enjoying their chat.

The direction of personal, subjective interpretations of good also is important. The evaluation can refer to feelings that a person ascribes outside herself – other evaluation – or to herself—self-evaluation. Earlier we described positive-negative as a global evaluation, approach-avoid as a behavioral or action evaluation, good-bad as a moral evaluation, and pleasant-unpleasant as a sensory-oriented evaluation. Some psychological studies use the related terms optimism-pessimism instead. Any of these terms can be used to refer to other-evaluation or self-evaluation. When a person uses those first terms to refer to something outside herself, she indirectly is indicating that the thing in question is reinforcing to her. When she attributes any first term of these pairs to herself, she is indicating a benign self-state. For our purposes all of the terms have a good-bad underlying semantic structure describing an evaluative decision that we apply to that which we apprehend and to ourselves.

Vladimir A. Lefebvre (1992) painstakingly investigated the details of human "reflexion," which he considered to be the human tendency to make good-bad evaluations. After extensively reviewing the literature and conducting scores of experiments, he concluded that, when given a bipolar choice, people typically label stimuli or events as positive approximately 62 percent of the time. And, the less objective the information that they have to make their decision, the more likely the 62 percent result. He cited data showing this is true whether people are evaluating beans or moral scenarios.

Lefebvre's results accord well with the more general "Pollyanna principle" that Christopher Peterson (2000) alludes to when he says, "Margaret Matlin and David Stang (1978) surveyed hundreds of studies showing that language, memory, and thought are selectively positive. For example, people use more positive words that negative words, whether speaking or writing. In free recall, people produce positive memories sooner than negative ones. Most people evaluate themselves positively, and in particular more positively than they evaluate others." Wentura, Rothermund, and Bak (2000) further differentiate the inter-personal evaluation process, asserting that our evaluation of other persons depends in part on the perspective that we take relative to them. We can evaluate other persons in terms of how their characteristics affect them or in terms of how their characteristics affect us. Wentura and his colleagues, as expected, show that under both conditions, individuals automatically evaluate other's characteristics as good versus bad. However, individuals are faster and more consistent in approaching the good or avoiding the bad when the target person's characteristics are considered from the point of view of the observing person, rather than from the point of view of the target person. For instance, when aggression is seen as a characteristic of a target person, the observing person is more inclined to avoid the target regardless of how the target would be expected to evaluate himself. This inter-personal evaluation process is consistent with our discussion of the relentlessly expectant search that we have characterized as a **self-centered** tendency to approach GBH targets and to avoid targets that threaten GBH.

David C. Riccio, Vita C. Rabinowitz, and Shari Aaxelrod (1994) describe the familiarity effect by which people tend to more positively evaluate stimuli to which they have been previously exposed, even when they do not consciously recognize the familiarity of the stimuli. The effect, has particular relevance to good-bad discrimination because, according to the "differential decay hypothesis," after receiving a message with a discounting cue ("William has the most wonderful natural singing voice of anyone I have ever auditioned. He can sing almost anything – opera, jazz, rock, or country. I wanted so much to hire him, but I didn't because all the people who wrote references for him mentioned his poor work ethic."), we remember the primary message for a much longer period of time than we remember the discounting cue. As time passes, then, the primary message becomes more and more powerful in determining our good-bad evaluation and the hedonic tone of the evaluation tends to be less balanced.

Together, the concepts of reflexion, familiarity, and differential decay suggest that when people make a subjective, good-bad evaluation, they are unconsciously biased toward the good and toward the predominant affective tone of the message rather than discounting elements. This means that when asked about our conversations, we usually describe them in positive terms and that the positive evaluation is ascribed both to the message and relationship aspects of the encounter. But while the conversant's conscious, subjective opinion about the conversation is an important explicit measure of whether she views the conversation as having been good or bad, the good-bad significance of conversation is much more complex than is a simple conscious decision by the conversant.

As we discussed earlier, in addition to referring to the conversant's personal, subjective evaluation, a good-bad evaluation also can be made regarding the objective behavioral effect of the event on the conversant. In other words, it is possible that an individual subjectively would say that the message from her conversational partner was good and their relationship was good, yet the objective effect on the individual could be bad. For instance, during a conversation, when a best friend very pleasantly describes how well everything is going for her, the listening partner might truly believe that she feels good for her friend. That same listening partner, however, could leave the conversation feeling bad because her own life is going poorly when compared to her friend. In deciding good-bad effects on an individual, then, we cannot depend solely on the explicit opinion of the conversants. We need an implicit measure as well, meaning a measure by which we can objectively infer how they have been affected by the conversation. For instance, we might decide the effect on them by rating the hedonic tone of the comments that they make during the conversation.

To be more specific in assessing the subjective and objective influences of conversation on an individual, we need to consider whether the effects are:

Good versus Better versus Homeostatic: As discussed previously, all volitional behavior, including conversation, involves people's engaging in a selfish, relentlessly expectant search that is not limited to what is good (G/GBH) but also to what is better or more homeostatic than the preexisting condition—that is, BH/GBH satisfaction. Sleeping in winter on a pavement heating grate does not feel good, but it is better and it affords more homeostatic relief than does sleeping with no heat source at all. Similarly, conversing with an unpleasant person may not make one feel good, but it may be better or it may afford more homeostatic relief than does having no one with whom to talk. Never underestimate the psychological significance of feeling "better." Karney and Frye (2002), describing feeling better in terms of a change over time, explain:

> "Thus, even if the current quality of an experience is less than desired, a sense of adequate or better than expected progress toward a goal can still give rise to positive affect, and a sense of inadequate progress or decline can still give rise to negative affect. In a series of studies that directly compared the relative importance of the two kinds of information with evaluations of ongoing experiences, Hsee and his colleagues (Hsee, Abelson, & Salovey, 1991) confirmed that when an outcome is changing over time and is intrinsically desirable (as opposed to a means of achieving some extrinsic reward), evaluations of the

experience are influenced more strongly by information about change over time than by the average level of the outcome across time (see also Wilson & Ross, 2000)."

Physical versus Mental: Happily, we only have to differentiate physical GBH or mental GBH when the satisfaction of one precludes the satisfaction of the other. Is your physical lust for a second chocolate éclair stronger than your mental desire to resist all that delicious fat? You can't both eat the éclair and satisfactorily resist it. In this case of gustatory lust versus dietary stoicism, physical GBH is inconsistent with mental GBH. Under normal circumstances though, physical GBH enhances mental GBH and vice versa. Physically stimulating conversations usually are mentally stimulating and the reciprocal relationship obtains for physically relaxing conversations as well.

Message versus Relationship: Sometimes our relentless expectant search for GBH is a search for pure message or pure relationship satisfaction. As with the physical versus mental dichotomy, however, message versus relationship fortunately is an infrequent choice that occurs only in those rare situations that require us to sacrifice message GBH at the expense of relationship GBH, or the converse. An example of the former would involve your having to "kiss up" conversationally to your despised boss in order to get the promotion that you covet. The latter would happen if you attempt to "fake" a conversation about an unfamiliar topic so as to win the favor of an attractive member of the opposite sex.

Personal Self versus Social Self in Relationship: Relationship GBH concerns the self-view that one independently holds of himself, his personal self, and the self view that he believes his conversational partner holds of him, his social self. In the best of all possible worlds, the needs of the personal self are congruent with the needs of the social self. But they can be at odds, as when the individual considers himself to be talking honestly (personal self), but presumes that his conversant partner considers him to be talking duplicitously (social self). Under these circumstances, the person in question must decide, usually unconsciously, whether he is willing and able verbally to defend the integrity of his personal self or to shift to what he perceives as the socially correct stance. Thus, there are times that the individual's search for relationship GBH is fueled by his desire to feel more positively about his personal self, and to do so he speaks according to his own standards. At other times the relationship GBH search is fueled by a desire to feel more positively about his social self, and to do so he speaks according to the standards that he believes others hold for him.

Constant versus Changing: There is no constant state of good, better, or homeostatic, for even homeostasis describes a condition that fluctuates within a trait-defined range. After any satisfaction there is a refractory period, a time during which the individual will not be positively reinforced by the satisfier. Banana splits are great but not for three meals a day, seven days a week. A satisfier also is not constant because of the "hedonic treadmill" effect that we mentioned before, referring to the fact that people eventually become acclimated to a certain level of pleasure, set that level as a new baseline, and then seek more or different pleasures. Once again, the analogy to drug dependence is relevant—drug tolerance causes addicts to use more and more of a mind-altering substance to achieve the effect that was experienced at earlier, lower doses.

Immediate versus Delayed: GBH obviously can occur immediately or after an activity has concluded. In the case of conversation, delay usually is deadly. Conversation is driven primarily by GBH that occurs during the ongoing discussion. This is true because the expectant search for GBH during conversation is mostly unconscious and the unconscious does not tolerate delay. Conversation not afforded either immediate message or immediate relationship GBH is conversation that will be resisted and aborted at the first opportunity.

This is not to say that delayed satisfactions never play any part in sustaining conversation. There are some instances in which delay, itself, may be coveted, such as when a person speaks about one thing in order to avoid speaking about something else, or **speaks** about an issue so as to avoid physically **acting** on it. In other circumstances, one could endure an acrimonious confrontation with a conversant in the expectation that it will ultimately lead to future message or relationship GBH.

Promotion versus Prevention: How do we account for delay of gratification in GBH terms? In large part, it is a matter of regulatory focus. As Higgins (2000) explains it, individuals can seek GBH by a **promotion** focus that represents an **eagerness** for reward, or a **prevention** focus that amounts to **vigilance** to avoid pain. The latter situation can prompt one to delay approaching, or even seeking, a GBH target in order to maintain currently acceptable homeostasis in the hope that GBH later will be attained more easily or more safely.

People primarily can have a promotion or prevention focus in conversation. The former occurs when we converse to get message/relationship GBH and the latter when we converse to avoid that which would interfere with GBH. In the case of the former: I'm talking with you because you have the information I need to complete my work project or because through my relationship with you I can get to do things I never could do otherwise. In the latter: I'm talking with you because I'm afraid I'll make a work-related mistake and you can tell me how to avoid it or you are my boss and I want to keep on your good side to avoid being axed.

Regulatory focus (approach reward versus avoid pain) also affects conversation because when the process or outcome of our conversation matches my regulatory focus, I feel better about it and remember it better. Expressed concretely, if I have a promotion focus and we are talking about ways that I can better reach a reward, I am more likely to feel good and remember; contrariwise, if I have a prevention focus and we are talking about ways that I can better avoid a feared outcome, I am more likely to feel good and remember.

Accentuate the Positive, Eliminate the Negative

GBH primarily is physical GBH for most animals, an inclination to move toward a more optimal level within and/or between bodily systems. Animals' expectant searches for GBH are mostly repetitive, instinct-driven actions toward simple, familiar targets that satisfy the most basic physical needs. When targets are attained, life is promoted; when targets are not attained, life is compromised, and the promoting or compromising can be objectively observed – an animal who fails to find food dies of starvation; an animal unable to secure shelter dies of exposure. We presume that animals do not search for independent mental GBH in any way comprehensible to us as humans. For most animals, mental GBH is inseparable from physical GBH; mental GBH is weak, secondary, and presumably limited to a vague, global sense of reduced tension however it is mentally represented.

For humans, the GBH scenario is more complicated. As a kind of animal, we, too, require physical GBH as expressed by adequate equilibrium within and/or between bodily systems, and we, too, desire physical change in the direction of a more optimal level. In short, we engage in the expectant search for physical GBH. But contemporary human society is such that most of our elementary survival needs are satisfied with little or not effort on our part. Much of what we covet by way of physical GBH is bodily gratification far in excess of that necessary for survival. In fact, we often desire physical satisfaction at odds with survival as when we want to eat too much. We also differ from most animals in that while physical GBH satisfaction does enhance our mental GBH status, we have a drive toward some mental GBH satisfactions that have minimal direct physical GBH accompaniment, or even for mental GBH satisfaction at the expense of physical GBH. An example of the latter would be physical discomforts tolerated by Olympic athletes who drive themselves to exhaustion for years to prepare for a single contest that they probably will lose. No matter how unrealistic though, the person who deliberately renounces immediate physical pleasure does so in anticipation of other pleasure. The Olympian derives at least some satisfaction either from the training or from fantasies of its benefits. Volitional behavior that eschews immediate physical pleasure is explainable in terms of the relentless search for GBH; it merely is an expectant search for mental and/or delayed physical GBH.

The disconnection of human physical and mental satisfactions is possible in large part because language can facilitate verbal movement toward an abstract mental GBH satisfaction that has no readily perceivable connection to survival, perhaps not even a readily perceivable connection to reality. Even more incredible when considered purely by animal standards, communication, itself, can be the mental GBH satisfaction that is coveted. This is because conversation is a powerful secondary reinforcer that it is associatively linked to primary reinforcers. For instance, talking to you about food gives me some fancied oral satisfaction by evoking memories of past gustatory pleasures or imagining future ones, but it is mental satisfaction without any true physical satisfaction.

It is important to add, parenthetically, that the GBH search is not limited to non-deliberative activities. Overskeid (2000) suggests that the GBH search lies at the very heart of conscious human problem solving decisions. In his words, "When people solve problems, the criteria they use in evaluating alternative solutions cannot in themselves motivate the choosing of an alternative. On evaluation, each alternative elicits a feeling that can be placed somewhere along a hedonic continuum. Whether rational or irrational, and even if the problem solver regards another alternative as correct, the alternative that produces the best feeling will always be selected as the solution to the problem." The position of Overskeid, then, is that we not only search for GBH, but also actively resist information and decisions that threaten our expectation of GBH satisfaction.

The flagship journal of the American Psychological Association, the *American Psychologist,* began the new millennium with a special issue devoted to happiness, excellence, and optimal human functioning – an issue celebrating the importance of "positive psychology." Most of the articles found that positive/pleasant/optimistic self-evaluation or other-evaluation were associated with physical and/or mental advantages. For instance, the physical advantages of optimism were emphasized by Shelley E. Taylor and her coauthors (2000) who said,

"Our work on cognitive adaptation to life-threatening events and on positive illusions (Taylor, 1983; Taylor & Brown, 1988), however, suggest that normal human perception marked by a positive sense of self, a sense of personal control, and an optimistic, even unrealistically optimistic, view of the future, may represent reserve resources that not only help people manage the ebb and flow of everyday life, but that assume special significance in helping people cope with intensely stressful and life-threatening events. Consistent with this perspective, in several studies researchers have found a relationship between dispositional optimism and reports of positive changes, benefits, or 'growth' following stressful events (Curbow, Somerfield, Baker, Wingard, & Legro, 1993; Davis, Nolen-Hoeskema, & Larson, 1998; Tedeschi & Calhoun, 1996; Tennen, Affleck, Urrows, Higgins, & Mendola, 1992). In the case of life-threatening illness, these resources may act as buffers against the reality of advancing disease and death to the point that people face such experiences not only with psychological benefits but also with more resilient physical resources as well."

In the same journal issue, the mental advantages of optimism were chronicled by Christopher Peterson (2000) who noted that "Research by a number of psychologists has documented diverse benefits of optimism and concomitant drawbacks of pessimism. Optimism, conceptualized and assessed in a variety of ways, has been linked to positive mood and good morale; to perseverance and effective problem solving; to academic, athletic, military, occupational, and political success; to popularity; to good health; and even to long life and freedom from trauma." The optimism of which Peterson speaks is essentially a mental tendency to expectantly search for the good and better – a selective attention toward good and away from bad.

Conversation that facilitates optimism, then, literally is good for us. When we seek optimism-enhancing conversations, instinctively we are engaging in the expectant search for GBH. Christopher cautions, however, that optimism can be elusive and subjective – that, to a certain extent, optimism is in the eye of the beholder. I respect his concern and suggest that optimism as facilitated by conversational messages ultimately is defined not only by their denotative content but also by the connotations that they hold for the conversants and that it is the connotations more than denotations that determine the subjective and objective effects of conversational content on the conversing pair. This is conversational optimism as embodied in message. However, optimism also can be present in the relationship between the conversants. Relationship optimism occurs when the conversants interact in ways that affirm each individual's wants and needs such as by mutual efforts to afford the other an opportunity to fulfill his GBH desires and to tell his story. This is a kind of self-serving altruism that is absolutely essential in making extended conversation possible.

Masochism and Other Harm-Seeking Behaviors

All this good-better stuff ignores an obvious fact – some people, such as ascetics and stoics, do not seem to be pursuing GBH, at least not as defined by the masses. I contend, however, that self-deniers do derive GBH from their actions, and that the GBH is mental in nature, related to pleasures associated with enhanced self-esteem, self-identity, and self-morality.

While, from our point of view, ascetics and stoics suffer inadvertently from their standards, some people deliberately do things that they, themselves, acknowledge as causing them direct, actual harm. Masochists, who intentionally seek out physical or emotional pain, epitomize this condition. When masochists converse, they might do so to be emotionally, or even physically, tortured.

As mentioned earlier, few, if any, behaviors can be attributed to one source. Masochism, of course, is multidetermined. However, masochistically self-abusive behavior frequently occurs because of the "homeostatic" link in the good-better-homeostatic explanatory chain.

Used in this sense, homeostasis designates a physical or mental state that has become an individual's norm, the level to which he has adapted, the level that is "natural" or customary for him, even if that level looks pain-inducing to the observer. Mental homeostasis in large measure is acquired through conditioning and through expectations embodied in the self-concept.

Swann (1992) could offer one explanation for the pain-seeking by saying that the masochist maintains emotional homeostasis by moving toward situations and people that enable him to keep a consistent, coherent negative self image. This happens because, like all of us, the masochist wants a stable personal sense of self. Perceiving himself as debased, he expects and elicits negative, not positive, ideas and interactions that promote that identity. In essence, the masochist's homeostatic need for consistent self identity exceeds his need to feel good. Given such a tendency, masochistic persons would not have survived in prehistoric times.

But what about "normal people" who want to talk about tragedy, death, and destruction? They don't appear to be conversing to feel GBH. To understand this bias toward unsavory subjects we must remember that GBH can derive from the message or from the relationship. From the message side, conversing about topics like death actually can make the conversants feel more alive or more appreciative of being alive. It can decrease my own fear by finding a reason why the dreaded event couldn't happen to me, or it can help me become more aware of ways to avoid the event. From the relationship side, conversing about an unsavory subject can be a way for me to demonstrate to the listener how empathic or sympathetic a person I am, and thus raise my relationship value. Alternatively, I may want to talk about the unsavory subject because I can use it as an exciting topic for conversation with someone else later.

The Magic of Thought and Language

Embodiment in All Mental Processes

Increasingly, experts from virtually all fields that study the human condition are realizing what may be obvious to laypersons – that all mental processes are vitally dependent on the body that houses them. "Embodiment" is the new buzzword that describes this phenomenon. To mention only a few examples: Some philosophers (e.g., Lakoff & Johnson, 1999) suggest that most essential concepts proceed from a few fundamental metaphors that are rooted in our bodily experiences. For instance, our concept of knowledge, itself, is equated with vision (I see what you mean.) and touch (I have a grasp of the subject.). Some neurologists regard decision making as being greatly influenced by unconscious visceral reactions that occur when we evaluate alternative courses of action. This position asserts that all decisions literally are gut-level decisions. Damascio (1999) goes so far as to say that consciousness only occurs when we perceive a bodily change in response to the environment. A sociologist, Jack Katz (1999), talks about emotion not only as having obvious visceral concomitants (e.g., a quickened heart rate when we are anxious) but as occurring when we shift attention from the external world to our bodily self. He notes that embarrassment epitomizes this since it wrenches us away from our ongoing, objective pursuit, and toward our physical self, such that we want to hide our face, if not our entire being. The fundamental concept of temperament principally describes bodily-oriented aspects of personality, such as excitability (Chess & Thomas, 1996).

Embodiment and the inextricable connection of body with mind, I suggest, also is central to understanding the thought that underlies conversation. Internal multi-sensory-motor-visceral representation is an essential fact of all mental life. Ivan Pavlov, the renown Russian psychologist, began his famous animal conditioning experiments because he noticed that his experimental dogs began salivating as soon as they heard their food-toting handlers arriving. Pavlov knew that salivation was the physical component of the dogs' mental anticipation that "meat powder" soon would be placed in their mouths. The Pavlovian studies showed that, at minimum, vague thoughts comprised of multi-sensory-motor-visceral components move at least some animals toward sources of GBH. Multi-sensory-motor-visceral thought also steers the overt behavior by which people attempt to achieve both body/mind and mind/body GBH. We readily appreciate that people think in every sensory modality. You can think about the *feel* of whacking your crazy bone, or the *taste* of chocolate ice cream. In fact, most thought is highly integrate as well as multi-sensory-motor-visceral. When you think about barbecued chicken, you very well might see it, smell it, hear it sizzling, and imagine yourself standing by the grill discussing baseball with your family. When you see, smell, and hear 4th of July fireworks in your mind, many of the same neural circuits "light up" as they do when you do actually see the sights, smell the smells, and hear the sounds at the real event. The multi-sensory-motor-visceral impressions that constitute this and all thoughts exist simultaneously, in parallel. However, because of the limited capacity of our working memory, a serial processor that enables us to focus on only one to nine "chunks" of information at a time, we only are consciously aware of a small fraction of the total thought gestalt.

Mental Representation

Like animals, humans strive selfishly and relentlessly toward internal GBH and toward environmental situations that cue GBH. And, like animals, people are subject to powerful conditioning forces. Unlike animals, we have language which we can employ to mitigate conditioning influences and selfishness, on the one hand, or to amplify them on the other.

Language is so automatic and ubiquitous in our daily lives that we rarely think about it in the abstract. Only in extraordinary situations does the significance of language become an issue. Travel to a foreign country is one such situation, especially when we cannot speak the native tongue. At that time, we become acutely aware that language powerfully determines communication.

But while language's communicative function is central to our social competency, there is an even more fundamental language function—that of language representation. Before we can understand how language communication affects GBH strivings, we must first understand mental representation, self-other representation, and language representation.

Bickerton (1990) describes representation as a physiologically-encoded awareness of experience in response to a perceived stimulus of any kind. He sees each awareness as a pattern of neurological activity, a kind of neuropsychological map and says that some features of a species' "primary representational system" (PRS) are phylogenetically-rooted, the result of its evolutionary heritage, while some are ontogenetically-rooted, the result of an individual's learning and experience. Bickerton means that a mental representation is an organically-based, sensory-motor-visceral, reliably repeatable, neurological experience that coincides with perception of a stimulus whether the stimulus is an internal or external aspect of the individual or of the environment, and that some of these neurological experience-stimulus equivalences are inborn and some are acquired. An organism can have a mental representation of its own beating heart or of its entire being, of a fluttering leaf or a swaying tree. Awareness is achieved because the organism, more or less reliably, perceives co-occurrence of its own patterned neurological activity in the presence of the internal or external referent with which it is associated.

We are speaking here of the basic life processes of interoception and exteroperception. Interoception refers to unconscious and/or conscious awareness of what is going on inside the boundary of our skin, including awareness of our body (muscles, viscera, and so forth) and of our thoughts and feelings. Exteroception refers to unconscious and/or conscious awareness of what is going on outside the boundary of our skin, including awareness of the inanimate and animate environment, awareness dependent on information coming to us through our sensory receptors, such as through our eyes and ears.

Life depends on coordinated, integrated intero- and exteroception. Through interoception we are alerted to internal needs that must be satisfied for us to survive and thrive. Through exteroception we are alerted to external, environmental resources suitable for facilitating health, growth, and self-enhancement. Interoceptive and exteroceptive scanning are simultaneous and continuous. When the interoceptive focus – typically prompted by our body, thoughts, and feelings – occurs coincident with an environmental target related to the focus, the target's GBH value is assessed and the target is tagged accordingly, prompting approach or avoidance. The entire process is mostly unconscious and automatic, although conscious and deliberate elements can be involved as well. Thus, we are motivated to act volitionally when interoceptive awareness of internal need coincides in time with exteroceptive awareness of external environmental resources offering the possibility of need satisfaction.

All interoceptively and exteroceptively guided activity is multi-sensory-motor-visceral: visceral because we literally are driven by "gut-reactions," including our hormonal fluctuations and emotions, and we have gut-reactions to that which we experience; motor because we use our muscles to act upon ourselves and upon the world, and because our muscles relax and tense in response to our experiences; and sensory because our sensory receptors are always sampling the environment and always adjusting to it.

As we shall see, body, environment, thought, and feeling (BETF) are four essential, constant targets and influences of mental life. The inside-the-skin awareness is awareness of the body, thoughts, and feelings and the outside-the-skin awareness is awareness of the environment. We are always being affected by BETF and always striving to derive satisfaction from them. BETF press continually upon our minds, virtually burning their associated experiences into our neurological circuits. It is because our nervous systems are hard-wired for continuous intero- and exteroceptive scanning that mental representation can occur. The concept of multi-sensory-motor-visceral representation, then, assumes that mental experiences occur as the result of a holistic, mostly unconscious process of relentless scanning, interoception, exteroception, and good-bad evaluative tagging.

Bickerton points out that not just people but virtually all animals, even insects, are capable of at least simple, short-lived mental representations, such as ones coincident with a fleeting perception. Hobson and Leonard (2001) agree that animals are capable of mental representation, although they refer to representations as elements of consciousness, as follows:

> "If we go back to our definition of consciousness as awareness of information processed by the brain, we can see why thought isn't needed. For your brain processes lots of things -vision, hearing, language, thought, emotion, and so forth- of which thought is only one. You can be aware of any of these items, but you need not be aware of any particular one to be conscious. Blind people and deaf people are conscious, and so are people when they are startled by lightning flashes, consumed with rage, or serving tennis balls—not just when they are engaged in higher thought."

> Of course, accepting this definition implies that virtually all other creatures are conscious too. That's because nearly all have some sort of brain, and nearly all act as well-coordinated individuals. So nearly all must have some brain system that registers awareness of what the brain is finding and manages a unified response. That means humans, apes, and dolphins are not alone. Dogs and cats are conscious; so are mice; and so are snakes and rats. Indeed, according to our definition it seems likely that even cockroaches are conscious.

> That doesn't necessarily affect our regard for any of these creatures, because the nature of any creature's consciousness depends on the nature of its brain.

> For example, one cannot imagine a consciousness employing language as we
> know it that does not possess the ability to make internal speech."

Hence, a fly may represent you merely as a large, looming, nonfly, nonfood
visual image. And once you are gone, presumably, so is his representation of you.
In that case, Terrence Deacon (1998) would describe the fly's representation as
an "icon"—the least elaborate representational token—to be contrasted with the
more information-rich "index" and the most information-rich "symbol." In Deacon's words,

> "When we say that something is "iconic" of something we usually mean that
> there is a resemblance that we notice. Landscapes, portraits, and pictures are
> all iconic of what they depict. When we say that something is an "index" we
> mean that it is somehow linked to something else, or associated with it in time
> and space. A thermometer indicates the temperature of water, a weathervane
> indicates the direction of the wind, and a disagreeable odor might indicate the
> presence of a skunk...Finally, when we say something is a symbol, we mean
> there is some social convention, tacit agreement, or explicit code which estab-
> lishes the relationship that links one thing to the other. A wedding ring sym-
> bolizes a marital agreement the typographical letter 'e' symbolizes a particular
> sound (or, sometimes, as in English, what should be done to the other
> sounds); and taken together, the words of this sentence symbolize a particular
> idea or set of ideas."

As far as we know, only humans can think symbolically. Non-human living
creatures are restricted to representations at the iconic and indexical levels.
Accordingly, the most basic mental representation of the simplest creature would
be an iconic representation of itself and non-self. Kendrick and his associates
(2001) demonstrate that a sheep, a mammal derided for its "stupidity," is capable
of iconically representing and remembering over 50 other sheep faces for periods
in excess of 2 years. Ruys and Schilling (2002) believe that Jackdaws (European
crows) iconically can represent its essential relationships as enemy versus companion – a good versus bad distinction—and its companions as flight companion,
love companion, and mother companion.

Please be aware that despite the term "icon," iconic representations need not
be visual. The critical condition is "a resemblance that we notice" and one that is
essentially static. The resemblance could be in any and many sensory modalities.
Rather than seeing in our mind's eye, we could hear in our mind's ear, feel in our
mind's hand, and so forth. An insect might dimly "sense' or "feel" where it begins
and ends and where a salient feature of the environment does.

Representations are the tokens of thought. We think by apprehending, evaluating, juxtaposing, comparing, and contrasting one or more mental representations with one or more other mental representations. What matters for representation is not how objectively well a representation matches the object that it represents; what matters is the extent to which an organism **perceives** similarity between the referent being represented and the mental representation itself (Gardenfors, 1998). On the human level, someone visually impaired might misperceive a coat rack for a person and ask that "person" a question in a manner absolutely identical to how he would have asked the question had the rack been a real person.

Stephen Kosslyn (1994) contends that mental representation evolved with perception. While asserting that this co-evolution probably occurred in all sensory modalities, to illustrate, he mentions that the contemporaneous development of visual representation and visual perception permitted organisms adaptively to "imagine" seeing obstructed portions of physically present objects, as when a monkey "sees" an entire lion although only the very top if its ears and head are visible in a cluster of dense bush. Zorzi, Priftis, and Umilta (2002) espouse an isomorphism of the visual mental image and visual perception by showing that stroke patients who are deficient in their ability to use a pencil to bisect a physically-present number line also are deficient in their ability to decide the bisection point of a mentally imagined number line. The intimate connection of mental representation to perception and even to action is supported by research finding that mentally imagined auditory images tend to disrupt auditory perception more so than visual perception and that the reverse is true for visual images (Kosslyn, 1994) and that verbal responses occur at a faster rate to an auditory stimulus than to a visual one (Elsner and Hommel, 2001). In a remarkable experiment, Carmena and associates (2003) show that macaque monkeys, with implanted brain electrodes connected to a brain-machine interface, can learn to use a robotic arm to reach and grasp virtual objects on a computer screen, presumably by thinking the required physical actions.

Like physical actions, mental representations are constructed in context, meaning that they have spatial and temporal aspects, assembled from elements of contemporaneous intero- and exteroceptive experiences. To say that mental representation is constructed is to imply that it depends on characteristics of the constructing person. The mental representation that I create must be different from the mental representation that you create, since our mental representations reflect our idiosyncratic physiologies, experiences, and attitudes. Moreover, because mental representation is constructed, it is constructed at a particular place and point in time. The mental representation that I construct today can not be identical to the mental representation that I will create next month, because I will not be the same then; my body, experiences, and attitudes will have changed to some extent, and the mental representation that I construct will change accordingly.

So, mental representation is always interoceptive-exteroceptive, context-specific, and always constructed rather than merely recalled or summoned. Elements of the construction of a given mental representation are recruited from a limited array of accessible multi-sensory-motor-visceral impressions. For instance, when I mentally represent my car, I recruit from a particular pool of multi-sensory-motor-visceral impressions (e.g., blue, cozy, responsive, and warm) and not from others (e.g., red, cold, unresponsive, and inhospitable). That is, the elements recruited are not a random sample of all elements potentially available to me. The mental representation is never just exteroceptive-sensory, not even when a stationary, inanimate object is depicted. The mental representation always has some interoceptive-motor-visceral elements because, at minimum, motor-visceral elements are extant within me, influencing the way that I form the representation, and motor-visceral elements comprise a part of my reaction to that which I am mentally representing, including both the target item and its context. The "body language" that accompanies conversation is an observable motor-visceral concomitant of mental representations underlying that which we say to ourselves and to others, and our reactions to that which we hear from others.

To reiterate and underscore my basic position: Despite laboratory studies of single-type mental representations, such as experiments that purportedly involve only an isolated visual or auditory "image," I contend that real-world experience is contextualized, multi-sensory-motor-visceral. When we mentally represent, the mental representation does not exist as a picture from a gallery in our mind. We do not search for the one immutable picture that expresses our idea and then gaze passively at it. Rather, a mental representation is akin to a mental meal created from an unlimited buffet of foods displayed on tables. We wander from table to table, choosing each morsel. Some morsels are chosen for their taste, others for their smell, texture, sound, "crunch quality," visual presentation, or other multi-sensory-motor-visceral qualities. The meal that is our mental representation is an aggregated collection of chosen relevant morsels laid out in the appropriate quantity and in the appropriate position upon the plate of our minds. We actively ruminate our mental meal to make it digestible.

If I were to ask you to consciously mentally represent something as mundane as a dog, you would not just "see" a dog in your mind, as though it were an inert, prototypic line drawing on an otherwise blank page of a book. Considering only the visual aspect of the representation first, the dog would have an orientation – such as facing toward or away from you and his image would suggest a particular level of motor tension – such as alert or relaxed. The dog probably would be perceived in some kind of setting – outdoors or indoors. You also might imagine the dog in motion. In addition to these visual-motor aspects, the dog mental representation could involve his odor, fur texture, friendliness or aggressiveness, bark, or other distinctive multi-sensory-motor-visceral characteristics. Equally important, your mental representation of a dog includes you – your experiences and attitudes regarding dogs. In the process of mentally representing a dog, you actively, mostly unconsciously, select multi-sensory-motor-visceral bits and pieces of impressions consistent with your dog experiences and attitudes. You make your selection in accordance with your mental state at that moment in time. If you are feeling angry, you might mentally represent an aggressive, snarling dog confronting you, or a defenseless, cowering one that you could kick. Your initial efforts toward developing an incipient composite mental representation also affect your physical and mental self. To think of a dog, for instance, could cause you to undergo increased or decreased motor tension, more or less emotional positivity, and so forth, and those personal changes can instigate further modifications to the final form that the mental representation takes. Your mental representation of a dog, then, is a multi-sensory-motor-visceral amalgam of the imagined dog and of you at the time that you fashion the representation.

It is critically important to realize that in our day-to-day lives we do not represent a single sensory impression – not a single, static mental picture or single, denotative mental word. We mentally represent ideas. We don't think "dog;" rather, we think "wild dog," "friendly dog," "dog following me,' or "dog on the step." Our thoughts are more like mental phrases than individual words. But, strictly speaking, mental representations are neither words nor phrases. Words and phrases are vehicles that abstract out knowable features of multi-sensory-motor-visceral mental representations that we use in our private, including unconscious, thoughts and in our public communications with others. Language helps us combine relevant bits and pieces of a mental representation, bringing an interoceptive-exteroceptive mental experience to consciousness so that it can facilitate our GBH search.

We live by, and therefore converse by, these multi-sensory-motor-visceral mental representations. When people chat, each contributes her language-abstracted, multi-sensory-motor-visceral representations such that what emerges is a synergistic co-constructed dialogue revealing both the uniqueness and consistency of the conversants as individuals and as members of a conversing dyad. We will have much more to say about this later.

To summarize this section, all overt action and all mental representation proceeds from multi-sensory-motor-visceral intero- and exteroception that includes the self as well as the object (s) being acted upon or being mentally represented. This is true for opening a letter, watching television, painting a door, driving a car, thinking about work, daydreaming, or conversing with a friend. The essential lesson of our discussion can be distilled to a single sentence that should be meaningful and memorable to you now: We register, represent, and respond to evaluatively-tagged interoceptive inside-the skin and exteroceptive outside-the-skin experiences in a holistic, multi-sensory-motor-visceral, self-oriented way that is automatic and inevitable.

Self-Other Representation

The primordial mental representation of all creatures is self versus nonself. Self-representation consists of a multitude of sensory-motor-visceral awarenesses—awarenesses that internal sensations, physical movements, and body parts and boundaries are mine. Once the self is represented, the nonself is represented by default as everything that is not part of the self. This is not to say that animals have a self concept, enabling them to be aware of their past and of anticipating their future. But mobile animals, at minimum, must have sufficient self-nonself awareness to move consistently and adaptively through space, and animals that mate must be able to represent members of their own species and to differentiate them sexually.

Referring specifically to human representation, Steven Pinker (1999) suggests that cognition flourishes partly due to our having inherited the primate visual system which split "...the visual flow of information into two streams: a 'what' system, for objects and their shapes and compositions, and a 'where' system, for their locations and motions." I would add that the "what" system began with the self-nonself distinction and the "where" system began with the here-there distinction: a self that could approach or withdraw from the nonself. Newberg and D'Aquili (2001) believe that this self-in-environment capability is located in the "orientation association area" of the brain's neocortex within the posterior parietal lobe.

Even a dim awareness of self–versus-nonself provides a creature the opportunity to make finer discriminations critical for survival. Quin and Eimas (1997) review research illustrating that for human beings these self-nonself representations begin in infancy as perceptually-based, just as all animal-based self-nonself representations are, but that for people they gradually progress to conceptually-based representations. Spelke (2000) also sees animal to human representational continuity followed by animal-human differentiation, believing that the most complex cognitive skills of human beings are an outgrowth of very basic underlying "core knowledge systems" which she defines as

> "...mechanisms for representing and reasoning about particular kinds of eco-logically important entities and events- including inanimate, manipulable objects and their motions, persons and their actions, places in the continuous spatial layout and their Euclidean geometric relations, and numerosities and numerical relationships. These systems serve to build representations of objects persons, places, and numerosities that encompass quite abstract prop-erties and relationships, such as the persistence of objects over occlusion (objects whose mental representation remains despite their having been hid-den from view) and the goals of perceivable acts. Infants' core systems appear to be very similar to those of many nonhuman animals, suggesting that they have a long evolutionary history."

Language Representation: Verbal Contents of the Mind

A human being always has a host of multi-sensory-motor-visceral mental repre-sentations in the form of icons, indexes, and symbols swimming about in her mind. But while our thoughts are multi-sensory-motor-visceral, the most elabo-rate ones most often are visual and auditory. The very architecture of our brain, in fact, attests to the special significance of the visual and auditory senses – each of which have been estimated to engage about 40 percent of the brain when actively processing information (Whitlock, 1998). Of these two special senses, vision is the more private and personal. Despite our scientific advances, we can-not determine whether your visual experiences are the same as mine, not even whether the green that you see is the same green that I see. At the level of thought, the idiosyncratic nature of the visual image is even more pronounced. If I ask two persons to "think about" a car, one might conjure up the visual equiva-lent of a boxy stick figure while the other sees the most detailed image of a Ferrari 360 Modena with dual air intakes, wire wheels, Connolly leather seats, and 40 valves. The more elaborate the personal visual image, the more difficult it is to communicate this picture to someone using only visual means. Only an artist can come close to adequately expressing the rich details of her visual thoughts.

Raw auditory images are no more communicable than are raw visual images. Do you and I hear the very same robin song? Who knows? However, there is a special class of auditory images uniquely suited for intra-personal and inter-personal communication—language. Many animals can see, smell, hear, and integrate their sensory impressions as well or better than we, but, as far as we know, they do not have language-based capabilities.

While not provable at this time, it is reasonable to believe that one must first be able to use language to mentally represent to oneself before being able to communicate with others via conventional, sophisticated verbal language. The words of a language can function as icons, indexes, and/or symbols. But words are the quintessential symbols and it is at the symbolic level that they confer greatest representational advantage. This is so because a symbol readily can condense enormous information into a manageable mental survival-enhancing instrument.

As we said earlier, vision and hearing are special senses that account for the overwhelming majority of our survival-relevant information processing. At the sensory level, vision is limited to one less-than-180 degree scene at a time oriented in the direction that we are facing, and each time that we blink the scene disappears. By contrast, we are capable of simultaneously hearing all the sounds within our human capability at 360 degrees, and hearing is always "on-line," whether we like it or not. At the representational level, when I view a scene, such as a scene populated by apple trees, my associations tend to be (but need not necessarily be) concretely-linked to what I am seeing. Though suitable for indexical or symbolic thought, visual scenes are biased toward iconic representation. On the other hand, words provide abstract representation as readily as concrete representation. An abstract word, such as "agriculture," evokes limitless associations that can generate limitless thoughts and associated GBH strivings.

Language representation, of course, is not merely hearing representation. Effective language representation occurs only among humans who are spoken to by language-competent others. Because receptive ability precedes expressive ability developmentally, infants presumably employ some primitive internal language representation before being able to communicate with others. We will have much more to say about language acquisition in the section entitled "Conversation as Self-Talk." For now, consider that young children regularly talk aloud to themselves and this is prima facie evidence for internally-directed, private speech. Children, as adults, talk principally to pursue their GBH goals and they begin by practicing on themselves before being able to communicate with others.

Language Communication: From Thoughts to Conversation is So Degrading

The richness of our shared, verbal language, the elaborate way in which we can transmit our thoughts by it, profoundly separates us from every living creature. Although language begins as internal representation, this is internal representation uniquely suitable for sharing. An individual's words, phrases, or sentences are communication only when spoken aloud to and embraced by someone who can respond to them. When private, personal language representations become publicly shared language communications, their power to promote personal GBH grows exponentially and the communicating person literally has the power to change the course of history.

But given the multi-sensory-motor-visceral complexity of thought, imagine the challenge that conversation presents to us. We must abstract out from the totality of our thought gestalt some kernel to express in words. If you ask me, "So how was your trip to Italy?" what shall I say? Your comment sends an electric-like charge through my body and mind. Instantly, I re-experience Florence—Michelangelo's David, Raphael's Madonnas, Boboli Gardens, Piazza della Signoria, Palazzo Vecchio…A thousand thoughts compete for attention. What shall I say?

My decision primarily will be made unconsciously and immediately. As always, my conversation, like yours, will proceed from an automatic tendency to use discourse to satisfy my current needs for GBH. It will be based on what I am able to comfortably say at that precise moment, and on what I believe you are willing and capable of receiving at that precise moment.

The link between language as representation and as communication is especially important regarding the thought-to-conversation transition. The "audience design hypothesis" (Clark and Murphy, 1982) suggests that a speaker mentally represents information differently if when initially exposed to it he believes that he will use the information in conversation than he does if he believes he will not be doing so.

The better I know you, the longer and more refined our conversational relationship, and the more I anticipate that I will be discussing a topic with you, the more adequately I will be able to speak with you on that topic. But in the grand scheme of things, my remarks always are an anemic distillation of my thoughts. Whether verbalized outwardly as social communication or merely internally-directed as private speech, the richness of mental experience necessarily is degraded when it is condensed into an exclusively verbal code. It is when we make a conscious, deliberate attempt to speak our multi-sensory-motor-visceral thoughts aloud – such as when we wish to express our condolences to the loved one of a deceased person—that we realize how inadequate words are. Consider the proverbial brilliant scientist who is an incompetent teacher. His thoughts are an intricate amalgam of equations, scenes, charts, graphs, time sequences, weights, tones, symbols, definitions, and phrases, each element articulating with the other to form a coherent gestalt. It is his ability to amalgamate the multi-sensory-motor-visceral components coherently that makes him extraordinary. He cannot communicate his complicated ideas verbally for the same reason that he is brilliant – apparently disparate and disconnected mental representations integrate seamlessly and unconsciously in his mind.

Basic Body Structures, Basic Mental Structures

As discussed previously, to survive, an animal capable of moving about the environment, at minimum, must be able to differentiate self from nonself. Having categorized something as nonself, the organism then has a choice: If the target of perception is static, the perceiving animal has the luxury of approaching or withdrawing at its own pace. If the target is moving, the perceiving animal must approach or withdraw with dispatch. To adaptively choose either to move toward or away, the perceiving animal needs to enact an elementary "valuing process" – a good versus bad assessment of the target that had been perceived through the senses. Scherer (1984) concurs with this position, strongly asserting that all organisms must perform some at least elementary evaluation of their environment.

Strange as it may sound, strictly speaking, the valuing process is applied not to a sensory target per se, but to an individual organism's mental representation of a sensory target. Thus, animals ascribe value to their mental icons and indexes and humans ascribe value to their mental icons, indexes, and symbols. Most important for considering conversation, words, our most powerful and most frequently employed symbols, have value attached to them. Some words are biased toward good or bad connotations due to the very structure of language and others are so biased because cultures sanction some words as good and others as bad. But, in the end, the good-bad value of a word for an individual is determined by that person based upon her own unique experiences: it is the indiveme aspect of a word that ultimately dictates whether a word connotes good, favoring approach, or bad, promoting withdrawal.

In describing the valuing process, I am postulating a basic mental structure across animal minds similar to that which has been found regarding basic animal body structure. Nobel-Prizewinners Edward B. Lewis, Christiane Nusslein-Volhard, and Eric F. Wiechaus and their associates (1995) recently demonstrated that specific genes control early embryonic development across most animal species. They showed that "hox genes," master gene regulators, control the basic body plan of the overwhelming majority of animals on earth – that basic body development control mechanisms are virtually the same from insects through the phylogenetic scale all the way "up" to people. Even more astounding, Walter Gehring (2002) demonstrated transferability of gene regulator control from one species to another when he removed the eye-development gene of a mouse, transplanted it into a fruit fly, and the fruit fly grew a fruit fly eye.

Ehret and Riecke (2002) extended the notion of a basic body plan to a basic communication plan, discovering that the vocal calls of baby mice to their mothers contain three separate tones of different frequencies, sound characteristics similar to the pattern of human vowel sounds. Moreover, with mice, as with humans, the lowest frequency of the three tones was found to be most essential for baby and mother mice to understand their communication.

These and a host of other studies strongly support the notion that a basic body plan, and, perhaps a basic communication plan, exists in the animal kingdom, and that the specifics of animal body construction, and perhaps of animal communication, are mere elaborations of the basic plans.

Analogously, the valuing process, I contend, is an across-the-animal-kingdom basic mental plan, like the basic body plan or basic communication plan, that guides all volitional behavior, and some non-volitional behavior as well. Animals ascribe good versus bad value to targets, triggering approach or avoidance. It is value that couples an animal to the target of its perceptual search; the target becomes reinforcing or threatening only in accordance with the value that the animal has assigned to it. In every instance of self-nonself discrimination, from those of insects to humans, volitional action does not proceed until the valuing process has concluded and a good-bad, approach-avoid decision, whether conscious or unconscious, has been made. The valuing process has as its end a decision that promotes life, health, and GBH.

For "lower" animals, some sensory targets might be hard-wire encrypted as "good" or "bad" and, thus, automatically elicit life-enhancing approach or avoidance by way of a limited repertoire of relatively rigid, fixed behavioral patterns – such as we find with "instinctual" behavior. Humans, however, have more varied options. Bickerton (1990) mentions that the human capacity for emotion frees us from most immediate stimulus-response connections. We can perceive a stimulus, delay, experience an emotion, and then respond.

A person's ability to delay assigning value, itself, can become destructive, however. Preschoolers, obsessive compulsives, and persons experiencing extreme stress sometimes ruminate about a good-bad decision to the point that he does not respond to the target with adequate dispatch. GBH becomes thwarted by a paralysis of indecision. Iyengar and Lepper (2000) suggest that good-bad decisions become especially taxing and protracted when "abundant options" are available. In such cases, emotion that could have been adaptive becomes maladaptive instead.

Although human beings unconsciously process experience simultaneously along parallel, multi-sensory-motor-visceral channels, the conscious mind is a serial processor, focusing on one limited part of the totality of the available information at a time. The valuing process functions as a basic mental component of human consciousness by reducing complex experience to a form amenable to a simple good-bad judgment. This is true whether the target of evaluation is inanimate or animate. In contrast to all other animals, humans alone also are capable of becoming aware of their own value as an elaboration of the action tendency toward or away from an environmental target. People, in effect, can take themselves as a target, a self-directed valuing process by which we tag our own behavior, including our verbal behavior or our entire being, as "good" and, therefore, to be approached (developed, exhibited) or "bad," to be avoided (rejected, secreted).

Words and Thoughts: Valenced and Automatic

Language and Valuing

As we implied above, to move toward the life-enhancing and away from the life-threatening, animals must have some elementary ability to recognize and to differentiate the good from the bad – to make valenced judgments. The philosopher Simon Blackburn (2001) agrees that the ascription of value is an essential feature of consciousness, itself. I would say of life, itself. The valuing process comes to us along with muscles, bone, and blood, as part of our animal inheritance. Valuing is synonymous with living in that it is the mechanism that directs life's volitional movements.

If language is a secondary method for both sensing and moving, it is subject to the same survival-enhancing requirements as physical, primary sensing and moving. Just as physically-based multi-sensory-motor-visceral impressions must be coded as good-bad in order to adaptively guide physically-based movements, language-based impressions need to be coded as good-bad so that language-based movements can be taken that will promote survival. It is perhaps for that reason that words, our most important and informative symbols, have at their core a pervasive and powerful evaluative dimension that profoundly influences our experience of the physical and social world.

The evaluative, or connotative, dimension of words contrasts with the denotative dimension. The latter has the dictionary as its principal accuracy arbiter. Any Merriam-Webster readily can provide the denotative definition of "mother." To communicate with any degree of reliability, we tacitly must accept some basic denotative features of "mother." But this word, and the overwhelming majority of words, has innumerable connotations as well. For some persons, "mother" is a virtual god; for others, she's the devil. Bartsch (2002) suggests that associations within the connotative dimension are organized around self- interest whereas associations in the denotative realm are organized in terms of feature sharing. By this reasoning we would expect that an individual's connotative associates of mother proceed from his experiences and feelings about how a mother has treated him and an individual's denotative associates of mother depend upon how closely the associated word matches dictionary-based defining features of mother such as "woman,' age relative to me, kinship, and so forth.

Extensive intra-cultural and cross-cultural research has affirmed that the good-bad continuum of connotative meaning is the single most powerful non-denotative dimension for explaining the significance of words, accounting for two-thirds of the variance between people (Osgood, 1957). That is, we automatically perceive most words as connoting something good or bad and there is substantial, although certainly not perfect, agreement about the affective valance of a given word across people. This, of course, is generally not true for syntactic function words such as "of," and "by" which, when seen isolated from context, are relatively connotation-free.

To better understand the connotative dimension of words, let's consider a small, informal experiment in which seven women (w1 through w7) and three men (m1 through m3) evaluated the words religion, salesman, clamor, siege, aroma, soft, music, steep, military, settled, Algeria, and snow. They were instructed to "rate the following words on a 7 point scale in which 7 represents 'good' and 1 represents 'bad'." No other directions were given and no one expressed any reservation about performing the task. As the chart means listed below indicate, the subjects rated music and aroma as most good, and siege and clamor as least good. The greatest evaluative agreement among the raters, as represented by the smallest standard deviation (sd), a measure of average variability, occurred for the word "music," and the least evaluative agreement, as represented by the largest standard deviation, occurred for the word "siege."

word	w1	w2	w3	w4	w5	w6	w7	m1	m2	m3	avg.	sd
religion	7	6	7	5	6	4	4	6	7	7	5.57	1.20
salesman	3	5	4	5	4	2	4	2	2	7	3.8	1.62
clamor	4	4	2	3	3	5	4	2	2	6	3.5	1.35
siege	1	7	4	2	1	1	3	1	2	7	2.9	2.38
aroma	7	7	4	7	7	6	7	6	7	7	6.5	0.97
soft	7	5	5	6	7	2	7	6	7	5	5.7	1.57
music	7	7	7	7	7	6	7	6	7	7	6.8	0.42
steep	1	4	4	7	4	6	7	2	4	3	4.2	1.99
military	7	4	4	6	4	4	4	2	4	6	4.5	1.43
settled	7	6	6	6	6	3	4	6	5	7	5.6	1.26
Algeria	4	4	4	6	4	4	4	3	4	5	4.2	0.79
snow	4	6	5	7	6	5	7	5	5	7	5.7	1.06

You could reasonably argue that any of the above listed words could represent something either good or bad. Music, the most favorably rated word, could be bad, if it is rap or classical, depending on your preference. Siege, the least favorably rated word, could be good, if it leads to a tyrant being deposed. In fact, as the chart shows, two persons rated "siege" as a 7, the maximal good score, while four persons rated it as a 1, the maximal bad score.

It also is possible that the affective valence of a word could change. The word 'skiing' might readily bring to mind tremendously positive connotations for you before, but perhaps not after, you suffer a compound fracture on the slopes. Yes, it is true; any word can represent something good or bad, and affective valences can change. It's a matter of indivemes within baseline consciousness, the latter being an inexorable river of thoughts and feelings that flows ceaselessly through our minds.

Baseline Consciousness

For our purposes, baseline consciousness refers to thoughts and feelings, derived from multi-sensory-motor-visceral representations, that stream through our mind when we make no effort to direct it. Thus, baseline consciousness designates the specific mental content that we inadvertently are processing and reacting to at any given moment. When external sensory impressions are minimized, as when we lie quietly, we can become aware of some mental representations within base-line consciousness. Mazoyer and colleagues (2001) have demonstrated by neu-ropsychological imagining (PET scan) and self-report that persons at rest with eyes closed evidence as much or more brain activity than they do when deliber-ately engaged in mental calculation or mental imagery. The subjects of the study, for instance, mentioned spontaneous occurrence of autobiographical memory and inner speech.

The content that is baseline consciousness includes elements of our cognitive and emotional mind that currently are active. Mental representations that are recent, primary, or salient in our physical or mental economies most powerfully affect our baseline consciousness and are most likely to instigate conscious thoughts and/or feelings.

Some constituents of baseline consciousness cycle through frequently because they are essential to physical survival; food related thoughts and feelings are an example. Other constituents cycle through frequently because they are necessary for basic emotional or mental well-being; thoughts concerning social status exem-plify this. Mental representations that persist signify an ongoing concern or goal. But some constituents of baseline consciousness have no enduring value, passing through infrequently or perhaps only once. These could be thoughts or feelings associated with a minimally interesting or fleeting impression, as when we think about a colorful bird that zips across our visual field. We use the term "perma-nent residents" for content frequently present in baseline consciousness; "day-trippers" for those that remain for a significant but limited time; and "passers-by" for those that stay only briefly.

Baseline consciousness is basic mentation, exerting its influence every second of our lives, whether we are awake or asleep. Regarding the latter, Nikles and associates (1998) show that nocturnal dream content can be influenced by wak-ing suggestions, but only when the suggestions involve issues of current concern to the individual being influenced. Cartwright, Newell, and Mercer (2001) find that the dreams of clinically depressed persons contain more negative affect and negative affect of higher intensity than do the dreams of those who are not clini-cally depressed. Stickgold (2002) asserts, "I think sleep is involved in rehearsing, restructuring, and reclassifying our existing world-view to allow us to function better," a clear endorsement of baseline consciousness as relentless and critical. And Watson (2001) unambiguously links thoughts while awake with thoughts while asleep when he says that there is evidence to support "…a *continuity* model of human consciousness: People who are prone to interesting, vivid, and unusual experiences during the day also tend to have them at night (see

Blagrove & Hartnell, 2000 ; Claridge et al., 1997 ; Watson, 2001b)." In short, day and night thought processes are inextricably linked and baseline consciousness is a primary determinant of both.

Imagine yourself home alone secluded in your favorite chair – no radio, television, or other distractions. If you let your mind wander, baseline consciousness becomes manifest in thoughts and/or feelings that spontaneously arise concerning, among other issues, your body, environment, mood, most recent activities, current aspirations, or persons and things important to you; they continue in baseline consciousness when they are associated with GBH strivings.

That which frequents your baseline consciousness is that which has cathexis or value to you. Do you often spontaneously think about music? If you do, music frequently is invested with cathexis. During conversation you are more inclined to introduce topics from baseline consciousness that have high cathetic value and the discussion of which you expect can result in GBH. Thoughts and feelings connected to primary reinforcers flow within the baseline consciousness of most of us and exemplify content common to human mentation. On the other hand, some elements of baseline consciousness are highly idiosyncratic, reflecting what is unique about individuals. For instance, Nobel Prize-winning chemist Richard Smalley in *Technology Review* (2001) discloses contents of his personal baseline consciousness that both set him apart from you and me and that drive him conversationally when he says, "I have to admit that I'm just obsessed about carbon nanotubes. It's hard for me to go for more than ten minutes without talking about them. I think they are the coolest thing…"

I underscore baseline consciousness at this point in our discussion precisely because it operates inadvertently and silently in collusion with directed thought while the latter typically gets full credit for ideas and conversations that are expressed overtly. Baseline consciousness provides raw associations that must be refined in order to facilitate directed thought used in concentration, problem solving, and conversation. Unrefined baseline consciousness rarely is communicated because unrefined baseline consciousness is mostly incomprehensible to others. Rather, during communication, baseline consciousness and directed thought continually interact, reciprocally influencing each other. Especially in casual conversation, the discourse that emerges is more spontaneous and earthy when baseline consciousness predominates and more considered and intellectualized when directed consciousness does, but virtually all communication results from a blending of the two. Hupet, Chantraine, and Nef (1993) allude to the untoward consequences of a radical imbalance of the two modalities when they suggest that some conversation errors of normal, elderly adults are inadvertent intrusions of raw baseline consciousness elements into directed thought, a deficit in refining conversation-relevant associations and excluding conversation-irrelevant ones. Disorganized Schizophrenic speech discloses a similar failure to censor.

Over time, we all develop context-specific habits toward more baseline or more directed conversations – predilections, respectively, for more spontaneous or more deliberated self-expression. For example, we tend to have a characteristic way of responding to the inquiry, "What's happening?" When a stranger asks, my habitual, defensive response might be, "Nothing much." If pressed, I might choose by a very directed process to disclose some trivial fact about my day. On the other hand, when asked the same question by a significant other, I might say much of what is on my mind at that moment, even coming close to disclosing some relatively raw contents of baseline consciousness. The effect of habit on speaking behavior is not all or none, however. Habitual responses can be strung together with spontaneous ones. Since conversations typically contain some more baseline and some more directed features, when a stranger asks, "What's happening?" I might begin with directed, trivial facts, become comfortable, and eventually disclose some significant baseline issues, and with my significant other, I might begin with significant baseline issues, have second thoughts, and move toward directed, trivial facts. Ouellette and Wood (1998) imply that directed thought should predominate over baseline consciousness in contexts where speaking habits are not well established, because intention is necessary to guide non-habitual behavior and intention, by definition, is non-automatic.

The topics that a person introduces into conversation from baseline consciousness indicate what he pays attention to, what moves him, what he believes he has the ability to say, and what he trusts that you will accept from him. The more consonance between what conversational partners pay attention to, what moves them, what they believe they have the ability to say, and what they trust that each other will accept, the greater the chance that they will converse often and easily. The greater the consonance between partners, the more likely that a topic simultaneously is active in each person's baseline consciousness. To share topics in baseline consciousness is to be connected intimately with one another cognitively and/or emotionally. It is why spouses find themselves saying the same thing at the same time and why they remark to each other, "I was just about to say that!"

Flavell (1977) cautions, however, that baseline consciousness also can work at cross-purposes to communication because our own viewpoints and preoccupations, circulating within our minds, continually threaten to distort that which our partner says.

Baseline consciousness and GBH strivings reciprocally influence each other and conjointly determine directed thought and conversational choice. Consider the topic of food – a perennial favorite topic of human beings. Since food is a primary reinforcer, we all seek it to feel physical and/or mental GBH and the issue of food, therefore, often rattles around in our baseline consciousness. No one would be surprised to have her conversational partner bring up food (if you'll pardon the expression), such as by asking, "What are you having for dinner?" The GBH mental goal of the question can vary such as when:

> An obese person asks because food is his major, perhaps only, enduring, reliable route to feeling good (G/GBH)

> A tense person asks because she is attempting to avoid an anxiety-arousing topic that is being discussed at the moment. That is, she asks in order to feel better (B/GBH).

> A homemaker asks because he is preoccupied with planning the family meal – a mental homeostatic benefit H/GBH).

Homeostatic mental benefit occurs when an item in baseline consciousness is released and mental pressure is reduced – catharsis. It is a variation on the theme, "I have to talk about this or I'll explode." A drive toward homeostatic catharsis could cause people sometimes to talk about topics that superficially do not appear to offer promise of a "good" or "better" feeling, at least not in the short term. Homeostatic catharsis also offers one explanation for the compulsion of some people to confess a guilt-provoking thought that will not leave baseline consciousness.

In addition to catharsis, homeostatic mental benefit occurs when an individual actively maintains his modal level of mental stimulation or thought – the level of mental stimulation or thought to which he has acclimated. In the realm of global self-concept, "self-verification" describes an individual's efforts to maintain his general sense of self (Schwann, 1992). To do so, he might feel compelled to reject another person's comments about him, if the comments conflict with his customary overall conception of self, even if it means that he must continue to believe some global personally-accepted negative feature of self identity. Individuals can be driven to maintain mental homeostasis concerning more specific features of their personality as well. For instance, many psychologists believe that the basic components of personality involve relatively stable levels of personal openness, conscientiousness, extraversion, agreeableness, and anxiety (Saucier & Goldberg (1996), and that personalities high on the first four factors and low on the fifth one are personalities in relatively good mental health. Yet, some people become so accustomed to their own self-perceived standing on these factors that they not only resist acting outside their range, but they can not tolerate anyone suggesting that outside-the-range behavior is possible for them. They cannot rest cognitively or emotionally until their baseline mental representations of personal openness, conscientiousness, extraversion, agreeableness, or anxiety are affirmed, whether good or bad. Such persons want to be assured by others that their own overall personality and its specific constituents are as they believe they are: They need to say and to hear the words that confirm their concept of self identity.

Emotion-Word and Word-Emotion

Consider for a moment the multifaceted, fluid relationship that governs the denotative and connotative features of words in our mental lexicon. As a constant in mental life, emotion is a powerful factor in words. Some words clearly are emotion-words, words that describe feelings. These can be found in a standard thesaurus and include terms like angry, hatred, gloomy, love, compassion, and hopeful among many others. Psychologists have used emotion-words to explore the nature of emotions and of personality, pointing out that emotion-words and words to describe personality often are identical or at least very similar (Plutchik, 1997), as when we use the word "anxious" to describe a type of emotion or a type of person. The joint exploration of emotion and personality through words led to the discovery that emotions and personality characteristics can be related graphically by plotting a circular configuration which begins by placing two polar opposite terms on a diameter (Wiggins & Trobst, 1997). Then terms relevant to the bipolar dimension are added onto the circle's circumference such that adjacent terms are more similar to each other, and nonadjacent terms are progressively less similar to one another, as in the following example adapted from Wiggins (1959):

Dominant

Arrogant   Gregarious

Cold   **Warm**

Aloof   Unassuming

Submissive

The overwhelming majority of words have both denotative aspects that are relatively emotion-free and connotative aspects that at minimum have a good-bad quality to them. For instance, if one hears a non-emotion word, such as "chair," he likely will think about sitting, seat, couch, and so forth. But "chair" would more readily have the negative emotional connotation "death," if he just left San Quentin and the positive emotional connotation "prestige," if he just left an auditorium in which his colleague was elevated to the chairmanship of a professional organization.

Word association is a complex process. When we hear a word, it activates numerous associates not only of the word per se, but discrete sound units of the word (John-Steiner, 1985). Thus, if one hears "chairman" words related denotatively and connotatively to "chair" and to "man" are energized and, therefore, more quickly available to consciousness than they would have been prior to hearing "chairman." This at least partially explains why we can have slips of the tongue that represent phonemic or semantic variations of any part of the word that we had intended to say.

Between emotion words and words with minimal emotional denotations are words denoting relatively straight-forward non-emotional information but connoting rich emotional associations. One such word is "candle," a word whose associations we will explore later when we discuss a study using it. Denotatively, nothing could be blander than a candle – merely wax and wick. However, "candle" is rich in affective significance as indicated by such common sayings as "He couldn't hold a candle to her;" "If everyone lit just one little candle, what a bright world this would be;" and "She was a candle in the wind."

To better understand words and their associates, think of each word as being affixed to the top of a container partially filled with round spheres. An individual sphere represents an associate of the word. Association spheres in full conscious activation shine brightly; association spheres in baseline consciousness shine dimly; and association spheres in the unconscious do not shine at all. Some association spheres are denotative and are colored white. Some are connotative, with positively valenced words being green and negatively valanced words being red. The number of association spheres in a container is a quantitative measure of the associations to a target word. Common words, such as "chair" have many association spheres in their containers; uncommon words such as "cerebellum" have few. The closer the sphere is to the top of the container, the more accessible it is to our directed consciousness and the quicker it is reflected in our directed response to a target word. The closer to the bottom, the less accessible it is to our directed consciousness and the less quickly it is reflected in our directed response to a target word. Under ordinary conditions, words at the bottom of the container may not accessible at all to our directed consciousness.

Continuing the analogy, recall that the container is only partially filled. There is room for a remixing of the association spheres. A mental shake of the container might cause some more common association spheres to roll their way toward the bottom and some more uncommon association spheres to roll their way toward the top. Any personal thought, feeling, or experience could cause the realignment, such as was mentioned about visiting San Quentin or attending the inauguration of a chairman.

One very important caution must be introduced here: We have been talking about associations between words because the focus of this book is conversation and conversation uses words. Holism, however, requires us explicitly to state that associations are not merely verbal. Words do not link only to other words. Words are epiphenomenona. Always, always mental life consists of multi-sensory-motor-visceral elements, the gestalt of which is so complex and ineffable that it never could be expressed as words. When I say a word, it lights up your multi-sensory-motor-visceral mind, not just your verbal mind, and you sort through all the impressions available to you.

The Unconscious: Cognitive and Emotional

In the early to mid 20th Century, the Freudian unconscious was regarded as the repository of the overwhelming majority of our thoughts. Unconscious desires, it was said, determined most of our ideas and such ideas could not be accessed volitionally due to intrapsychic, emotionally-defensive barriers against the raw animal instincts – especially sexual and aggressive—that fueled them. This once popular notion lost favor, beginning in the 1960s. Instead, psychologists sought to explain thought in terms of rational processes, as by reference to computer models that demonstrated input-output relationships.

While computer models did help clarify some facets of deliberate, rational thought conducted in experimental settings, they were woefully weak in accounting for spontaneous, everyday thought and everyday conversation. The more that natural thought and language was investigated, the more undeniable became the central role of unconscious processes. But psychologists were reluctant to use the simple term "unconscious," considering it to be replete with unwanted Freudian-like connotations. Therefore, the term "cognitive unconscious" was coined to give respectability to the field.

Kiehlstrom and associates (1992) define the cognitive unconscious in terms of mental processes that cannot be brought into full awareness. They believe that the evidence for unconscious mental processing is uncontested, but suggest that controversy remains concerning the existence of unconscious mental contents. Thus, they accept that unconscious mental processes account for your ability effortlessly to drive an automobile while talking on your cell phone, but they question whether your unconscious thoughts or feelings about past events affect your current functioning. Theirs is a minority opinion, however. For instance, Erdelyi (1992) has no doubt that unconscious contents are powerful and pervasive. He particularly notes that inaccessible memories have "…far-reaching influences on the thoughts and behaviors of the unawares subject." Piatellit-Palmarini (1994) goes so far as to say that even the content of our most deliberated reasoning can be affected deleteriously by the unconscious mind. These "inevitable illusions," in fact, are common "mistakes of reason," misunderstandings that sometimes persist even after their errors are meticulously pointed out to us. For instance, the common reasoning error called probability blindness, reproduced in numerous studies, finds that people are less likely to take a medication that they believe "has resulted in fatalities in 2 cases out of a 1000" than a medication that "produced no fatalities in 998 of 1000 cases." And Piatellit-Palmarini does not limit herself only to logical versus illogical numerical understanding. She speaks also about affective results; among her examples is what she considers to be "misplaced regret" as in the following: Baker and Jones, who have separate five o'clock flights, share a taxi to the airport. Due to traffic congestion, they arrive there at 6:30 to discover that Jones' flight left on time but Baker's left only fifteen minutes ago. In such a situation Piatellit-Palmarini expects that Baker to be much more upset than Jones despite the practical, objective equivalence of their misfortune.

Langer (1997) approaches unconscious influences in terms of blocks to learning which she terms "mindlessness," deep-seated, automatic mental sets that cause people to perceive situations without sufficient conscious deliberation, especially by limiting their thoughts to old categories, old information, and single rigid perspectives.

Please note that despite the pejorative connotations, mindlessness is not necessarily a sign of personal failure or inferiority. Mindlessness regularly affects all people, not just those with Attention Deficit Hyperactivity Disorder, or subaverage intellectual functioning. Empirical studies have shown mindlessness to be a significant determinant of natural, everyday conversation (Langer, Blank, and Chanowitz, 1978; Kitayama & Burnstein,1988).

Consider the family physician with medical chart in hand who met with a female patient whom he had not seen in almost a year. He recognized her, but only dimly. In reviewing the newly updated medical history, the doctor noted that a few days earlier a specialist physician had diagnosed the woman with Raynaud's Disease, a condition characterized by markedly decreased blood flow to extremities exposed to the cold. After advising her about the illness and then completing a full physical examination, the doctor began to schedule a follow-up meeting at which point the patient advised, "That month is no good. I'll be back in Minnesota then." Taken aback, the doctor exclaimed, "Why would you go there? That's a terrible place for someone with Raynaud's Disease!" She answered, "My husband works there." To which he countered, "What kind of work does he do?" She replied, "He's a professional athlete." The doctor followed-up, "What does he play?" When she answered "football," the doctor flushed, realizing that his patient's husband had been the most valuable player in the Super Bowl only two weeks earlier.

My daughter recently gave me the following example of mindlessness: When e-mailing her girlfriend, Megan wrote the body of her text and then added, " BTW, I might be able to visit you in June. I'll let you know by the end of this month." Meg's girlfriend replied to the e-mail and after the body of her text she added, "By the way, what does BTW mean?"

A personal example also is instructive. Recently when vacationing at the beach, I went for a run each day immediately upon awakening and I took an out-door shower upon returning. Rather than having me go into the house for a towel, my wife would drop one down from the porch above. She and I just "fell into" (if you'll pardon this pun that undoubtedly came from my baseline con-sciousness) the habit because that behavioral sequence occurred the first day that I ran. She did not complain about getting my towel, but it was a minor inconve-nience for her to do so and for me to have to wait. It was not until the third day that I "thought of" the obvious: Take my towel with me upon leaving the house and place it in the shower to be there when I returned. One certainly would not call this heavy duty problem solving, yet I had to be "mindful" to change the rou-tine that my wife and I unthinkingly had stumbled into. Believe Langer and me, mindlessness is a very common feature of daily life!

Memes spread in part due to our mindlessness tendency, as when we accept and pass along an idea primarily because a prestigious person has articulated it. Even the ubiquitous non-advancing, blinking time display on a videocassette player can be understood in terms of a mindlessness plus cost-benefit analysis explanation: it is not that individuals are so "technologically-challenged" that they could not figure out how to set the time display; it is that they do not do not think mindfully about setting the clock, because setting the clock lacks sufficient GBH value to compensate for the effort.

Most psychologists regard the cognitive unconscious as a "fundamentally adaptive system that automatically, effortlessly, and intuitively organizes experience and directs behavior...most information processing occurs automatically and effortlessly outside of awareness because that is its natural mode of operation, a mode that is far more efficient than conscious, deliberative thinking." (Epstein, 1994). The information processing of which the definition speaks includes the act of conversing. Having emphasized the cognitive, rational nature of the unconscious, some psychologists then ignore the non-rational. However, there are exceptions. Epstein (1994) goes on to say that the rational system is complemented by an interacting emotionally-based experiential system. Arthur S. Reber (1996) concurs. He believes further that the unconscious system is primary and that a variant of it even exists in relatively primitive, invertebrate organisms and allows for the survival-oriented moving toward the good and away from the bad "choices." Speaking specifically about humans, Bargh, Gollwitzer, Lee-Chai, Barndollar, and Trotschel (2001) endorse and amplify Reber's view, offering empirical evidence that a holistically-organized pursuit of a habitual goal often is initiated and conducted without conscious intent. They assert:

> "Our argument is that goals can be triggered outside of awareness and then run to completion, attaining desired outcomes (Bargh, 1990, Bargh & Chartrand, 1999, Bargh & Gollwitzer, 1994). No conscious intervention, act of will, or guidance is needed for this form of goal pursuit. In this view, nonconsciously activated goals will cause the same attention to and processing of goal-relevant environmental information and show the same qualities of persistence over time toward the desired end state, and of overcoming obstacles in the way, as will consciously set goals. Thus, at its core, our hypothesis is that however a goal is activated, either by conscious or unconscious means, it will operate effectively to guide a person's goal-relevant cognition, affect, and behavior from that point on."

In applying these ideas to human discourse, I conclude that the cognitive and emotional unconscious cannot be separated, if we are to understand real people engaged in real conversation. Not only do our ideational containers include objective features of words (white spheres) and their emotion-based connotations (green and red spheres), but the relationship between the objective and emotion-based dimensions are fluid, with thought, feeling, and action being both consciously and unconsciously directed. In casual conversation, and even in most formal discourse, the unconscious influences on thought are especially powerful and automatic. This is why we speak so effortlessly and why the things that we say sometime surprise us. At any point during a discussion, we unwittingly can say something with a strongly positive or strongly negative emotional connotation, despite our best efforts to remain objective and rational.

I recall two relevant examples from my own life, coincidentally organized around the same theme—bodily integrity. At a conference that I attended in an unfamiliar setting, I tentatively entered the room and randomly chose a seat. The man next to me also was alone and new to the area and within a few minutes we were chatting like old friends. As we exchanged "I'm so busy at work" stories with each other I exclaimed, "I have a list of assignments on my desk as long as your arm!" He smirked and at that point I noticed that he was missing his left upper extremity. This "Freudian slip" had come straight from my emotional unconscious. His missing limb was positioned away from me and before making the remark I had absolutely no conscious awareness of it. Fortunately, he was totally at ease with his impairment and we both had a good laugh about my awkward remark. My second example concerns statements by my conversational partner, not me. I went to my local home improvement center intent on buying a storm door and hanging it myself. The fact that I never had done so before did not deter me. (Perhaps it should have.) I quickly located a knowledgeable salesperson eager to assist. He pulled an appropriate-sized door from a stack, stood it against the wall, and described how to do the job. Grasping the door and struggling to steady it, he said, "You'll need another hand to do this." Just then, I saw that three digits on his left hand were gone. Neither of us smiled. He was straight-faced and in no way joking. We then went to the order desk where he placed a shiny catalog on the table and commented, "This is brand new. Untouched by human hands." The salesman seemed totally oblivious to the irony with which he spoke. His statements issued from the interface where unconsciousness, baseline consciousness, body image, and word associations meet.

Associations between Words

The structure of language, itself, facilitates associations between words. Using a thesaurus, Adilson Motter and colleagues (2002) investigated the associative links among 30,000 English root words (common, generic words such as "house," rather than "mansion."), demonstrating that almost any two of them could be cross-referenced one to the other within three thesaurus citations. They suggested that this is true because language evolved to make thinking as interconnected, efficient, and effective as possible.

Whether you accept Motter's results or not, you undoubtedly know from your own everyday experience that any two words certainly can become linked as indi- vemes in the mind of a given person. To illustrate both the common and unique aspects of word association, I offer to you another finding from the same "small informal study" of 7 women and 3 men mentioned earlier. For this part of the study, the ten participants were told:

> "On each of the 7 lines below, write one word that comes to mind when you think of the word '**SOFT**.' Write each word in the order in which you think of it. Do not censor your answers. Write anything that comes to mind. You **MUST** write 7 words."

As explained previously, with "w1" designating woman number one, "w2" designating woman number two, "m1" designating man number one, "m2" designating man number two, and so forth, their responses, in the order in which they wrote them, were:

w1	w2	w3	w4	w5	w6	w7	m1	m2	m3
fluffy	squishy	cotton	skin	comfort	squishy	cuddly	weak	pillow	delicate
pillow	small	baby skin	petals	fuzzy	easy	water	fragile	not tough	blanket
clouds	furry	cashmere	baby	pink	ice cream	hard	sponge	cotton	warm
cashmere	kitten	pillow	skills	rice	weak	blanket	towel	toilet paper	precious
cotton ball	baby	down feather	country	baby	cushion	ball	feather	soft drink	tender
puppies	skin	warm water	book	not stat firm	pillow	skills	bird	cloud	pillow
hair	smooth	dolphin skin	heart	not hard	pushover	safe	egg	soft sell	cotton

The persons in the study were seen at their common workplace. They were of the same socioeconomic class (upper middle) and race (Caucasian). They had similar educational backgrounds (approximately 18 years of formal education). Because of and in spite of their similarities, they aptly demonstrated that people have both common and unique associations to everyday words. Twenty percent of the total of 70 associations were shared among two or more people, the most frequent association being "pillow," mentioned by fifty percent of the group. However, only two respondents shared the same first association to "soft" which was "squishy" and fifty percent of the 70 associations were given only once.

The next study was designed to further elicit word associates and their good-bad ratings by using the word "candle," a non-emotional word that, nevertheless, can become richly linked to other emotion-laden words. I also chose to include the word "romance" to contrast with "candle" because "romance' is so blatantly and heavily emotional. Stacy, a 50 year-old mother, and her 23 year-old daughter, Sax, each independently first wrote 20 associations to the word "candle" and then 20 to the word "romance." Subsequently, each independently rated all of their own word associations on the same 7 point scale as mentioned earlier, with 7 representing 'good' and 1 representing 'bad'." The words, in the order in which they were written, appear below. The numbers indicate each word's 7 point rating. The upper case letters P (positive), N (negative), and O (neutral) designate the affective valence of the mother's word ratings with N being given for ratings of 1 and 2, O for 3, 4, and 5, and P for 6 and 7. The same scheme applies to the daughter's ratings, except that lower case letters are used. (The letter "z" appears as a filler in the Romance Table for Stacy and for Sax because one association from each of them needed to be removed to ensure confidentiality. Accordingly, despite their having given 20 romance associations apiece, only 19 are reported for each of them.)

Candle Stacy					Candle Sax	Romance Stacy					Romance Sax
Light	7	P	o	4	Fire	love	7	P	p	7	Lover
Wick	1	N	o	5	Bright	man	7	P	z	z	Z
Burn	6	P	o	3	Flame	woman	7	P	p	6	People
Blue	7	P	p	7	Romance	z	z	Z	p	6	Candle
Scented	7	P	p	6	Wax	couples	7	P	o	4	Fire
Birthday	7	P	p	6	Dancing	February	2	N	p	6	Dancing
Candelabra	7	P	p	6	Dinner	Valentine's Day	7	P	p	6	Dinner
Pink	6	P	p	6	Bedtime	weekend	7	P	p	7	Love
Yellow	1	N	o	5	Smell	kiss	7	P	p	6	Perfume
Stick	1	N	n	2	Burn	intimate	7	P	p	7	Caring
Unscented	1	N	p	6	Perfume	moment	7	P	p	7	Marriage
Leaded	2	N	p	6	Warm	dinner	7	P	p	7	Children
Votive	2	N	o	4	Lights out	dancing	7	P	p	7	Vacation
Candlelight	7	P	p	6	Candleholder	anniversary	7	P	p	6	Togetherness
Pretty	7	P	p	6	Candelabra	wedding	7	P	p	6	Flowers
Bright	7	P	o	5	Buy	vacation	7	P	p	6	Gifts
Smoke	2	N	o	4	Midnight	getaway	7	P	p	6	Wedding
Fire	5	0	p	6	Purple	movies	6	P	p	7	Anniversary
Warm	6	P	p	6	Family	holidays	7	P	o	4	Years
Romantic	7	P	p	7	Friends	Christmas	7	P	p	7	Family

Looking first at the candle data, we find that both Stacy and Sax each gave associations that were exactly 60 percent positive. Thirty-five percent of Stacy's associations were negative and 35 percent of Sax's were neutral. Therefore, 5 percent of Stacy's associations were neutral and 5 percent of Sax's were negative. The two participants shared 6 of their 20 associations or thirty percent of them. Now considering the romance data, we see that 95 percent of Stacy's associations were positive and 89 percent of Sax's were positive. As was the case for the word "candle," the two participants shared 6 of their 20 association, or thirty percent of them, for the word "romance. (This calculation included the confidential, nonreported words that were expressed as zs in the Romance Table.) Also, as had been true for "candle," for "romance," their rating style for non-positive associations was opposite to each other: Stacy's associations were 5 percent negative with none neutral, and Sax's were 11 percent neutral with none negative. These percentages, however, were misleading because Stacy had only one non-positive association to "romance" and Sax had only two.

The candle data is especially informative because it demonstrates that a common word such as "candle" can be meme-like in its publicly shared denotative meanings, yet indiveme-like in its idiosyncratic connotative meanings – the meanings that make a difference in the day-to-day lives of individuals. It is because words always have person-specific connotative-affective associations that we need the concept of indiveme to underscore the critical role of the individual in determining the practical significance of society-wide memes.

The romance data shows that some words with heavy affective valence share so much connotative-associative-affective meaning that it is not necessarily in associations but in usage that we observe the indiveme nature of a word. Thus, two people can share a great preponderance of connotative-associative-affective meanings in their minds, but one converses easily and often about a concept such as "romance," whereas the other speaks hesitantly and rarely about it.

The studies described above demonstrate once again that virtually any words can be associatively linked to yield an indiveme, that most everyday words have good or bad connotations attached to them, and that individuals have both shared and unique associations to everyday words. The fact that the words, presented in isolation, were so effortlessly rated by the study's participants bears testament to the almost instinctual nature of our good-bad rating tendency. We automatically and unconsciously rate virtually everything that we experience in terms of good-bad, because good represents survival enhancement and bad represents survival threat. This is not theory. It is fact, fact that has been shown repeatedly in research that exceeds one hundred years. So what? What does this mean for conversation?

It means that when we converse, even casually, our words inevitably express our personal values, and that the persons with whom we speak are exposed to those value denotations and/or connotations. As they speak, they obviously express and expose their values as well. There is, then, a reciprocal value-based transaction occurring during conversation. But before we can determine the benefits of such transactions, we need to better understand the costs associated with them.

Physical and Mental Energy

Ego Depletion, the Unconscious, and Mindlessness

The relentless search for GBH and omnipresent baseline consciousness exact a price in personal resources. To be active is to expend energy. Animal cells use energy to maintain their own health and vitality and to function as part of larger work assemblies that make up organs and systems. Even at rest animals utilize energy as defined in the concept of basal metabolism, meaning the amount of calories consumed by a quiescent body to maintain itself. Movement needs to be executed in ways that efficiently promote survival. Too much action depletes life resources; too little and an animal fails to secure the raw materials necessary to actualize life potentials. The greatest percentage of actions must produce positive results when subjected to a cost-benefit analysis. Consider, for instance, that a cheetah, the lightening bolt of the animal kingdom, is exhausted after little more than a 100-yard sprint. A cheetah that consistently expends 500 calories chasing down scrawny gazelle calves that provide 400 calories of nutrition literally will run itself to death. (For your information: A survey in 13 American zoos showed that cheetahs consumed an average of 1.32 ± 0.4 kg of food daily with an energy value of 1800 kcal/kg to maintain an average bodyweight of 36.7 ± 1.0 kg. Wild cheetahs in the Serengeti take in an average of 1.3 kg food/day : Referenced from: Big Five Veterinary Pharmaceutical Company, 2003)

Animal species endure because they have evolved mechanisms that allow maximum movement at reasonable cost. At the physical level, the automaticity of action is foremost among these survival-promoting mechanisms. Willingham (1998) speaks in terms of the "dual mode principle," saying that motor acts can be executed either in an unconscious, automatic mode, or a conscious, effortful one, with the latter demanding more attention and energy than the former. When an individual **first** performs a task, the unconscious mode cannot be used, so performing a new task is more energy-expending. The task must be practiced for the sequencing, perceptual-motor integration, and dynamic processes to become tuned to it. The attentional demands of a task decrease **only** when one uses the unconscious mode, not merely as a result of rote practice or training. The conscious mode can participate in skill acquisition at any time, because it is available at any time, provided there is enough surplus energy available to power it. Once learned, motor acts can be executed in either the conscious or unconscious mode, and the active individual can shift from one mode to the other. But, if the conscious mode is used after the unconscious mode already has achieved dominance, the efficiency and effectiveness of performance decreases dramatically. When organisms behave in non-automatic, non-habitual ways, they expend increased energy, among other things, because they need to attend and concentrate more, and, therefore, their actions are more organismically costly than habitual actions are. Animal survival and animal action clearly are biased toward the unconscious, automatic mode.

Willingham's ideas help us to understand the dynamics of actions required for the relentless, expectant GBH search that is highly unconscious and automatic: Imagine a wild pig that stays in a circumscribed section of the forest where he successfully forages for roots and grubs. Because he is so familiar with the area, and because the forest is relatively constant, he continues in the automatic mode for as long as the food source holds out. He wanders unconsciously through his domain and achieves the GBH that he desires. When he exhausts the resources of his immediate area, he moves slowly and tentatively in widening circles around his base of operations. Initially he needs to use the more energy-expending conscious mode to explore and to find food, and, as he does, he subjects himself to greater environmental risk. Once he satisfies his new GBH requirements in the expanded area, however, he is able to resume the unconscious, automatic mode, dwelling in the new vicinity until it too is found wanting. Then he begins another slow, tentative territorial-expansion process.

There is experimentation to support the general notion that animals maintain consistent, automatic actions when they are satisfied, but vary their movements when their customary actions fail to produce GBH. Neuringer, Kornell, and Olufs (2001), for instance, found that when laboratory rats were deprived of food they at first repeated their previously successful food-seeking behavior, but eventually they engaged in very different, uncommon actions in an apparent attempt to secure the nutrition that they craved.

The pig, rat, and animals in general, are fortunate since, absent extraordinary events, such as floods and forest fires, their environments tend to be fairly static, changing minimally and/or slowly over their lifetime. The sameness of an animal's life space and of their basic GBH needs make their overwhelmingly unconscious, automatic lifestyle adaptive and survival-promoting, because first line automatic, habitual behavior tends to be both effective and energy-conserving.

In addition to the cost of overt physical, muscular action, energy is consumed due to mental activity itself. From the perspective of human beings, we know that a relatively quiescent brain requires 40 percent of the body's blood glucose and 15 percent of its oxygen. When the human mind exerts itself, as when integrating, analyzing, and/or synthesizing information, metabolic activity in the working brain areas accelerates beyond 25 percent of the energy required to fuel the entire body (Miller, 2000). The reds, yellows, and greens of positron emission testing, the PET scan, graphically illustrates the metabolic cost of brain function.

It is obvious to us each day that we have a limited store of physical energy—that we become fatigued both as a result of using up our limited energy resources and because of the accumulation of noxious byproducts of action, such as the build up of lactic acid during exercise. It may not be so obvious that we have a limited store of mental energy. Much of the research involving PET scans involves comparisons of areas of metabolic activity in the brain at rest versus doing a targeted mental task. These scans confirm what we all on occasion have noticed—that mental exertion during studying or testing can be more taxing than doing physical labor. Many psychologists believe that there is a limited pool of mental energy from which we draw continuously. Freud (1938) referred to this as "libidinal energy" which he considered to constitute a kind of life force. Muraven and Baumeister (2000) postulated a similar notion saying, "There exists a resource that the self uses for a broad variety of volitional activities. These activities include overriding response tendencies such as habits or impulses, making conscious or deliberate choice, and initiating action (as opposed to being passive). In broad terms, the self's executive function, including all acts of controlling or altering the self and all acts of decision making and initiative, depends heavily on this resource." When the pool of energy resources is drained so too is our ability to perform mental tasks, a condition they term "ego depletion."

Our hominid ancestors inherited the energy-conserving unconscious, automatic mode and it worked just as well for them as for other animals. We, too, have acquired the automatic modus operandi for both physical and mental actions. This is the mindlessness about which Langer (!997) spoke. Like animals, we operate mindlessly most of the time, because doing so is energy-conserving. And, like animals, we benefit most from the automaticity of mindlessness when we operate in relatively simple, repetitive situations and seek simple GBH goals. To behave deliberately and consciously is to tax our energy resources. Moreover, this energy-robbing process is cumulative.

Ego depletion theory explains that whenever an individual acts in a non-habitual mode and this is followed by another non-habitual act, the latter is even less efficient and effective than it would have been had it occurred without the preceding non-habitual act. Thus, not only must we pay initially for consciously-directed behaviors, but also pay doubly, if we are so bold as to follow a consciously-directed behavior with another consciously-directed one. This cost seems reasonable if one consciously-directed behavior is followed by another of the **same** type, as when we play two hotly contested games of chess in rapid succession. But research suggests that even **unrelated** subsequent consciously-directed behavior are more energy-robbing when they follow a previous consciously-directed one. Baumeister and his associates (2000) found that a variety of acts of self control undermined a variety of other acts that bore little overt resemblance to the preceding act. For instance, people who tried to control their emotions during an upsetting video evidenced less stamina on a succeeding task of endurance (Muravan et. al, 1998) and persons subjected to unpredictable noise performed worse on a succeeding tasks involving proofreading, frustration tolerance, and ability to inhibit overlearned responses than did persons subjected to predictable noise, controllable noise, or no noise (Glass and Singer, 1972).

As proto-humans incrementally developed language skills, the potential for mindfulness increased exponentially. And our primate ancestors became less and less dependent on overt physical action and more and more capable of mindful mental action.

Language-based mindfulness enables contemporary humans deliberately to do things and go places experimentally in their "heads," forgoing the ego depletion and danger coincident with physically doing things and going places. But mindfulness is both an asset and a liability, conferring potential dangers as well as advantages. To be mindful of financial limitations and to budget accordingly is to promote financial responsibility. On the other hand, to be so mindful of finances that one literally counts his pennies is to be obsessive-compulsively impaired. Considered this way, a map of an individual's areas of mindfulness is a map of his personality.

As convoluted as it sounds, mindfulness is helpful only when it is used mindfully. Willingham (1998) suggests that an individual is able to use a mindful, conscious mode to learn a new task only when he both has explicit knowledge of some skill that is relevant to executing the new task and knowledge about how to apply the preexisting skill. Mindfulness is ego depleting when one uses the conscious mode for an unconsciously efficient process, since he not only uses more attentional energy when behaving mindfully, but also takes that energy from somewhere else that it ordinarily had been used to facilitate GBH strivings.

Mindfulness can be ego depleting too when we multitask—attempt to perform two or more unrelated actions simultaneously, such as balancing a checkbook while cooking Sunday dinner. Although such multitasking commonly is done, each task usually is performed less well and less efficiently than it would have had it been done separately (Just, 2002). The cost for each task switch depends on the particulars of the tasks being performed. For example, Rubinstein and associates (2001) suggest that more energy is expended in switching from a familiar to an unfamiliar task than vice versa.

All but the most superficial conversation also suffers when we attempt to converse and perform a non-habitual task simultaneously. Despite being mostly driven by unconscious processes, authentic conversation is cognitively-affectively-interactively dense, involving our whole physical and mental being. The demandingness of conversation accounts for the fact that when speaking on the telephone we usually know when the other conversant isn't involved in our discussion; we can sense that he is not devoting enough energy to be meaningfully connected to us (McCusker, 2002). Elderly adults often withdraw from conversations because they must expend too much energy to listen, comprehend, and remember that which is being communicated to them (Schneider, et al., 2002).

Whether due to multitasking or to other demands, ego depletion is stressful. An ego-depleted organism is an organism less capable of achieving GB/GBH. It is more inclined to seek H/GBH to regain its strength, so that the relentless pursuit of GB/GBH will be more effective when it is resumed. An ego-depleted organism works with less intensity and less persistence in an attempt to reduce energy consumption in a self-protective, survival-enhancing way. Therefore, an ego-depleted organism is even more likely than usual to operate in a reflexedly defensive, unconscious, mindless manner.

Danger: Conversation in Progress

Conversation is a wonderfully efficient and effective device for pursuing GBH goals in relative safety, but it is not totally without risk. Ego depletion, the unconscious, and mindlessness affect conversation as well as overt physical action, and they help answer the question, "Why do we prefer to talk to the same people about the same things?" Think about it this way: The risk of conversing with a new partner clearly is greater than conversing with our usual partner. Compared with our habitual speaking partners, when we talk to somebody new, among other things, we must expend more energy giving them background information, helping them to understand our intentions, and worrying about how they will interpret what we are saying. Obviously, ego depletion is far greater with a new partner. And, after all that effort on our part, in cost-benefit terms, we need a more robust GBH result to offset our greater energy outlay. If the new partner shrugs off our conversational input or gives us minimal GBH satisfaction, we unconsciously, or perhaps consciously, conclude that we wasted our time and are dissuaded from future conversational overtures.

It is reasonable to believe that sometimes people don't want to talk because they expect that payback won't be worth the effort. When you have acquired a comfortable conversational habit as a result of discussing a topic in a certain way with a particular conversational partner, you are reluctant to devote the additional energy necessary to develop a completely new conversational style with someone else. Accordingly, you tend to employ the original style with a new conversant partner. When she successfully accommodates to your style, the conversation flows. When she do not, you unconsciously make a cost-benefit analysis, determining whether the GBH benefits of the potential conversation are worth the conversational effort required. This preference for the habitual biases us toward conversational modes resistant to change.

The threatening, ego-depleting nature of nonhabitual conversation is especially obvious in some situations. People who are quite comfortable with automatic, routine, work-oriented conversations on the job often are uncomfortable when having to converse with coworkers outside of work, as at a party. We all have had occasions when we protect ourselves from an ego-depleting discussion by saying, "I just don't feel like talking about it right now." And, no matter how much we would like to talk an emotionally-charged issue through, we usually refrain from pressuring our conversational partner to do so when we realize that he is feeling overwhelmed at that particular moment.

It is true that those under emotional pressure are especially vulnerable to mindlessness. Dolinski (2001) describes situations in which one first experiences a state of arousal, as a state of joy or fear, and then that state suddenly vanishes, such as when initial joy in believing that one has won a prize disappears when he realizes that he has not, or initial fear that one has lost his wallet disappears when he finds it on the car floor. Such "emotional seesaws" cause the subject to respond to subsequent unrelated events in an automatic, unthinking manner. Dolininski shows, for example, that following an emotional seesaw, subjects are more likely to comply with extraordinary or unwarranted requests by strangers because the subjects simply did not have the cognitive resources available to process and/or resist the request. We, then, should expect emotionally pressured persons to converse in an especially mindless way.

In addition to ego depletion, conversational danger can be of a physical type. Public speaking raises heart rate and blood pressure in presenters, regardless of the their basic personalities (Fichera and Andreassi, 2000). Tardy and Allen (1998) demonstrate gender-oriented differences in physiological response to speaking, with men having higher vascular reactivity increases and women, higher heart reactivity. Edith Chen and her associates (2002) show that

> "...women, who have more relationship-oriented goals, show greater CVR (cardiovascular reactivity) to a disagreement task, whereas men, who have more achievement-oriented goals, show greater reactivity to a task that ostensibly taps their verbal abilities (Smith et al., 1998). Individuals who have more feminine personality traits exhibit greater increases in BP (blood pressure) during a task in which they are instructed to persuade rather than empathize with others on a controversial topic. In contrast, individuals who have more masculine personality traits exhibit greater increases in BP when told to empathize with rather than persuade others about a controversial topic (Davis & Matthews, 1996). Finally, individuals who score highly on the trait of *John Henryism* (e.g., a strong disposition toward striving to excel) and who are in situations in which achievement is difficult (e.g., low SES) are more likely to develop hypertension (James, Strogatz, Wing, & Ramsey, 1987)."

Research by Bongard, et al. (1998) concludes that the extent of a person's baseline hostility interacts with their anger-out tendencies to determine their cardiovascular reaction to public speaking. Somewhat surprisingly, however, James J. Lynch (1985) finds that the mere act of speaking during casual conversation raises conversants' blood pressures, regardless of the content of the discussion. Fortunately, for most people, listening then lowers their pressure back to or even below its original baseline. But for some hypertensives, blood pressure remains high, even to a detrimental level. Blood pressure of elderly persons can be elevated by words connoting negative stereotypes about aging (Levy, et al., 2000). Other studies (e.g., Broadwell and Light, 1999) suggest that during casual conversation men are especially vulnerable to deleterious cardiovascular effects, and that both genders are more cardiovascularly reactive when talking about private aspects of themselves than about nonprivate aspects (Lyons, et al, 2000).

All in all, these studies convincingly demonstrate that conversation can pose an actual physical danger to some people some time. If deleterious cardiovascular effects occur, then some persons may avoid conversation due to a conscious or unconscious awareness of the danger and/or discomfort coincident with speaking.

Beyond the physical affects, conversation presents a potential threat to some people because to converse with someone is to subject yourself to their behavioral influence, an influence that can be automatic and insidious. Social norms theory (Haines, 1998) posits that people unconsciously alter their behavior to comply with what they believe is normative behavior, whether or not it is truly normative. The conversing person tries to determine and deliver socially "proper" verbalization; this is ego depleting and, as we discussed early, it amounts to sacrificing the integrity of the personal self for acceptance of the social self.

Children and adults, alike, are affected merely by being in the presence of a conversational partner (Pasupathi, 2001). Toddlers as young as eighteen months of age naturally copy elements of parent conversation (McLaughlin, 1998). In fact, all people tend to unconsciously mimic their interaction partner's expressions, mannerisms, and postures, a condition that Charten and Bargh (1999) describe as the "chameleon effect."

Conversation also affects our emotions. Conversing persons in long term relationships tend to become more emotionally similar to each other over time, and this usually occurs due to greater changes in the less powerful member (Anderson, Keltner, & John, 2003). Hatfield and Struck (1993) show that even such short term influences as a speaker's vocalized emotion tend to induce that same emotion in the listener. When a conversational partner states an emotion-charged idea, it primes the listener to think along similar lines, bringing related, personal, emotion-charged ideas to mind that can persist long after the conversation has ended (Wegner, 1994). Since research repeatedly has found that verbally expressing ideas that fuel negative emotion can reduce both the emotionality and underlying physiologic stress associated the ideas (Lepore, Ragan, & Jones, 2000), conversing about one's distress clearly can have adaptive value for the person who initiates her distressing topic (Petrie et al. 1998). In fact, Taylor, Klein, Lewis, Gruenewald, Gurung, and Updegraff (2000) believe that the inclination toward tending (nurturing) and befriending (affiliating) can have adaptive value for the tending and befriending person and her target, and may even have a biological basis in stress reduction, at least in females. Accordingly, if, in searching for her own GBH, a person introduces a dysphoric topic and this prompts her conversational partner to successfully deal with her own related dysphoric issue, both can benefit. However, Neumann and Struck (2000) discovered an insidious, pervasive mood contagion potential by demonstrating that a speaker's negative emotion can be induced in the listener without the listener's becoming aware that the inducement occurred. Such a listener does not benefit. Instead, she is left with an undesirable mood change in search of its source. One could imagine a telephone conversation in which a depressed person "infects" her listening partner with dysphoria such that the listener hangs up, feels "down," and declines her spouse's invitation to take their customary evening stroll. Her partner, in turn, wonders what he has done to be so rejected, doubts himself, and so it goes. Inter-personal relationships and emotional well-being, then, can be undermined by the noxious influences of some conversations in which the needs of conversants are discontinuous and/or even harmful to one or both speakers.

Equally important, research strongly suggests that some persons have an attentional bias toward negative information that causes them to be especially vulnerable to anxiety (McLeod, et al., 2002). They have enough trouble dealing with their own personally-induced and personally-focused problems. They are too sensitive to anxiety-producing cues to tolerate being burdened by the problems of others. Negative conversations can be toxic to them especially since other's problems can cause these persons to imagine their conversant partner's problem happening to them. A related problem occurs when one person receives from her conversant partner some bit of destructive gossip about a third person. Since most of us poorly retain the source of any information that we hold (Schacter, 2001), once we accept an item of gossip, we are unlikely to be able to check the reliability of the slander. To compound the situation, as Ruscher and Hammer (1994) have demonstrated, conversants spend more time discussing negative than positive revelations about a third, non-present person. Thus, destructive gossip becomes uncritically and deeply incorporated into our storehouse of associations, undermining our relationship with the victim of gossip without affording them "due process."

What about our self concept and self esteem? Could conversation threaten the very core of our being? Previously we said that all living things are programmed to relentlessly search for physical GBH as an essential physical survival mechanism and that a similar GBH- seeking mechanism facilitates mental well-being in the form of positive bias as explained by Lefebvfre (1992). Koole et al. (2001) believe in the existence of an automatic, unconscious tendency for individuals to positively value anything associated with the self. Pelham et al. (2002) refer to this as "implicit egotism" that purportedly explains such obscure findings as the fact that people disproportionately choose to live in cities whose names are similar to their own first or last names, such as someone named Johnston living in Johnstown. In a similar vein, Oates and Wilson (2002) demonstrate that people have a greater tendency to answer a stranger's e-mail request for information when the e-mailer has the same first and/or last name as the e-mail receiver. In fact, when we do not think too deliberatively, we instinctively prefer our particular family, religion, cereal, even the letter initials of our name, to others' (Kitayama. & Karasawa, 1997). Such a positive, self-valuing mechanism might be an inborn defense against depression and discontent.

Under ordinary circumstances, this automatic positivity bias is so expected and so fundamental to our well-being that Frijda (1988) considers it to epitomize "the law of greatest gain: Whenever a situation can be viewed in alternative ways, a tendency exists to view it in a way that maximizes emotional gain." However, when we move out of the automatic, unconscious mode and into the deliberate, conscious one to ruminate about items or resources associated with the self, we may decide that such items or resources of ours are lacking. Conversations with some people can invite just such rumination and discontent. If this happens occasionally, it can cause minimal, transient problems or even be incentive to improve what objectively is lacking in our lives. But some people are chronically negative, exhibiting unhappiness, dissatisfaction with life, low self-esteem, and non-clinical depression that is reflected in maladaptive social interaction, negative behavioral response by others, and negative social reputation (Furr & Funder, 1998). Depressives, for instance, are pathological primarily because they don't pursue GBH intently or consistently enough. Such persons model pervasive pessimism. To converse with them on a regular basis is to run the risk of being "contaminated" with an overly deliberative, overly critical view of life, of one's own self, and of that which is associated with the self, and, in so doing, to weaken one's own inherent, automatic, unconscious positivity bias that helps us to defend against our own personal depression and despair.

Conversation also can threaten our sense of self-control, at least in the short run, because the role that our partner adopts in conversation often directs us toward a complementary role. If he makes a request, I become a request satisfier or denier. If he offers a joke, I become a jocular comrade or sober antagonist. Thus, conversation threatens self-control by inviting me to dance a conversational dance with my conversant partner whether I want to or not. To converse, I open myself up to someone's conscious or unconscious agenda. Maybe he'll try to "hit" me for a loan. Maybe he'll subject me to another rendition of his tired, old fraternity adventures. Alternatively, it is possible that I don't trust myself to converse with him. Perhaps he irritates me such that I'm afraid I will be rude or short with him, since he is forever saying "the wrong thing." Some people are afraid to dance certain dances, or to dance certain dances with certain people. Some people are afraid to dance, period. It is important to recognize too that dancing requires timing. People can pursue GBH through overt physical action or mental verbal action. To conversationally dance, both partners must place at least some restraint on unilateral physical GBH pursuit in deference to bilateral verbal pursuit, and they must do so in a coordinated way that provides each partner some modicum of satisfaction. We instinctively express this when to someone's conversational overture we hastily retort, "Sorry, I can't talk now. I'm right in the middle of something."

The ultimate conversation threat to self-control is Folie a Deux, or Shared Psychotic Disorder (American Psychiatric Association, 1994). This psychopathology occurs when one person, usually an inter-personally dominant one, passes his well-established delusional system onto a significant other, usually an inter-personally passive, but relatively more mentally healthy, one. For the latter person, GBH probably is relationship-based. He derives satisfaction from endearing himself to a powerful other, but pays a heavy price, relinquishing his sanity in the process, literally allowing himself to be talked into craziness.

Baseline Consciousness as Conversation Tyrant: Why We Sometimes Strenuously Avoid Talking About Obsessive Thoughts

Rather than specifically fearing other people's influence, some individuals avoid conversing about certain topics active in baseline consciousness because they regard the ideas as generally threatening to their self. They fear that exposing these baseline consciousness preoccupations could render them physically or mentally vulnerable to dangers as limitless as their own imaginations.

Wegner (1989) studied thought suppression extensively and in a way consistent with many of the concepts we have already discussed. He focused especially on two particular aspects of baseline consciousness: automatic versus controlled thinking and object-level thought versus metacognition. Automatic thoughts, he felt, were unconscious and not limited to one-thought-at-a-time whereas controlled thoughts were conscious and produced serially. Wegner asserted that while object-level thoughts were statements about the world, metacogniton described thoughts about thoughts. And he believed strongly in the importance of the good-bad connotative dimension as it pertained to the way in which we evaluate our thoughts, saying "All possible metacognitive statements can be summarized at one level, as they impinge on one kind of influence: At the metacognitive level, the mind registers what is okay, or not okay at the object-level. Metacognitions are preferences for our minds, wishes about what we might think."

Metacognition suggests that people are self-conscious thinkers who evaluate thoughts as good or bad. And since conversation flows from thoughts, metacognitive evaluation of thought profoundly affects what we are willing to submit for conversation. When our baseline consciousness, then, is populated by an unsavory or otherwise threatening idea, we must resist the virtual reflex tendency that seems so adaptive—to seek homeostatic satisfaction (H/GBH) by releasing the pent-up, activated thought through conversing about it. And this suppression frequently is neither easy nor pleasant.

Wegner posited that typical thought suppression of items in baseline consciousness is doomed to failure and inherently paradoxical because in his thought-suppressing attempt the individual brings into consciousness the very thought that he wants to avoid. In investigating thought suppression, Wegner built upon work of the legendary William James who almost one century earlier asked subjects to try **not** to think of a white bear. Like James, Wegner discovered that the forbidden thought intruded into the consciousness of the suppressing persons. When the same individuals were subsequently ask **to** think about the white bear, they reported doing so at a significantly higher rate than did persons who were told to think about a white bear but who never had been instructed previously to suppress white bear thoughts. Wegner concluded that thought suppression increases the intrusion power of thoughts beyond their usual strength.

Wegner's experiments mean that under ordinary circumstances when a thought is pressing relentlessly on our baseline consciousness, we would do well to converse about it at that moment and so be able then to move on from there. But there are complicating factors that work against that facile solution when suppression is being attempted. Again referring to James, Wegner alludes to fact of baseline consciousness by pointing out that thoughts usually flow smoothly one to the other and that it is only when our thoughts are halted by a "bad" or unwanted thought that we actively try to suppress that thought. The unwanted thoughts, he opines, are obstacles of three major types: something we do not want to do, to say, or to feel. Wegner explains, "In each of these cases, thought precedes something we wish not to have happen, and so we stop it. Doing, saying, and feeling are all public, irrevocable signs of our thoughts."

A conversation is the worst possible setting for inadvertently leaking a suppressed thought, then, since it places the speaker squarely at the center of attention at a time when he is most vulnerable to follow-up questions by his speaking partner. Accordingly, a suppressor strenuously avoids conversing with persons who have an interest in the unwanted thought being resisted. If you took a "mental health holiday" on Friday, your boss is the last person you want to chat with on Monday, even if she never would question or even inquire about your absence. This is true not simply because you fear punishment, but because you instinctively know what Wegner has shown – that the more you try to suppress the thought of having done something wrong, the more uncomfortable you will be and the more effort you will have to expend in hiding any hint of it during your conversation.

In an ideal world, no one should need to suppress any thoughts. Unfortunately, we live in a less-than-ideal world. While "keeping secrets" in matters of great seriousness can be psychologically damaging, psychological damage is not inevitable for keepers of secrets (Vrij, et al., 2002). After reviewing relevant theories and research, psychologists Kelly and McKillop (1996) conclude that "Although confessions may be 'good for the soul,' given that they can wreak havoc with one's network of friends and supporters, some things are better left unsaid. Thus, we recommend that only if a person is particularly troubled by a secret should the person risk telling others about it. In addition, the person should scrutinize potential confidants for their ability to keep a secret and to offer new insights into the secret without being judgmental. In those cases, secret keepers should reap the benefits of revealing secrets so often touted by researchers" Apparently, many Americans intuitively know that some secrets should remain thus. An Ipsos-NPD telephone poll conducted in March, 2001 of 1000 married persons found that 42 percent of men and 36 percent of women admitted to keeping secrets from their spouse (Lague, 2001).

Intra-Personal and Inter-Personal Determinants of Conversation

Is it All in Your Head?

Since conversation begins in our minds, intra-personal mental factors profoundly influence what will be said. But conversation is not purely intra-personally-determined. The inter-personal environment, too, determines conversation, because conversation always is co-constructed collaboratively, on-line, and relative to the person with whom we speak. These intra-personal and inter-personal factors seamlessly and automatically both constrain and enhance each other as they combine to make conversation possible.

Accessible Material: CAMM and TAMM

Some intra-personal factors issue from organizational principles of the mind. Earlier we conceptualized each word in our mental lexicon as sitting atop a container partially filled with round spheres, the spheres representing the target word's associates. When we retrieve the target word, we retrieve some of its associates too. But not all target words are equally retrievable, and here, too, mental organization is important.

In attempting to express an underlying, multi-sensory-motor-visceral idea, we reach into our mental lexicon and pull out the word that comes closest to achieving that purpose. One part of the mental lexicon, the chronically accessible memory material (CAMM), contains words, ideas, and feelings that **always** are readily accessible to our consciousness. The other part, the temporarily accessible memory material (TAMM), contains words, ideas, and feelings that only **occasionally** are accessible to our consciousness. The CAMM contains important, frequent, and/or over-learned material, as well as some material that achieves CAMM status for a wide variety of reasons as when it was a first experience – a phenomenon that psychologists call "primacy." The TAMM contains **currently, but not permanently,** salient, moderately novel, and/or recently experienced material. However, CAMM and TAMM material influence each other in that words, ideas, and feelings activated from the CAMM can cause an individual to be especially receptive to cues which activate the TAMM, and vice versa. A person with computer expertise has a rich matrix of computer-oriented CAMM ideas and, accordingly, is particularly attuned to new transiently available TAMM computer information. Conversely, someone who is not expert with computers but who is attending to computer-oriented TAMM material will have whatever computer-oriented chronically available CAMM material that he does possess activated by the TAMM material.

Unlike a word in the CAMM, a word in the TAMM requires special circumstances in order to be activated. For instance, ordinarily you might say, "I have a lot of options for my vacation," lot being the CAAM-stored word that you typically use colloquially to designate a large quantity. But when leaving English class you might say, "I have a plethora of options for vacation," plethora being a TAMM-located word you ordinarily do not use in conversation but that was cued by material read in class. Thus, while the always-present, CAMM stored words usually are the most reliable influences in determining our associations, TAMM-stored words, cued by the immediate environment and most recent experience, can work their way to the top of our word containers and assume temporary dominance over the CAMM-stored ones. It is also possible that items which begin as TAMM-stored can become CAMM-stored through repeated use and processing.

Lewis Carroll's oft-quoted "Words mean just what I want them to mean, nothing more and nothing less" has much merit. Words do mean only what people use them to mean, and words in conversation mean only what the conversing persons understand them to mean. Willard V. Quine (1977), a preeminent language philosopher, seems extreme in claiming that there is no intrinsic meaning behind words. But he does underscore the fact that dictionaries are insufficient to capture the meanings of words in conversation. When I use a word while conversing, if I am using a conventional dictionary definition at all, I am focusing only on one small part of it at that moment when I am trying to communicate my thought. This is especially true because the word I choose always will be an insufficient expression of my total thought gestalt. To converse adequately with me, you need to ignore all the other meanings listed in the dictionary to react appropriately to mine. And the only way our meanings will match is if we share enough mental content, baseline consciousness, and speaking standards that permit us to communicate the all-important nuanced meanings of what we want to say.

The Self and Conversation

When first discussing mental representation, I indicated that the primordial mental representation is physical self versus nonself – that mobile animals must have at least some vague, visceral sense of their physical being that enables them to differentiate themselves from the physical world in order to move adaptively through space and time. The human social self, analogously, is a mental representation by which we distinguish ourselves from other persons so that we can move adaptively through social space and social time. A mental representation of the physical self exists to define a person in a physical environment; a mental representation of the social self exists to define a person in a social environment. In both cases, the individual organism is defining itself and is being defined by its surroundings.

Of all that defines the social self, nothing is more important than social comparison of the self with other people. Stapel and Tesser (2001) suggest that mere activation of a personal sense of oneself promotes his social comparison, and a search for what makes him both separate from and similar to the social field. In their words,

> "...often people's goal is 'being the same and different at the same time.' That is, people derive their sense of self or identity from a fundamental tension between their need for validation and similarity to others (being the same) and a countervailing need for differentiation and individuation (being different). Individuals are concerned with obtaining a certain level of being the same and being different, called *optimal distinctiveness (Brewer, 1991)*. From the present perspective, self-activation is thus likely to activate optimal distinctiveness concerns. Such concerns can only be addressed by reference to other people, that is, by social comparison."

Social comparison is endemic in social relationships (Kelly, 1955). We automatically compare and contrast ourselves with significant others as well as with strangers, and we react affectively based on our conclusions, especially in terms of the extent of self-relevance of that which has being evaluated. Beach and colleagues (1998) found that when a married person compares himself or herself with their partner, they are less likely to be bitter about the partner's superiority or less likely to gloat over their own superiority than they would in comparisons with strangers. For dating couples, by contrast, pleasure in the partner's superiority, if present at all, is most likely to be restricted to comparisons of low self-relevance. An intense attachment seems necessary, if we are to be "charitable" in our self-other comparisons. Moreover, when social comparisons involve decisions, we incline toward a "person sensitivity bias" by which we ascribe too much credit to others when things are going well and too much blame to them when things are going poorly (Moon and Conlon, 2002).

According to Rusbult et al. (2000) people maintain a positive sense of self in part by selective attention, encoding, and retrieval of self-reinforcing information, by interacting with others who support one's positive beliefs, and by having a broadly-based corpus of readily retrievable positive self facts. And similar processes are employed in the attempt to maintain a positive sense of one's inter-personal relationships. Concerning the latter, Rusbult and his colleagues emphasize several social comparison strategies including: Downward comparison by which one views her relationships by contrast to others deemed less positive; dimensional comparison by which one focuses on particular aspects of her relationships that are especially salutary; manipulation of surrounding dimension which finds reasons to discredit the attractive features of others' relationships; and avoidance of comparison which blinds her to anything that depicts her relationships as inferior to those of someone else. However, as Stapel and Tesser (2001) note, we are two selves – a personal self, with a tendency to look within for self-centered, often secret, GBH goals and desires, and a social self, with more broadly shared, outwardly-directed goals and desires.

The dual character of personal self definition and of social self definition in relationships is critical in conversation wherein the individual both contributes thoughts and feelings and reacts to the thoughts and feelings of her immediate social environment, that is, of her conversational partner. The dual character also is apparent in the subpart of the self that we call "self esteem"—a subpart that remains prominent in all conversations. Heine and his colleagues (1999) assert that, in Western culture, "People have a need to view themselves positively. This is easily the most common and consensually endorsed assumption in research on the self (e.g., Allport, 1955 ; Epstein, 1973 ; James, 1890 ; Maslow, 1943 ; Rogers, 1951 ; Steele, 1988 ; Tesser, 1988). In fact, positive self-regard is thought by many to be essential for achieving mental health (e.g., Baumeister, 1993 ; Leary, Tambor, Terdal, & Downs, 1995 ; Taylor & Brown, 1988)."

Tafarade (1998) states that self esteem is comprised of the individual's contributions –self competence– and the contributions of the wider society – self liking. He regards self competence as an individual's assessment of his ability to "impose his will on the environment," meaning the veridical and presumed environment, and, as such, it is an autonomous, personal evaluation. By contrast, self liking is seen as "one's worth as a social entity with reference to internalized standards of good and bad" that derive not so much from the individual's autonomous values but from values embraced by people in his reference group. In conversation, then, an individual's self esteem derives from the extent to which he can talk himself into getting whatever GBH that he wants (self competence) while abiding by the social mores of proper conversational behavior so that he can mentally represent himself as being inter-personally appropriate (self liking).

Although language as representation is a totally private mental process, language as communication must be public, requiring disclosure of personally owned mental contents to at least one other person. As such, communication necessitates disclosure of self. Conversation, the gold standard of communication, presents the self as subject – the person doing the speaking – and object – the target for a listener's reaction. At minimum, the speaker in conversation must risk self disclosure in order to pursue GBH.

This means that a person evaluates herself along a good-bad continuum, just as she evaluates non-self targets. The capacity to regard herself as an object to be scrutinized and evaluated, self-reflexiveness, is at the root of the self concept: People decide whether they like the self that they see and hear, and whether they want to move mentally toward that image or away from it. Nowak and associates (2000), in fact, assert that a differentiating, inner-directed self evaluation of subparts of the self lies at the heart of our sense of self and is the agent that provides us a sense of personal coherence. They say:

> "There is reason to think that evaluative coherence provides the basis for integration in the self-system. Evaluation, after all, is arguably the most important global variable in the mental system (Tesser & Martin, 1996), and evaluative consistency is widely recognized as providing the basis for organizing social judgments generally (cf. Abelson et al., 1968 ; Eiser, 1994 ; Fiske & Taylor, 1991 ; Heider, 1944 ; Wegner & Vallacher, 1977) and self-concept in particular (cf. Duval & Wicklund, 1972 ; Showers, 1995 ; Tesser & Campbell, 1983). The evaluative dimension can provide integration for low-level elements that may be quite disparate with respect to cognitive content and means—end relations (Vallacher & Nowak, 1994 , 1997 ; Vallacher, Nowak, & Kaufman, 1994). Donating money to charity and helping a child with homework are clearly distinct elements, for example, but are similar with respect to their reflection on one's sense of self as a socially responsible person."

But the highly refined human self concept requires a conception of others as well. The meaning of self always occurs in an inter-personal context, even if the context merely exists in our minds, as when we incorrectly believe that people regard us in a particular way when they do not. The self is evaluated and perceived in terms of the behavior of other persons and vice versa (Sullivan, 1953). We consider ourselves to be good by contrasting what we regard as our virtuous behavior with what we see as the dastardly behavior of someone else (Kelly, 1955).

The Self and the Other

When people converse, each is conscious of himself and of the other with whom he is conversing. Anything that affects one's sense of himself or his understanding of the other will affect conversation.

Humans are highly self-conscious creatures. A sense of self is demonstrably present at least as early as two years of age (Harley & Reese, 1999). We constantly think about the impression that we make on others—how we are "coming across" and what people think of us (Goffman, 1967)—and there is reason to believe that this process operates unconsciously (Koole, et al., 2001). While adolescents have been perceived as especially sensitive to the presence of an omnipresent "imaginary audience," Frankenberger (2000) presents research to suggest that adults at least as old as thirty years are similarly affected. This self-consciousness attaches to any aspect of our being, from the way we dress to the way we walk.

Conversation, however, is uniquely and automatically self- conscious, because conversation always is public, and therefore, subject to explicit or implicit criticism, and because message and relationship elements have the self at their core. We relentlessly pursue message and relationship GBH to make our physical-mental "self" feel GBH. Moreover, the self is always involved in conversation because we always are trying to "save face" when conversing (Goffman, 1967). Even when I ask the most straightforward, objective, message-oriented question, it is obvious to myself and to all listeners that I am responsible for asking it. Was it a dumb or a smart question? Was it relevant to the topic? Should I have known the answer? Relationship-oriented remarks clearly involve the self in a way that invites evaluation of the speaker. If I say or imply that I like or dislike someone, I betray my preferences and my preferences represent much of what constitutes my personality.

Thus, during conversation, we not only are trying to communicate objective ideas, but also to position ourselves (Drew et al 1999) favorably in order to get GBH—message or relationship. We are trying to make the presentation of ourselves such that it enhances our GBH efforts.

Because conversation is vastly more self-conscious than is self-thought, conversation sometimes makes me especially sensitive to the words that I use when expressing myself. The word sensitivity could be word sensitivity concerning the objective meaning of words, as when I feel that I have not expressed myself clearly enough. But, more often, it is word sensitivity in the sense of the social-positioning implications of our word choices – concern about how I as a "self" am "coming across" to my conversational partner. If I say that I am a "cosmologist" or "cosmetologist," the message conveys the same essential objective fact about me – my job title. However, the effect on the listener, the social positioning or social fact, is vastly different for me to call myself a cosmologist than it is for me to call myself a cosmetologist, since my conversational partner will make very different assumptions about me as a person based purely upon the two job titles.

The converse of self-awareness is other-awareness. For conversation, an especially important aspect of the latter involves what psychologists call "theory of mind" (ToM). At base, ToM refers to the human ability, and perhaps, controversially, the ability of only one animal – the chimpanzee – to think about the thought of others.

Conversing partners need a sufficiently clear ToM of their counterpart as a prerequisite for developing the "empathic accuracy" (Icker, 1993) necessary to read correctly the thoughts and feelings of the partner. Those who lack adequate empathic accuracy are prone to giving either too little or too much detail to their counterpart when conversing. While all conversants are vulnerable to empathic inaccuracy, those having more intimate and more long-term relationships are less so.

ToM makes conversation both possible and complicated. Since conversation is a non-obligatory behavior initiated for GBH purposes, an individual starts to chat in the **expectation** of satisfaction. He does so because through use of his ToM faculties he believes that he knows generally how his conversation partner will react to his overture. At minimum, he expectantly hopes that by conversing on his chosen topic he has a fighting chance to attain GBH, message or relationship. The complication that arises is that ToM capabilities permit some individuals sometimes to perceive conversation as a zero sum game, meaning that he imagines that his GBH gain can only occur as a result of a loss on the part of his conversation partner. Such a mindset promotes destructive, duplicitous conversational games in which each person is intent not only on satisfying his own needs but on undermining the needs of the other. The Transactional Analyst Eric Berne (1968) wrote about these games, such as the "Now I've Got You, You Son of a Bitch" game in which the purpose of conversation is to expose the other's lie or foible. The GBH for the "snagger" perhaps is the satisfaction coincident with being one-up on the person with whom he is speaking.

To summarize, the self-conscious tendency is a direct consequence of the valuing process by which we automatically tag stimuli, experiences, and the self as good-bad, and we have at least an unconscious awareness of our own evaluating proclivity and of a similar proclivity by others. The self-conscious self is at the center of conversation. The speaker is conversing in an expectant, self-centered search for GBH, "arguing" for his position and "arguing" for his "self conscious self" in order to obtain GBH. The speaker's desires and preconceptions determine what he will say. As he speaks, he, at least unconsciously, wonders what his partner's response will be. His anticipation of the partner's understanding and response to it is biased toward what the speaker believes and against whatever ideas that he does not share with the partner. The partner, usually unconsciously, wonders, "Why is he saying that now?" The partner eventually becomes the speaker who operates according to the very same dynamics that the previous speaker had. It sounds tedious and complicated, but it usually works effortlessly and effectively, simply because it is so automatic and unconsciously orchestrated.

The Conversational Triangle

In addition to being self-conscious, conversations are context-dependent. Just as three converging lines define every triangle, every discussion is defined by three main vectors, one representing each speaker and one representing a topic. The speaker, his conversant partner, and the topic are powerfully influenced by each person's beliefs about what the other knows.

The speaker, his coversant partner, and the topic are most powerfully affected by the knowledge that each person ascribes to his partner regarding the topic being discussed. Nickerson (1999, 1998) suggests that people often erroneously presume that their conversational partner knows more of what the speaker knows than is true, and that this is at the heart of many communication problems. Citing the work of Nickerson et al. (1987), Rainer Bromme, Riklef Rambow, and Matthias Nückles (2001) describe his three central hypotheses:

The correspondence hypothesis. It states that one is more likely to impute a bit of knowledge to others if oneself has it than if oneself does not have it. We call this the correspondence hypothesis because it says that the estimations will show some sort of correspondence with the estimator's own knowledge.

The overestimation hypothesis. This one says that persons tend to overestimate the commonality of their own knowledge.

The expertise hypothesis. The third hypothesis indicates that persons who possess an extraordinarily high level of knowledge in a certain domain will tend to overestimate what other persons know about this domain.

Fortunately, the deleterious affects of the correspondence, overestimation, and expertise hypotheses often are reduced among frequent conversational partners. Although the entire universe of ideas connected to a topic is open to the conversants, their conversation is unconsciously restricted according to their relationship history together regarding the topic. History powerfully channels conversants toward some topics and some topical details and away from others. For instance, I ask my colleague, "Eugene, How's your brother, Keith?" and Eugene replies, "Great, his practice is going well." I did not specifically ask about his brother's professional/financial life, but that is the response I received; in fact, I was most interested in knowing how the brother was doing physically and recreationally. Eugene has an extensive past and present with his brother to whom he is emotionally very close. He could have gone anywhere with my interrogative. In the past, Eugene and I have mostly spoken about his brother in his professional capacity. Eugene's response to me suggests that when he and I speak about his brother, the fact that he is speaking to me activates associative links to his brother that focus on the brother's professional/financial life. In this case, it may be because his brother and I are both psychologists. It would be informative to know how Eugene would respond to the very same question, "How's your brother, Keith?" asked by his fishing partner. If Eugene responded to the fishing partner with the very same answer, then the associative links of brother equals professional/financial issues would be more pervasively tied to Eugene's own internal psychodynamics rather than to Eugene's conversational relationship and topic history with me.

Conversational Templates and Fingerprints

The example of Eugene illustrates that any given conversational triangle can be very restricted and template-like, or very freewheeling and fingerprint-like. And, once again, the histories of conversants singly and together are central. I bet you have conversed with certain people who tell you something, often verbatim, that they have told you or someone else before. This kind of template discussion signifies that they hold the topic in their baseline consciousness. Your presence may have activated it into consciousness, in which case it would be TAMM located, or it already may have been activated when you arrived on the scene, in which case it would be CAMM located. In less extreme cases, the template is not narrowly topic-centered but more broadly subject-centered, as when your conversational partner always tends to reminisce with you in a non-verbatim way about "the good old days" in high school.

Conversational templates say volumes about the conversing partners. For one thing, they indicate the CAMM and/or TAMM of the person introducing the topic. But the fact that the receiving person embraces the topic means both that the topic is in her CAMM and/or TAMM too and that she, like the introducing person, is expecting to achieve GBH from the topic. Templates also show how the conversants define themselves vis-à-vis each other: whether they are persons together interested in family, sports, politics, religion, or whatever. The quality of the templates discloses the depth of their relationship: regardless of their topic, do they treat it lightly or gravely, cooperatively or contentiously? Perhaps most critical is whether the partners have the desire or temerity to step outside the boundaries of templates and to relate in terms of conversational fingerprints, whether they can discuss new issues or old issues in new ways. If they can, each individual has an opportunity to grow conversationally and personally and, if either does, so can their relationship.

The Conversational Meadow

Have you noticed that you tend to have conversations about the same things – conversational template-like- with the same people? This is rather astounding when you think of it. You and he literally could talk about anything from the most remote past to the most remote future. You even could discuss fantastic ideas that defy classification. That you tend to be repetitive is more evidence in favor of the view that you and your partner are not just conversing to converse, but are looking for GBH in the places where you expect you will find it together. You could go anywhere but instead you hang around the same area, just like the wild pig we spoke about who prefers to stay in his familiar territory.

The conversational terrain is like a huge, unobstructed, fully-accessible meadow that can be entered from any direction and traversed in any way. When

addressed or when addressing, each conversant can wander anywhere conversationally, so long as she can make some reasonably relevant connection among the
ideas presented. Yet conversations between frequent speaking partners typically
follow familiar, historically-salient routes. Just as Eugene always responds to my
question about his brother by focusing on the bother's professional/financial life,
most people have prototypical topics and topic development specific to their conversational partner. Why is this? It is because in addition to having our GBH
needs, we have expectations about where, and to what extent, our current conversational partner can satisfy them, and he has similar expectations about us. He
and we take the path of least resistance that offers the greatest promise of GBH
with the least expenditure of effort. This is due, in large measure, to our conversation history with this person and to the rewards that we have enjoyed in the past.
To take another conversation entry point or to traverse a new route is to place
ourselves at risk, to jeopardize the GBH satisfactions that have kept us conversationally connected to this speaking partner in the past. But when we do take the
risk, we open ourselves, and our partners, to new potential pleasures. We will
have much more to say about conversational direction and consistency later.

Conversational Synchronicity

We need to stroll the meadow in time with our partner. In conversation, as in all
of life, timing, or synchronicity, is critical. For conversation to be sustained
beyond the briefest comments, there must be a synchronicity of conversants in
process and content. Conversation process synchronicity refers to conversants
volitionally engaging in discourse at the same moment. They need to be sufficiently committed to talk then and there rather than to any other "action" that
competes for their mental energies. Conversation content synchronicity refers to
conversants discussing similar subject matter then and there rather than to any
other subject matter. To be in synchrony, conversants need to be mentally
attuned to, or at least receptive to, certain mutually shared features of BETF
experience, although each will be so connected in an idiosyncratic, personal, my-
story kind of a way. Persons excessively focused on overt, physical action, rather
than on verbalization, and on narrow, esoteric topics, rather than on wide,
broadly held ones have a reduced probability of achieving the process synchronicity and/or content synchronicity that helps conversation unfold readily and
smoothly.

Conversation content synchronicity often takes the form of our mirroring the
talk of others by using their very words or metaphors. Two especially relevant and

common types of mirroring are lexical choice and conceptual pacts. In lexical choice mirroring, conversants use identical or tightly related terms to refer to the same concept, as when I say that I feel that I am a "ship at sea" and you advise me to seek a "safe harbor." Brennan and Clark (1996) demonstrate that in conceptual pact mirroring, conversants use their shared lexical choice conceptualization repeatedly in the current or subsequent conversations, even when other word choices would be more linguistically economical. Speaking specifically of dyads, Niederhoffer and Pennebaker (2002) suggest, "If one person uses a high number of positive or negative words, words that signal concrete thinking (e.g., articles) or sentence complexity (e.g., prepositions), the other does too." Over time, conversational partners often conjointly modify or abandon their conceptual pacts—another example of the ubiquitously co-constructive nature of conversation. Davis and Rusbult (2001) show that close conversants tend toward "attitude alignment," changing their individual opinion about a given subject when the issue is salient and central to the partner's self concept.

When discussed this way, the necessity for conversational synchronicity seems obvious and trite. Yet failure of synchronicity is a major impediment to effective, satisfying conversation. How often have you begun talking with someone only to lose interest because your partner was not "there" with you? She may have been doing something else, such as intently filing papers, and obviously not paying attention to your interaction (process), or her irrelevant or tangential comments may have signaled that her current issues were discontinuous with your own (content), such as when you speak about your job and she replies about her parents' new car.

In addition to process and content synchronicity– the conversation essentials—there is also the non-essential, but highly desirable, affective synchronicity. Whether our relentless, expectant search is for message or relationship GBH, we desire to speak with someone who is "in time" with us emotionally. If we are solemn, we **usually** want a serious partner. If we are effusive, we **usually** want an emotionally reactive one. It's a matter of "misery loves company" or "laugh and the world laughs with you." This does not mean, however, that we **always** want our conversant partner to mirror the exact same feeling that we do. Conceivably, there are occasions when we search for someone who evidences emotion at variance with ours in order to snap us out of our current mood. The synchronicity in this case is that we want our partner to do the "snapping" then and there, at the very moment that we need it.

Gendered Language and Conversation

There is a saying in the life sciences that similarities among people far outweigh their differences, and this undoubtedly is true. Biologists, for instance, agree that physical distinctions between races are minimal (Olson, 2002), and linguists assert that infants from every country begin speaking at about the same time and follow the same course of developing language competency (Lenneberg, 1984). The one area of significance difference that most life scientists concede is gender difference.

Gender powerfully dichotomizes the human species from the moment of conception to the moment of death. Provine (2000) flatly states that, "There are no gender-free human encounters." Males and females always will be different in some important physical, intellectual, and emotional ways. We are speaking now in terms of group differences. For instance, relative to the other sex, men usually have a higher muscle to fat ratio and women usually are faster processors of language, but some men have a lower muscle to fat ratio and some women are slower processors of language. Gender differences are such that normal men and women often perceive the social field differently (Gabriel and Gardner, 1999). D. Erik Everhart and his associates (2000) consider some of these fundamental differences to derive from disparate brain lateralization, citing their research showing that when identifying facial expressions, boys use their right hemisphere and focus on the whole face and girls use their left hemisphere and focus on the details of the face. Turhan Canli and his group (2002) present data showing that, under an incidental recall paradigm involving a two week delay between presentation and testing, females remembered 75 percent of highly emotional images to which they were exposed whereas males remembered only 60 percent.

In the 1960s the notion of behavioral or psychological gender differences was anathema, but in the new millennium we have accepted and even embraced the idea. In fact, at times we seem obsessed with it. The national best seller, *Men Are from Mars; Women Are from Venus* (Gray, 1992) inspired a television show of the same name. And when ABC aired "The View," a round-table all-female group discussion and interview program, NCB countered in the same time slot with "The Other Half," a round-table all-male group discussion and interview program. (Not surprisingly the studio audiences for both shows were overwhelmingly female.) Popular magazines of our day frequently address gender issues such as:

Boy? Girl? What's the Difference? (*Life* magazine, July, 1999)

"The War between Men and Women" (*Discover* magazine, May, 1999)

"Are Women Better Leaders?" (*U.S. News & World Report*, January 29, 2001)

"Why Do Men Act the Way They Do?" (*Reader's Digest*, September, 2000)

"He Says, She Says" (*Town and Country*, April, 1999)

"The New Gender Wars" (*Psychology Today*, November/December, 2000)

"Boys, The Weaker Sex? (*U.S. News & World Report*, July 30, 2001)

Taylor, Klein, Lewis, Gruenewald, Gurung, and Updegraff (2000) comprehensively review male-female differences in affiliation tendencies and conclude:

> "In a broad array of cultures, men have been observed to form groups for purposes of defense, aggression, and war (Tiger 1970). They tend toward larger social groups than is true of women (Baumeister & Sommer, 1997), and these groups are often organized around well-defined purposes or tasks. Although men orient toward and invest in a large number of social relationships, many of these relationships emphasize hierarchies of status and power rather than intimate bonding (Baumeister & Sommer, 1997; Spain, 1992). Female groupings tend to be smaller, often consisting of dyads or a few women, and although some such groups are focused around tasks (such as food preparation, sewing, or collective child care), these groups often have the establishment and maintenance of socioemotional bonds at their core, a characteristic less true of male groupings (Cross & Madson, 1997). Women in women's social groups show more affiliative behaviors, including smiling, disclosure, attention to others, and ingratiation (Baumeister & Sommer, 1997; Pearson, 1981), and they interact at closer physical distances than do men's groups (Patterson &Schaeffer, 1977)."

Christopher Moore (2002) suggests that the affiliation-independence dichotomy has a gender-dimorphic etymology in that religious Christian men traditionally went off to monasteries, "monastery" being derived from Greek and Latin roots meaning to live alone or be single, while religious Christian women joined convents, "convent" meaning to assemble together.

The aforementioned illustrates that male-female affiliation issues and even language, itself, has a gender-relevant structure. Female and woman are marked in terms of male and man, respectively, meaning that they are defined by their relationship to the masculine term, just as short and little are marked, respectively, relative to the terms tall and big. To understand "marking" as I am using it here, let's think about short and little first. No matter how short or little a person is, one usually would ask, "How tall is he?" or "How big is he?" We do so because tall and big are implicitly-valued terms, the "markers" by which we judge desirability on the low to high scale. Similarly, throughout history male and man have been the implicitly valued terms by which we judge desirability and by which females and women have been judged, rather than being judged as entities in and of themselves. In fact, according to the Merriam-Webster dictionary, etymologically, the terms " man" and "woman" derive from Old English with man meaning human being and woman meaning wife of human being. Tannen (1994) also refers to marking as important when applied to women, but she uses the term slightly differently than I have, saying "It refers to the way language alters the basic meaning of a word by adding something – a little linguistic addition that has no meaning on its own. The unmarked form of a word carries the meaning that goes without saying, what you think of when you are not thinking anything special." She specifically mentions that diminutives such as "ess," as in "poetess" mark words as female and so unnecessarily draw our attention to gender and to irrelevant gender associations, in this case to the gender of the poet rather than to her essence as a creator of poems. In a related vein, I note from the world of sports that we speak of the NBA and the "Woman's NBA;" the PGA and the "Lady's PGA"

While women have been defined as the marked, and usually inferior, version of men, the strengths of women also have been recognized by some. Even as early as 1952, Ashley Montague wrote *The Natural Superiority of Women*, emphasizing such now commonly recognized truths as women's greater heartiness at birth, greater longevity, and greater resistance to many illnesses and learning problems. Addis and Mahalik (2003) indicate that on average men die almost seven years younger than women. Sanjay Gupta (2003), a neurosurgeon, recently has come to appreciate that men's behaviors are no less important than their genes in explaining why they typically have shorter life-spans than females do. He notes that men have higher mortality rates in 14 of the 15 leading causes of death, the exception being Alzheimer's disease. According to him, men are more likely than women to smoke, consume alcohol heavily, abuse drugs, drive without a seat belt, and operate roll-over prone SUVs and motorcycles. Moreover, men more frequently suffer lightning strikes, drowning, and stress-related diseases, such as hypertension and heart disease. Ninety percent of on-the-job fatalities happen to men. Addis and Mahalik (2003) enumerate other maladaptive features of men's lives, citing research suggesting that even such well-educated males as medical students and university faculty are less inclined than their female peers to recognize and label nonspecific stress as indicating emotional problems. They add that men are less likely than women to seek help for medical and mental conditions, including conditions of stress, physical disability, depression, and substance abuse, and that this is true across age ranges, nationalities, and racial and ethnic groups. When men do visit caregivers, they ask less questions than women do.

Men's physical survival is less likely than women's in part because they resist accepting some of the realities of the natural world at the level of action (such as preferring to ride motorcycle without a helmet). Men's social-emotional survival is less likely than women's because men resist accepting some of the realities of the inter-personal world at the level of conversation, such as tending toward limited and dysfunctional conversation in areas that enhance social-emotional survival. Eugene Queenan (2003), a humorist, is not too far off when, tongue-in-cheek, he states, "If it wasn't for sports, men would have absolutely no emotional life."

To say that male behavior contributes mightily (an ironic choice of words?) to their death rate is to say that the related direct physical action tendencies of men are more often maladaptive than are women's. Since conversation is a verbal action tendency, it is reasonable to wonder whether males' conversations also are less adaptive than those of women. If women's documented higher rates of tending and befriending of which we spoke earlier (Taylor, Klein, Lewis, Gruenewald, Gurung, and Updegraff (2000)) and of pro-socially-oriented discourse (Lakoff, 1975) are any indication, the answer is a resounding "yes."

Female superiority also has been discovered concerning the structure of the English language when words are used to describe personality traits. Sankis et al. (1999) identified 1,710 personality terms (such as valiant, elegant, caring, sophisticated, and clingy) that were divided into 14 lists of 120 terms and 1 list of 30 terms, all arranged alphabetically. One thousand, three hundred, ninety college students rated the extent to which the terms applied to masculinity, femininity, and social desirability. Their ratings disclosed significantly more desirable female-linked than desirable male-linked terms, suggesting that, despite the dominance of men in positions of power, as a society we favor more traits stereotyped as feminine than as masculine.

The Sankis study implies that language can be used to distinguish feminine and masculine personalities. Wolfinger and Rabow (1997) find that the specific language employed by speakers also can differentiate males from females according to the style that they use when conversing. Five hundred forty nine UCLA undergraduate subjects were given transcripts of conversations with gender-identifying remarks removed. Of the eight transcripts rated, all but one was correctly gender differentiated by both male and female subjects. Women tended to be better raters than men were and personal characteristics such as socioeconomic status and race had minimal effects on the ability of the subjects to perform the ratings.

The abilities of women raters extend beyond mere gender differentiation. Montepare and Vega (1988) find that women who listen to telephone conversations can decide correctly whether conversing women are speaking to an intimate male friend or to a causal male friend merely by rating the conversing women's vocal and psychological characteristics. In addition to making such discriminations based on word choice and other lexical variables, there is reason to believe that vocal intensity may be used to determine the relationships between conversing persons (Welkowitz, et al., 1972).

Conversational style can distinguish women from men, but more important, conversational style can profoundly impact women and men both in terms of their intra-personal and their inter-personal experiences together. In tracking the development of positive communication skills from premarraige through one and one-half to five and one-half years post marriage, Schilling and her colleagues (2003) find that when men progress from more negativity in communication to more positivity there is a decreased incidence of marital distress and when women progress from more negativity in communication to more positivity there is a increased incidence of marital distress. They allege that this is so because women's increased negativity presumably occurs in ways that facilitate more honest expression of female discontent that allows more adaptive solutions to the problems that underlie it. The authors apparently presume, but do not state, that men who become more positive have no analogous problem in assertively expressing their discontents.

Earlier we mentioned play as an enactive form of thought expression that is more "primitive" than conversation and that can influence the development of conversational style. Gender-dimorphic play experiences differentially influence boys and girls and both reflect and contribute to differences between adult men and women. For instance, consider how boys' play frequently involves cars, dinosaurs, and other relatively non-social materials and activities and how girls' play frequently involves dolls, home environments, and relationships. It is possible, perhaps even preferable sometimes, for a boy to have a car or dinosaur play adventure that focuses largely or exclusively on physical, non-human events, thus reinforcing the establishment of pleasurable goals via object-oriented action and dominance over the inanimate world. By contrast, play with a doll or other human analogs must be social by definition. Even a girl sitting alone in her room combing a doll's hair is engaging in highly social behavior. Hughes and Dunn (1998) offer evidence indicating that girls ranging in age from 39 to 55 months already exhibit more frequent and more developmentally advanced talk about mental events and relationships than do boys of comparable age.

Cross, Morris, and Gore (2002) refer to the oft-cited research finding that women express more relationship-oriented thoughts than men do. They hypothesize that this is so because a woman's sense of self-representation is more likely to be based on interdependent self-construal—a sense of self that includes self as related to significant others and groups- as opposed to men whose sense of sense is more likely based on an independent self-construal – self-representation separate from the representations of others, including significant others and groups. Rusbult et al. (2000) explain that women also are more likely to exhibit "perceived superiority" in their communications about relationships. By this is meant that women, more than men, tend to regard their relationships as better than other person's relationships, or at least not as bad, as the relationships of others. Since the tendency toward perceived superiority of relationships is related to commitment to those relationships, one would expect women to have a greater sense of inter-personal commitment, and there is research that supports that contention (Taylor et al., 2000). In fact, it has been suggested that the value that men versus women ascribe to relationships is such that women's lies often are directed toward making their conversant partner feel good, while men's lies are oriented toward making themselves look good (Feldman, Forrest, & Happ, 2002). This female tendency, if true, does not invalidate our striving-for-GBH principle, however, since the women in question would attain GBH by making their conversant partners feel good.

Women and Men in Conversation

Left to their own devices in segregated uni-gender settings, women and men tend to converse differently and about different topics (Tannen, 1993). Our own common sense experiences and formal psychological and linguistic research overwhelmingly certify this. I do not wish exhaustively to enumerate male-female conversational differences, since many articles and books recently have been published on the subject, but brief consideration is useful to facilitate our discussion of conversation in general.

Primarily, men are described as using conversation more as a vehicle of competition, while women purportedly use it more as a vehicle for relationship building (Tannen, 1990). What does this difference imply? I illustrate by referring to an intense, largely one-sided discussion that I witnessed between a husband and wife, Dick and Jane.

Jane begins by asking Dick whether he followed her advice to ask his bowling partner, Ed, about his wife. Dick responds by supplying a few superficial wife-oriented comments, allegedly made by Ed. Jane counters by complaining, "Ed is your friend and you know almost nothing about him. How old are his kids? Where does he go on vacation?" Overwhelmingly dominating the discussion, she complains that men have no friends because they show no interest in each other's lives. She compares this with her belief that women talk about their desires, frustrations, husbands, children, and "so much more." Dick succinctly replies, "We talk about bowling, and work, and stuff." He does not try to defend himself, clearly not into this, "Our conversation is better than your conversation" thing.

Dick and Jane, though real people, could be characters in a primer about gender-dimorphic conversation as it relates to GBH. Jane presumes that women and men have identical goals for their conversations. She is right in the general sense that both strive for GBH in message and/or relationship when talking. But while both converse in ways to achieve their goals, she is wrong if she thinks that either the stereotypic female route that she espouses or the male route that her husband epitomizes is "the" correct alternative. It's more a matter of what GBH goal one specifically is pursuing and that specific goal need not be conscious.

Jane might argue, "You should know all about your friends, because that's what makes the relationship special; that's what friendship is." But that supposition may be the essence of the conversation difference between Dick and Jane, a difference rooted in the old-fashioned, but relevant, view of women as relationship leaders and men as instrumental leaders (Graves & Powell, 1982). Jane clearly is focusing on conventional markers of relationship as the primary purpose of conversation and factual information (message content) as the criterion of intimacy. However, in the male case, relationship GBH may have little, if anything, to do with objective, denotative conversation content and everything to do with subjective, non-content-oriented features of interaction. On the one hand, the teasing and taunting that characterizes much male-male casual conversation may be men's ways to achieve GBH via dominance as Tannen (1990) suggests, but, on the other hand, it also primarily could serve to fill a verbal content void while men get other GBH that they really seek, such as the "intimacy" of merely being together and "doing things" together. There could be a phylogenetic basis for this "let's just hang out" tendency, since male chimpanzees who hunt have been said to do so in large part to develop and solidify male bonding (Small, 2001). Equally possible, while such an objective might be heretical for Jane, Dick's conversation principally could be focused on attaining GBH of a purely non-relationship, message type, as when men converse with their golfing partners not so much to talk about family and relationship as to get the inside story on corporate life in order to move ahead.

Reasons for Gender Differences in Conversation

How can we explain gender-dimorphic conversation differences? Tannen (1990) summarized the opinions of many theorists by suggesting that women as a group tend to use talk to seek "intimacy"—comfort, support, and consensus—whereas men as a group tend to use it to achieve "independence" – increased status and decreased failure. She considered this mostly to be a consequence of differences in male-female socialization. Others, such as Susan D. Witt (2000), have emphasized that females and males are differentially reinforced for their gender-dimorphic behaviors and it is this that gives rise to their diverse conversation styles.

Whether powered by socialization, by reinforcement, or both, if men primarily have achievement-based relationships, this accounts for the popularity of boys who are strong, competitive, and athletic. But these very characteristics can be problematic for intimacy-based relationships. A dominant, achieving male can turn his strength against his friend; he can lose status if he fails to perform; he can inspire jealousy in males defeated by him—all zero-sum relationship effects. Women often are opposite when it comes to friendships. They frequently are popular precisely because they possess qualities associated with enduring social attractiveness, namely, women tend to value women who are "chatty," interested in others, helpful, and empathic – the very characteristics that promote intimacy-based friendships. Once again, it is a matter of women's placing more value on relating to others, because that is how women often measure success as mothers, daughters, and girlfriends, whereas men usually measure success by how well they are able to out-muscle other men.

I accept that both socialization and reward are powerful determinants of male-female differences and that we need to carefully consider the influences of both. However, socialization, meaning socializing effort, often is insufficient to force the direction of development—to "make" children do as we want them to do. Our control over rewards, whether through socializing agents or not, typically is no more effective. Consider schooling: In contemporary America, we are obsessed with student achievement, pouring billions of dollars into education and agonizing over our every education-related decision in an attempt to have children succeed. Unfortunately, even though we make special socializing and reinforcing efforts to turn all children into students, certain youngsters in general, and many boys in particular, are inclined to resist.

The issue is neither socializing agents nor rewarding agents. Rather, because the education-enhancing behaviors of students ultimately are volitional, they are naturally and vigorously pursued only when they cause the individual to attain GBH. Socialization and reward can be structured in an attempt to cajole and coerce, but they succeed only to the extent to which they cause children to adequately **value** education and adequately **experience** the GBH of learning and academic achievement.

The same is true of conversation differences between males and females. It is not merely that boys and girls are differentially socialized and differentially rewarded for their conversation orientation, it is that they experience GBH differently. For instance, what makes boys "feel good" may not necessarily be what makes girls "feel good." This may be due in part to socialization and reward, but other influences are likely as well, such as biological differences between the sexes. But even if there are biological factors that contribute to gender-related conversation differences, as we have explained earlier, the differences likely would be more quantitative than qualitative. Just as there is a range of muscularity, with some girls being more muscular than boys, there surely is a range of factors that affect how GBH is experienced.

Our daily lives offer ample support to the view that neither socialization, reward, nor biology can, in and of themselves, restrict conversation style to one gender-oriented direction. We all have known women who converse like men and vice versa. Those who do so naturally are those who truly derive GBH satisfaction from the conversational style associated with their opposite gender.

If the differences between those who adopt the stereotypically male or female conversation approach are differences primarily in GBH satisfaction, then reward salience and reward sensitivity are critical variables affecting an individual's conversational style, regardless of whether they are male or female. Reward salience is important: the more visibility and impact, the greater the reinforcing qualities of any reward. If two persons are given the same reward, but one recognizes and values it more, then she will be more likely to make a stronger behavior-reward connection and be more likely to repeat the behavior that occasioned the reward. Personality attributes may play a role in this. For instance, research suggests that the primary difference between introverts and extraverts is not that that extraverts obtain greater satisfaction from social situations per se but that they are more responsive to all pleasurable stimuli (Lucas & Fujita, 2000) Shy males and/or those excessively concerned about their masculinity are less likely than other males to enjoy positive reinforcement from conversation, because, for them, shyness and toughness concerns may be linked in a way suggested by Bruch (2002):

> "The pattern of these interactions is consistent with the previously mentioned rationale as to how the interaction between shyness and toughness may be related to greater emotional inexpression. Because shyness involves self-deprecatory thoughts arising from fear of negative evaluation and toughness involves the opposite concerns of acting strong and confident, the resulting tension between these needs may be associated with a greater degree of emotional inexpression. Thus, shy men who rigidly adhere to a norm of toughness may believe that the silent, rugged he-man role (e.g., John Wayne) is less likely to evoke criticism and is acceptable to more people. However, this role behavior may have a number of negative inter-personal consequences. Such role behavior is likely to involve little smiling and laughter, greater gaze aversion, and a tendency to show little interest in other people. Garcia et al. (1991) found that shy men who show an absence of these behaviors limit the amount of mutual gaze activity they have with their dyadic partners thereby reducing the amount of conversation time and the degree of satisfaction reported following an interaction. Consequently, adherence to a toughness role norm may compound a shy man's tendency to restrict his verbal—affective expression, which in turn may lower the effectiveness of his social interaction."

Remember that GBH involves an *expectant* search. Expectation can influence reward value, as we are well aware from the voluminous literature on self-fulfilling prophecies, but the impact of expectation extends far beyond reward value in and of itself. Whether they acquire the predisposition to GBH expectation through socialization, reward, biology, or all three, if males and females learn to differentially expect GBH from conversation, their conversation behaviors will be different.

If more males embrace the philosophy that "talk is cheap" and that "actions speak louder than words," then they will be inclined to resist conversation for conversation's sake, and their expectant searches for GBH more likely will focus on doing rather than talking. And if more females expect GBH from conversation for conversation's sake, then their expectant searches more likely will focus on conversation as an end in itself. By this process, the conversational differences between male and females will broaden and feed upon themselves in a self-sustaining fashion.

Women's tendencies toward the verbal aspects of casual conversation as primary and men's toward the verbal aspects as secondary might be summarized by the following extreme, but thought-worthy, generalization: When men get together to play cards, card playing tends to be the central focus and talking is peripheral; when women play cards, the opposite is the case. Goleman (1995) seems to agree with me. He mentions that

> "Ted Huston, a psychologist at the University of Texas who has studied couples in depth, observes, 'For the wives, intimacy means talking things over, especially talking about the relationship itself. The men, by and large, don't understand what the wives want from them. They say, 'I want to do things with her, and all she wants to do is talk.' During courtship, Huston found, men were much more willing to spend time talking in ways that suited the wish for intimacy of their wives-to-be. But once married, as time went on the men – especially in more traditional couples – spent less and less time talking in this way with their wives, finding a sense of closeness simply by doing things like gardening together rather than talking things over."

Although male-females conversational differences often merely affect our comfort level when we are with men versus women, at times the differences literally can have life or death implications. When Roter and her colleagues (2002) meta-analytically reviewed research of physician-patient communication covering the years 1967 to 2001, they not only found that women physicians engaged in more positive and more emotionally-focused talk, but that they also spent 10 percent more time with their patients. That was 10 percent more time for patients to express their true concerns and 10 percent more time for doctors to address them.

Is this conversation difference a matter of men being more inclined toward action-oriented GBH, with conversation as a secondary aid, or is it that women are more inclined toward conversation-based relationship GBH, with the content of conversation being secondary, or both? The answers to those complex questions are left for future research.

Conversation and Sexual Selection

One other explanation of male-female conversation differences warrants brief discussion. Geoffrey Miller (2000) believes that sexual choice shaped human nature and that conversation primarily is a means for promoting sexual choice and reproductive success. Among other things, he cites the fact that women have a relatively small number of ova that are present at birth and whose numbers dwindle markedly with the passage of time, while men continually produce an extraordinarily high number of sperm from puberty into old age. Throughout almost all of our species' existence, women had no choice but to "endure" their pregnancies and literally be saddled with infants, toddlers, and young children, while men could copulate and abscond. Because of these differences, the theory goes, a woman's sexual biology has inclined her toward relationship commitment. She has had the greatest chance of bearing and successfully rearing her few precious offspring when she has had an enduring relationship with faithful men (and women) willing to support her and her brood (Taylor et al. 2000). Men have had no such need. Combining this theory with that of Rusbult and colleagues' perceived superiority, we see that women have had many reasons to prefer commitment in physical-social relationships and, by extension, to commitment in conversational relationships.

From Miller's sexual choice and reproductive success point of view, male conversation is oriented toward self-promotion – boasting and preening—and toward fending off male competitors. Men seek to be the center of attention and to control and dominate during conversations, just as they seek to control and dominate in other social situations. Miller considers female conversation to be oriented toward understanding all people as potential partners. Women must be able to evaluate male verbiage, as well as plumage, to determine which men have the best resources and to use that information in mate selection. Women's prowess in general conversation and in understanding the broader social field is merely a secondary benefit of their learning to understand men.

Some might be offended by the "sexist," if you'll pardon the expression, nature of Miller's theory. But there is a larger criticism of his approach – it ignores the essential role of language as representation and conversation's role in using representation to promote the survival and comfort of individuals. The conversation of both genders proceeds from mental representations that I described earlier as being interoceptive-exteroceptive, multi-sensory-motor-visceral. I highlighted the fact that interoception includes experiences emanating from an individual's body, thoughts, and feelings, and that exteroception includes experiences emanating from the environment.

Conversation is more than a peacock tail to be fanned and more than a club-like weapon to be brandished. As we have demonstrated repeatedly, at its core, conversation enables men and women to confront all the basic exigencies of daily life. The survival-enhancing, comfort-promoting aspect of conversation involves social relationships, including gender relationships, to be sure, but it is much broader than that. Conversation helps all individuals to expectantly search for GBH wherever it affects their body, environment, thoughts, or feelings, even in relatively non-social, non-gendered areas, such as in controlling the pain of injury or in finding shelter from a storm.

Four Constants of Mental Life

Targets and Influences

Body, environment, thoughts, and feelings (BETF) are essential to mental representation because BETF comprise four unremitting sources of tension that we continuously target for improvement and that continuously influence our survival. These four constant interoceptive-exteroceptive targets and influences of life are always present, always interacting, and always affecting us to some extent. A change in any single element of the BETF system can produce a change anywhere else, although not necessarily at the same order of magnitude. Most often when we seek GBH, we desire to change BETF to a more optimal level. Think of it this way: In order to survive and thrive we focus inward to our body, thoughts, and feelings to discover our needs, and we focus outward to the environment to identify resources to satisfy those needs. To focus in this case is to mentally represent each BETF element in a multi-sensory-motor-visceral way. The centrality of our BETF focus is apparent in Clore, Ortony, and Foss (1987) finding that BETF are the four classes of psychological conditions that people most readily discriminate.

BETF elements singly or in combination drive us physically and mentally. Imagine the four as housed within a vehicle that is the self and that has four functional steering wheels. Any individual BETF element or combination of elements can steer the self while the remaining one or ones go along for the ride.

Each BETF element exists both as trait and state tension, but, to simplify our discussion, let's illustrate by talking only in terms of the body. Trait body tension refers to our modal level of physiologic tension – our usual resting level. Trait body tension differs from person to person, much as blood pressure does. For instance, a person who always seems "uptight" is high in trait body tension while a "laid back" person is low in trait body tension. Like blood pressure, however, body tension is not completely static for any single person. State body tension describes an individual's tension fluctuations within his trait-circumscribed range, temporary peaks or valleys soon replaced by his modal, resting level.

117

A resting level of trait tension represents readiness that permits us to quickly respond to everyday circumstances of life. An individual's resting level of trait tension can be subjectively comfortable or uncomfortable. In the latter case, the uncomfortable condition could be due such factors as physical pain, noxious environment, disturbing thought, or dysfunctional mood.

Regardless of the comfort or discomfort of the trait condition, our physical and mental selves periodically are roused from the complacency of this relatively stable, resting, trait level and moved into a changed state. Physical change is perceived by us when it exceeds a given biological threshold. The change can be caused by alterations in the internal milieu, such as when blood sugar or hormonal levels drop precipitously. Or it could be caused by an external source as when a cold blast of air chills our skin. Mental change is perceived by us when thoughts or feelings occur that are qualitatively or quantitatively different from the extant trait baseline. When any one of the constants deviates from its trait baseline significantly, the foregrounding of it that occurs amounts to increased "press" (pressure to seize our attention and/or to influence our behavior) for GBH satisfaction of the fore grounded constant. Tension advertises this press and rises as GBH "hunger" increases. As will be explained later, the changed thought or feeling state can be generated from inside or outside of the self, from conscious or unconscious stimuli.

The changed tone of the constant sometimes evolves slowly over time, as when people become less aggressive with age. Or the changed tone sometimes erupts into our consciousness, as when we are jolted by a leg cramp, surprised to see a sky that abruptly turns black and foreboding, alarmed to precipitously realize (think) that we forgot to turn off the oven, or overwhelmed by an unanticipated emotion. Moreover, the constants interactively influence each other. Sometimes there is conflict among them, as when through our thoughts we "talk ourselves" into engaging in overly strenuous physical exercise, pitting thought against body. But more often the constants achieve a harmonious amalgamation that is an individual in her milieu. For instance, happy thoughts typically occur in a context of relatively happy feelings, happy bodily conditions, and a happy environmental setting, any of which could have been prepotent in originally establishing the overall positive tone and then steering the other constants in its preferred direction.

When a changed state occurs from our current trait baseline, we habituate to it and establish a new trait-circumscribed baseline. We then perceive subsequent changes as deviations from this, habituate to the new condition, establish a new trait-circumscribed baseline, and so the dynamic process continues.

At any given moment in time, then, we experience any combination of bodily sensations, environmental stimuli, thoughts, and feelings (BETF), but they are not of equal strength and not at an equal level of consciousness. Most often only one or two of these is steering – is fore grounded. For instance, as I walk along the beach, I may be totally absorbed in and conscious of vacation-related ideas, and oblivious to my reddening skin, the roar of the surf, and my serene mood. At this point my conscious physical and mental life is steered by my thoughts. However, in the next second, I could slash my toe on a sharp seashell, instantly foreground my bodily self, background the heretofore engrossing vacation-related thoughts, and direct myself to restoring my body-oriented GBH integrity. My previous thoughts can be lost forever. Instead, I function at a reactive level of state arousal, become attentive to my bodily self, and direct my activities toward my injury, comfort, and safety. Subsequently, I habituate to the "shock" of my injury, establish a new trait-circumscribed resting level of bodily tension, background the concern about my toe, and foreground some other BETF element. In short, mental life can effortlessly move back and forth among BETF elements. Similarly, as one converses, his purposes can change—merge, split, fade, expand, and so forth.

The Four Constants and Conversation

Overwhelmingly, the impetus for conversation derives from the four constants as they exert their press on us. And press can be summated. For instance, if you have to urinate, that's press. However, if you have to urinate and you are talking with your boss about losing your job, that's double press, and, therefore, it has double the impact.

The quality of press also varies: The thoughts that continually stream through our minds are well-formed and conscious, or fragmentary and fleeting. Our emotional states may be full-blown and discrete, composite, or nothing more than vague comfort or discomfort. Bodily sensations sometimes are internally-based (e.g., the beating of our heart), externally-based (e.g., the chill or warmth of our skin), or both (e.g., our sense of equilibrium and proprioception). Environmental press (e.g., brightness or darkness, soft or harsh sounds) can be subtle or dramatic.

The four constants stimulate ideas that can be communicated. Bodily sensations are primary instigators of conversation. We could be in the midst of the most intense, ethereal discussion when I double up in pain. At that point all I would want to talk about is my discomfort and how to relieve it, and you undoubtedly would comply. By constantly impinging on us, the immediate environment also vies for space in our discussions. A sudden, booming thunderclap grabs us by the ears, drowns out our discussion, and demands that we at least comment about it. Previous thoughts are another major impetus for subsequent thoughts. Just as words tend to form associative chains, so do ideas. If we begin talking about a mutual friend who just was promoted, we may then move to talking about her spouse, our jobs, or other objectively linked ideas. However, the links between ideas need not be objective, for the emotional or connotative links between ideas are another source of conversation. Talking about the friend's promotion could cause you to think about money and the fact that I owe you twenty dollars. You could become irritated that the debt is months old and remind me of it right then and there.

In short, the four constants can affect our consciousness at any time, and become the raw material for conversation. These same constants have their own emotional tone and, as such, are themselves conduits for personal satisfaction and reinforcement. Conversational messages or relationships can facilitate in us a good or bad bodily sensation, environmental sense, thought, or feeling. Let's first be positive ourselves and consider the following:

GOOD INFLUENCE

Body	Dentist says, "I'm all done drilling." or Conversing partner's demeanor reduces my physical tension.
Environment	Boss says, "Let's open the shades; it's dark in here." or Conversing partner's presence makes a cold environment seem warmer.
Thought	Customer says, "I accept your proposal." Or Conversing partner engages me in engrossing discussion.
Feeling	Spouse says, "I love you so." Or Conversing partner is emotionally supportive.

Bad influences, obviously, can be illustrated by minor wording changes to the positive BETF influences enumerated above. More interesting is the fact that certain psychiatric disorders involve psychopathologies of the four constants and, therefore, identify conversational risks. For instance, bad conversations can occur due to a hypochondriac's bodily preoccupation, a paranoid's suspicion of the environmental field of which you are a part, an obsessive-compulsive's tedious thoughts, or an hysteric's excessive emotionality.

To return to our more positive orientation, consider that "normal" people differ in their **readiness** to become conscious of body, environment, thought, or feeling. Sharpeners (Hamilton, 1991) are those who are very attentive to subtle differences, emphasizing acute distinctions between two things that others may not even perceive. Depending on their orientation, they could be exquisitely aware of slight deviations in their baseline experiences of body, environment, thought, or feeling (BETF). And, prompted by that awareness, they might readily initiate or change a conversation. Levelers (Hamilton, 1991) are the opposite; unless the distinctions are blatantly obvious, they tend to see things as pretty much the same. These persons may struggle to introduce topics of conversation or to change the conversational direction because a BETF distinction does not readily "light up" to excite their interest.

Regardless of whether they are sharpeners or levelers, people also differ in the **exclusivity** and **intensity** of their focus on body, environment, thought, or feeling (BETF). The exclusivity and intensity of attentional focus, a result of complex, powerful personality forces, explains why some individuals are so quick to talk about some topics and so reluctant to talk about others. Sometimes a conversational predilection is obvious to all. We are not surprised to find a weight-lifter or handicapped person who makes repeated references to the body; a sightseer or combat soldier who speaks incessantly about the immediate environment; an academician or journalist who richly elaborates thoughts; or a psychologist or nursery school teacher who emphasizes feelings. However, all of us are predisposed toward our own unique combination of BETF sensitivities and associated conversations that are a direct result of our CAMMs and TAMMs.

Building Blocks of Conversation

Acceptable Speaking Standards: CASS and TASS

Our minds are flooded with ideas. We, of course, are unaware of the overwhelming majority of our thoughts. We could not disclose our every thought, even if we were conscious of them during conversation. Analogous to CAMM (which we earlier described as the part of the mental lexicon that contains words, ideas, and feelings that always are readily accessible to our consciousness), the chronically acceptable speaking standard (CASS) is our typical standard for discussing information. While CASS tends to be constant in a general sense, it varies according to topic and to our conversational partner. There are some topics about which you readily talk and others about which you never talk. There are some people with whom you almost reflexedly talk about certain things and others with whom you would never discuss the same thing. Analogous to TAMM (which we earlier described as the part of the mental lexicon that contains words, ideas, and feelings that only occasionally are accessible to our consciousness), the temporarily acceptable speaking standard (TASS) is one that depends on special conversational contingencies. Perhaps you never have discussed your sex life with anyone, but would have no reluctance to do so with a psychologist.

Conversation Executor

CASS and TASS, and all other components of conversation, are governed by a conversation executor that determines what is discussed and how it is discussed, both from the point of view of self as speaker and self as listener. The conversation executor is the conversation-specific subsystem of the more general executive functioning system of the self. Peter R. Giancola (2000) describes executive functioning as

> "...a higher order cognitive construct involved in the planning, initiation, and regulation of goal-directed behavior. The cognitive abilities subsumed within this construct include attentional control, previewing, strategic goal planning,

temporal response sequencing, self- and social monitoring, abstract reasoning, cognitive flexibility, hypothesis generation, and the ability to organize and adaptively use information contained in working memory (Kimberg & Farah, 1993 ; Lezak, 1995 ; Milner & Petrides, 1984 ; Stuss & Benson, 1984). From a biological level of analysis, the prefrontal cortex, particularly its dorsolateral aspect, is believed to be the primary neurological substrate that subserves executive functioning (Fuster, 1989 ; Goldman-Rakic, 1987 ; Luria, 1980 ; Milner, Petrides, & Smith, 1985)."

The conversation executor has one overarching goal – to achieve conversation-facilitated GBH as safely and efficiently as possible. Like most human processes, it primarily operates automatically and unconsciously, but is subject to at least some deliberate, conscious control. Because the conversation-oriented monitoring, censoring, and deciding must be made in real time regarding what to say and what not to say, if the executor were not mostly automatic, we would be paralyzed in our ability to speak. Should you ask me so simple a question as "What did you do the past weekend?" the conversation executor must enable me instantly and reflexedly to consider, among other things, how much you really want to know, how much time we have to discuss it, and what I am willing and able to disclose.

The conversation executor cues us to speak or to fall silent in order to increase our chances of GBH by permitting our coversant partner to strive likewise. The executor directs comments and questions in ways that further our message and/or relationships goals; it promotes responses to our conversant partner that satisfy the partner enough that she continues to be receptive to our goals. The intra-personal conversation executor, then, facilitates inter-personal conversation, functioning as a kind of referee in the virtual GBH tug-of- war that occurs whenever people converse. As each conversant exerts a force on the other, the conversation executor modulates the interaction to keep it moving and balanced. For discussion to continue, each conversant needs some slack to pursue personal needs and some resistance from her partner to keep the latter sufficiently engaged in pursuing her own needs. If one person speaks too much or too long, the other may despair of attaining GBH, let go of the conversational rope, and the discussion ends.

From the perspective of self-as-speaker, the executor relentlessly looks for an opening through which to introduce the self's GBH issues. From the perspective of self-as-listener, the executor searches for commonalities and concordances regarding partner-initiated verbalizations that the self can exploit to further his own GBH strivings. The executor seeks to satisfy the self's selfish desires in ways that contribute to the GBH search for self-competency while simultaneously maintaining the GBH search for the self-liking feature of self esteem that requires all of us to adhere to mores of "proper" conversational/social conduct. Accordingly, the executor facilitates some types of conversational behaviors with some people while discouraging other types of conversations with other types of people. It also is through the executor that we determine the extent to which the personality and behavior of others is consistent with our stereotypes of them based upon their references groups (e.g., gender, ethnicity, race, occupation, religion) and how much is to be regarded as due to their unique, individuated self-qualities (Macrae, and others, 1999).

In addition to promoting self-relevant topics, the conversation executor attempts to make sense of the conversational moves of his conversant partner. Whenever we converse, we wonder, "What is he getting at?" and "What kind of a response does he want from me?" This is the conversational equivalent of the psychological principle called "demand characteristics" – the automatic, general human tendency to try to understand all human encounters (Orne, 1962). Demand characteristics are central to virtually all conversation. Consciously or unconsciously, the self wants to understand the discourse strategies of his partner. On the one hand, by doing so, he is better able to structure the encounter toward actively reaching his own selfish goals. On the other hand, to understand the partner's strategy is at least to increase the likelihood of "getting through" a conversation with the least stress possible. In that case, the goal is to avoid conflict and to promote homeostatic comfort. Most casual conversations are relatively benign and grossly positive precisely because the conversation executor usually performs the latter function so well.

The executor is a useful hypothetical construct because it enables us to understand conversation as being directed—intra-personally and inter-personally, consciously and unconsciously. An analysis of the conversation executor reveals a great deal about the speaker and about his view of the listener relative to himself. It provides valuable insights into the kinds of things that are on the speaker's mind and those that are not. It tells us what he emphasizes and what he minimizes. The executor reveals the specificity or vagueness of the speaker, and how rational or emotional he is regarding the issues. We get a sense of the dynamics that determine when the speaker presses his case and when he reverses it. The executor discloses to us how the speaker is moving vis-à-vis his partner, such as whether he comes progressively closer to the other's position or further away from it.

From Mentation to Conversation

The conversation executor takes us from mentation to conversation. The executor searches the accessible content of mental life, surveys CAMM and TAMM, reviews baseline and directed consciousness, extracts that which is salient, determines what is communicable, evaluates conversational candidates through CASS and TASS, and ultimately selects topics to be pursued and the words by which to do so. The entire conversation-creating process can be summarized graphically as follows:

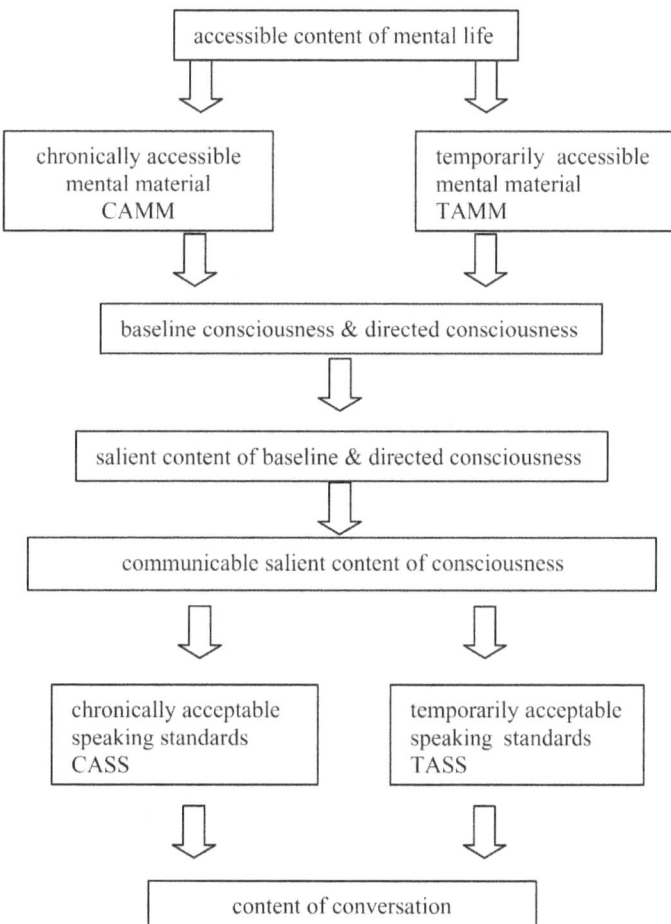

The Affective Dimension of Ideas in Context

Earlier we spoke about the connotative dimension of words. But more important for conversation is the connotative dimension of complete verbal thoughts – our own and others'. When we employ internal, mental language representation, we typically think in a series of connected phrases rather than in individual discrete words, and phrases are even more likely to be emotionally rich than are words. We use language to communicate similarly – mostly through phrases rather than individual words. And these mental or spoken phrases, singly and connectedly, overwhelmingly have connotative valence. Consider the nature of the phrases that we use in casual conversation. Most have overt, significant emotional tone. Ordinarily, I would not comment to you that, "I had dinner last night." To be chat-worthy, an otherwise mundane idea requires an affective spark. I would be eager to share that I had dinner at the White House last night, and you probably would be eager to hear that story. A conversationally-suitable idea, like the daily news, typically needs at least a hint of spice.

Moreover, while most phrases have some degree of positive or negative connotation inherently connected to them, context is critical in determining the connotation of any communicated idea. The context that influences verbal connotation includes body language, vocal quality, and many other variables beyond the scope of our discussion. Even restricting ourselves to verbal content issues, as we are in this book, we still must consider an array of variables to understand context as it affects connotations in conversation.

The first contextual connotation variable is the aforementioned conversational triangle—our personal history, the personal history of our conversational partner, and our shared histories concerning the topic. Every idea that we express derives its meaning from our idiosyncratic experiences with the notion that we are attempting to convey. Having been in the United States Marine Corps, my ideational "marine" container is deep and full of white, red, and green spheres. If you have not been a marine, you simply cannot have the associations to "marine" that I have. My task in speaking with you is to match my need and ability to explain my marine-oriented ideas with your desire and ability to understand them. Through my conversation executor, I unconsciously, intuitively negotiate this with you and you do likewise as we converse. The challenge is for me to say just enough to satisfy my GBH needs without interfering with your ability to satisfy yours. That job will be less ego depleting to me if you had been in the marines, or at least in the armed forces, or if we have spoken about the marines in the past.

A second contextual connotation variable is the current affective climate. How we feel at any given moment powerfully influences the emotional coloring that we experience and express (Bower, 1981). A positive mood promotes positive conversations; a negative mood promotes negative conversations. Consider my experience at work last week. A coworker returned from a much-deserved long weekend in New England, and I asked about it. He explained that it "sucked," and then detailed all of the undesirable aspects. Four hours later I heard him describe the same weekend to a female colleague. There was music in his voice as he mentioned having stayed at a plush home in an exclusive resort area. He quickly glossed over a few undesirable features of his stay, emphasizing instead the salutary ones.

What's going on here? Did he lie to me or to her? Probably neither. Surrounded by medical charts, all requiring notation, it was 8:00 AM when my coworker and I spoke at the nursing station. He knew that I had worked the weekend. When he spoke with our female colleague, his hectic morning was over. They sat relaxed in the lunchroom. She had just finished telling him about the wonderful Chesapeake Bay sailing experience that she had the same weekend that he had gone to New England. His conversation, as all of ours, was determined by his current emotion at the conversational moment, by the current emotion of his speaking partner, and by the environmental context in which he spoke.

A third contextual connotation variable is unconscious influence, the influence of baseline consciousness. Our unconscious tends to hold on to affectively significant ideas. These baseline consciousness ideas rattle around in our brains, just waiting for a chance to be expressed – whether directly or indirectly. If you had been working intensively all day on an especially challenging project, thoughts relevant to it do not stop abruptly as soon as you leave your place of business. They will continue to "press" upon your mind for an indefinite time, perhaps during your commute and at home, looking for any opening to erupt into consciousness and into conversations.

Finally, contextual connotation is dependent on conversants' shared realities at the moment of conversation. While being enacted, conversation is always provisional and subject to revision. We can never be sure what we are communicating until after we have said it and our partner has replied. This is true because everything that we say depends on our conversation executor, the listener's conversation executor, and the reactions of each to the other. For instance, if I say to my spouse, "I'm tired." She might reply, "You seem bored." and I might conclude, yes, I really am bored. We then might decide something to do together. I thought I was communicating my fatigue, but something else was transmitted, something outside of my awareness. In this case, my conversation partner was better attuned to my unconscious, underlying, affectively-based thought than I was; her response helped me introspect; and it drove subsequent conversation about how to spend our time.

To summarize, the affective dimension in conversation encompasses words and thoughts, speakers and listeners, and conversant's responses to his own remarks and to those of his conversant partner. Each level offers opportunities for and presents threats to GBH, and each opportunity and threat occurs in real-time contexts that powerfully determine the chances for good versus bad conversation outcomes.

Messages and Relationships

Obtaining Information and Bonding Inter-personally

Conversation occurs in an inter-personal context, proceeding through affectively significant words and ideas organized around topics. In part, the affective dimension of the words and ideas of the topics consists of emotion directly linked to the words and ideas being discussed. That is, the message-satisfaction is underscored. If while speaking with you I spontaneously tell about the role that I played in implementing a new work procedure, presumably I do so because talking about it causes me to feel GBH. The focus here is on the subject of discussion and how it makes me feel. There are many possible connections between GBH and any given message. In the case of the current example, I may be re-experiencing the tingle of excitement associated with success, or I may be verbally anticipating the benefits that the work success will bring to me.

But the affective dimension of conversation and the GBH that I seek through it does not have to be connected to the message per se. I am just as likely looking for GBH in my relationship with you. That is, relationship-satisfaction is underscored, anticipated relationship satisfaction associated with my desire to "get something" through my relationship with you. Again, there are many possibilities. Perhaps I admire you and covet the self-enhancement that goes with being your esteemed friend. Or, maybe I perceive you as powerful and hope that being in your good graces somehow can make my life better.

The essential point is that all conversation primarily is in the service of the self and its pursuit of GBH, not in the service of objective truth or even for the development of relationship merely for the sake of relationship. Sometimes the message provides the self -service, as when we are talking to someone in order to get something from him, and the getting or not getting, itself, is the essential sought-after message. Sometimes the relationship provides the self- service, as when we "feel good" talking with someone or want to endear ourselves to a powerful or attractive person. This merely is a Darwinian fact of life. We converse for the same reasons that we eat, drink, or mate—to feel good, better, or homeostatic (GBH). And, like our desire to eat, drink, and mate, our attempts to secure message GBH and relationship GBH tend to be unconsciously motivated.

The message- versus relationship-satisfaction distinction is real. Sometimes we willingly tolerate conversing with someone we do not like because of the message satisfaction that we derive from the topic of discussion. In other circumstances, we willingly tolerate discussing a boring or otherwise distasteful topic with someone because of the relationship satisfaction that we derive from the conversation. However, the ideal conversation is one affording us both message- and relationship-oriented GBH.

The person who initiates a topic and his partner ideally seek GBH from both the information that they derive and from their personal acquaintance, that is, from the message side and the relationship side of the transaction. In the language of self esteem that we used earlier, each wants to enhance his self competence and self liking. And most often this can be accomplished with relative ease, since each partner is more likely to achieve his conversational message and relationship GBH by facilitating, or at least not interfering with, that of his partner. For instance, even a high message orientation discussion, such as occurs when we call a telephone operator, proceeds best when it provides at least minimal relationship GBH to both participants, since both would prefer to achieve at least a "civil talking relationship" while transacting their business.

The message side and relationship side of a conversation each can have both overt and/or conscious and covert and/or unconscious features. Message-oriented conversation can have overt content that appears inconsistent with its underlying covert purpose, as when I casually ask about your job as though I am interested in your well-being when, in fact, I consciously or unconsciously am thinking about applying at your place of employment. Or a relationship-oriented conversation in which I solicitously ask about your vacation plans consciously or unconsciously could be my competitive way of scoring my lifestyle against yours. A covert attempt at message GBH also could be contained in our conversation: If I speak with you about how much I want a new DVD player, explain that I have no money, and then ask you to go out shopping with me, I may intend to ask you for a loan. Or, if you tell me that you have to hang-up the telephone and I keep prolonging the telephone discussion, I may be so desperate for relationship GBH that I, in a sense, am "refusing" to let you leave me.

When two people converse, they often are amazingly and automatically adept at finding their way to personal message and/or relationship GBH. Any combination of message or relationship satisfaction is possible. Each could realize both types of GBH or each could realize one type, even a type different from that of her partner. I am reminded of two girlfriends who love to criticize the one girlfriend's husband: the wife-girlfriend gets GBH from having an ally with whom to vent a negative idea lingering in baseline consciousness – message GBH—and the other woman, who is divorced, gets GBH from downward comparison relative to the wife's being married but dissatisfied – relationship GBH.

It often is useful to ask whether your conversation with someone is primarily message or relationship oriented. Time may be an indicator. Thus, if a coworker pops her head into your cubicle for one minute and leaves after having gotten you to promise to help her with her inventory job, then she likely was seeking GBH in the message, namely, that you would help. If someone is always around just "shooting the breeze" and never getting any significant information from it, her goal is probably relationship GBH.

We see then that conversation is a series of topics, often connected, each intended to achieve GBH, in message and/or relationship. Topics or conversations end when the initiator's goal has been achieved, thwarted, or deemed not worth the effort. Our expectations about achieving GBH determines in large measure whether we will venture into conversation at all. Consider the situation in which a spouse wants her partner to attend the spouse's office party. When offered a chance to go, the partner opines, "I have nothing in common with those people (anticipating that he will not realize any message GBH) and/or, "I don't feel like going. I don't know anyone there (anticipating that he will not realize any relationship GBH).

Passive Conversationalists

You might wonder about the situation in which one person verbally dominates a conversation. Where is the passive one's GBH? There are many possibilities: among them, since knowledge is power, the passive person could be deriving satisfaction from getting the "inside scoop" on her conversant partner, or the reticent person could be achieving GBH because her message needs are congruent with those of the verbose one, or she could be ingratiating herself to a powerful other. A lesson from animal research into GBH strivings is appropriate here. Held and her associates (2002) conducted a conditioning study of dominant and submissive pigs who were penned together. If either pig pressed the experimental lever at one end of the pen, some food pellets would be deposited in a trough at the opposite end of the pen. At the beginning of the study when both pigs were ignorant about the significance of the lever, each pig had equal access to it. During that period, the submissive pig sometimes pressed the lever. When he did, food appeared and he often was able to eat it. Soon both pigs made the connection between lever pressing and food appearance. From that point forward, whenever the submissive pig pressed the lever, the dominant pig would muscle him aside, eat the food, and the submissive pig got none. Before too long the submissive pig ceased pressing the lever. Instead, he lingered near the food trough and waited for the dominant pig to press the lever whereupon the submissive pig was able to eat a couple mouthfuls of food before the dominant pig raced down from the level location to the trough, brushing the submissive pig aside. Unlike the submissive pig, the dominant pig never ceased his lever-pressing behavior, preferring to work to get something to eat rather than starve because his counterpart would not press the lever.

Two other factors are significant in explaining how a conversationally passive person might allow others to dominate discussions, and still derive GBH. First, listeners can achieve vicarious satisfaction from some discourse primarily voiced by their conversant partner by identifying with the dominant speaker's satisfactions, provided that she shares with the partner enough meaningful story themes to make the discussion worthwhile. Second, the listener can realize GBH via downward comparison in which she lets the conversant partner dominate discussion while she, herself, finds message and/or relationship GBH in the discourse content that allows her to feel one-up on a verbally dominant speaker who inadvertently has disclosed his foibles and problems.

Conversational Movement

Whether pigs or people, most animals move to live and live to move. Animal movement is prompted from inside-the-body by inherent, internal forces, because movement is necessary, among other things, to facilitate an animal's respiration, circulation, digestion, and elimination. Animal movement also is prompted from outside-the-body by external forces, because movement inclines toward environmental elements that promote life and health and away from elements that contribute to death and disease.

At base, animals of most interest to humans are uncompromisingly active organisms in motion. Animals capable of movement, including the human animal, are not adequately described by the most finely detailed anatomical chart depicting static, isolated body organs or systems. Sheets-Johnstone (1999) assertively, elegantly, almost poetically, argues that, above all else, animals are integrated organisms engaged in expectant, relentless movement. She explains:

> "...Animate forms are the starting point of biological evolution. They are where life begins. They are where animation begins. They are where concepts begin. They are where emotions are rooted, not in something that might be termed 'mental life' (e.g., Cabanac, 1999, p. 184: 'emotion is a mental feeling'), a 'mental' that is or might be embodied in some form or other, but in animate form to begin with. *Embodiment* deflects our attention from the task of understanding animate form by conceptual default, by conveniently packaging beforehand something already labeled 'the mental' or 'mind' and something already labeled 'the physical' or 'body' without explaining—to paraphrase Edelman (1992, p. 15)—'how "the package" got there in the first place' (cf Sheets-Johnstone, 1998; 1999)....The hard problem is to give animate form and the qualitative character of life their due. More broadly, the hard problem is to see ourselves and all forms of life as intact organisms, living bodies, rather than as brains or machines. We come into the world moving; moving and feeling moved to move are what are gone when we die. Surely when we lament or fear our own death, we do not lament or fear that we will have no more information to process. We lament or fear that we will no longer be *animate* beings but merely material stuff—*lifeless, unmoved, and*

unmoving. Nature is 'a principle of motion', as Aristotle recognized, and kinetic form is its natural expression."

Sheet-Johnstone's assertions are centrally relevant to human experience throughout the life cycle. Consider, for instance, how self-feeding and self-ambulation enhances the satisfaction, independence, and viability of the infant and how lack of self-feeding and lack of self-ambulation undermines the satisfaction, independence, and viability of the infirmed elderly.

The active animal body includes an active animal mind, and vice versa, that directs the organism toward GBH enhancement and away from GBH threat. The human animal is impelled to do things and go places to fulfill the demands of life, as according to Maslow's hierarchy of needs, and to derive a sense of pleasure and balance. Yet, while only some people can be physically active and engaged frequently in pleasurable dancing, singing, drawing, or building, virtually all people, virtually all of the time, can be mentally active and engaged in pleasurable conversation.

Language is our specialized secondary system that enables people to sense and move without acting in an overt, physical sense. Language brings the self and the environment, especially the inter-personal environment, together in the mind to be sampled, tested, and manipulated. This non-physical action conserves life resources and protects bodily integrity—exploration and problem solving that is uniquely safe and efficient.

Conversation is language's premier vehicle for realizing the potential of internal mental representation and internal mental movement. Through it we achieve message GBH, seeing and hearing important information that others have seen and heard, and relationship GBH, comforting and allying with others to enhance our mutual survival. Such a view of language and conversation presumes that they are vitally connected with action – that language, conversation, internal subjective states, and overt movement are linked. This is just what Ushakova (2000) posits when he states,

> "According to our hypothesis-confirmed by many data collected in our studies—there exists a special mechanism, inborn in the human brain, that functions to **exteriorize internal subjective states** by means of **movement**, among which **vocalization** has an important place. The child's subjective impression is expressed in one or another form of movement, an adequate form employed by the human being most often the production of sound. As illustrated by the infants' cry, this form is predestined for this function by nature and manifests itself from the time the infants are born.

This natural "core" develops in childhood according to natural laws and acts during the whole life as a motivational and "intentional" basis of oral speech (see, e.g., Addeo & Buerger, 1974,). The social environment—the ambient people who employ an elaborated **language** system—help the infant to shape this core by offering convenient and adequate verbal forms for use. And this language system, undoubtedly, actively influences the internal language forces of infants."

The theory that Ushakova proposes is consistent with my belief that GBH is the driving force behind language. He asserts, as I have earlier, that language begins with the neonate's cry, a cry that is a plea for GBH, "asking" caretakers to reduce its hunger and other discomforts, and that all subsequent language and conversation proceeds from and elaborates upon this base. The neonate, then, as all of us, is inherently motivated to move toward circumstances facilitating objective and/or subjective GBH, and those GBH-facilitating movements can be overt, action-oriented or verbal, language-oriented.

Moving Toward the Good: Trying to Hit a Moving Target

Repeatedly we have emphasized that living things relentless **search** for stimuli that they **expect** will enhance their survival and comfort. They naturally strive for the "good," meaning that which is life enhancing. Regarding elemental physical needs, basic biological drives exert press for their satisfaction by invoking instinct-like actions, such as required for hunting. Because these instinct-like actions have evolved within an appropriate environmental context, the route to satisfaction is relatively straightforward. The successful hunter pursues, seizes, and devours his suitable prey. The search for that which is good for the physical self is satisfying only when it culminates in decreased physical tension. Emotional needs also press for satisfaction, but there is no simple, instinct-like action sequence that ensures satisfaction within a particular environmental context. The actions that lead to emotional satisfaction can be quite circuitous and complicated because emotional satisfaction is mostly subjective. The search itself for emotional satisfaction may be as satisfying, even more satisfying, than the goal that is sought. For instance, persons sometimes get more pleasure from preparing for vacation than from the actual vacation. Similarly, in conversing, arguing with someone may be more fun than is winning the argument.

Thus, that which is good can be the object of the search or the search itself. Moreover, what is good today may not necessarily be good tomorrow and what is good for one organism may not be good for another. There is no constant good. The old saying "variety is the spice of life" is apropos. What is required is a match between the readiness and need of the organism and the availability and appropriateness of the target at any given moment in time. Food normally is a powerful primary reinforcer, but not so for an animal who just has eaten his full; such an animal turns away from food and toward other sources of good. Raynor and Epstein (2001) found that people eat 44 percent more food when courses contained a large variety than when they contain a small variety. Considering secondary reinforcers now, a compliment means little when it comes from someone who compliments too freely or insincerely. This is why behavior therapy emphasizes that rewards be dispensed judiciously with an eye toward maintaining their reinforcing power. Hollywood knows this. Publicists carefully titrate the public exposure of their celebrity clients. There is a point at which overexposure becomes as career-debilitating as underexposure.

Emotional satisfaction also is very sensitive to the criteria that an individual uses to decide what is good, and these criteria can change. People often desire a goal and strive vigorously to attain it, but only savor the reward briefly before becoming discontented with it and upping the ante to a higher level. As we discussed earlier, this "hedonic treadmill" (Brickman & Campbell, 1971) tendency to move the satisfaction baseline explains why we experience short-term gratification after getting a salary raise, but soon decide, "If only I had a little more money, then I really could get what I want." What does this say about conversation?

Because conversation is an **expectant search** for messages and relationships, expectant searching drives conversation forward. We keep conversing only as long as we maintain the expectation of reaching GBH. When our initial topic results in GBH we move to another topic and resume the search. The relentless, expectant search during conversation is related to our general need for stimulation as a source of GBH. Stimulation as GBH explains why we keep clicking the television remote controller in search of a more perfect program, and why we are intolerant of being bored. It is why we attend sporting events and go to movies: They are ways to be active vicariously and to actively experience things without moving, and, therefore, without risking ego depletion.

When all of our conversation searches have achieved their GBH ends or when we finally conclude that they will not result in GBH, we cease conversing and look toward other GBH avenues, as via direct action. The nonconversationalist is a person with a trait-like conviction that conversing will not lead to GBH.

Although conversation usually is a means to achieve message and/or relationship GBH, being multi-determined, conversation, itself, can be a proximal (nearby) or distal (distant) goal. That is, the conversation qua conversation can provide GBH satisfaction. For instance, some persons sometimes want to converse because, in the vernacular, "Thy love to hear themselves speak." This is a special form of relationship GBH involving a search for self esteem enhancement, or enhancement of one's relationship with herself. Other persons at other times might converse to avoid action, as when one incessantly chatters about all the work that he plans to do that day, work that he never gets around to doing because he is talking too much. In still other situations, the conversational search, itself, may be reinforcing in that anticipation of the good by way of fantasizing/imagining/rehearsing about it sometimes is as rewarding as the good itself.

Inter-Personal Movement

Inter-personal movement per se is targeted by the science of proxemics, pioneered by Edward T. Hall (1966), who defined it as "man's use of space as a specialized elaboration of culture." Among other things, he popularized the now familiar idea that conversational partners must maintain a culturally defined "proper" speaking distance, if they are to feel comfortable. For instance, when speaking, the English normally stand closer to each other than do the French who, in turn, stand closer together than do the Dutch (Remland, Jones, & Brinkman, 1991). Sussman & Rosenfeld (1982) empirically supported Hall's ideas. They compared American, Japanese, and Venezuelan undergraduates during a 5 minute, same sex, same nationality conversation and found not only that Venezuelans sat closest together, Japanese sat furthest apart, and Americans sat at an intermediate distance, but also that foreign students' speaking distances better approximated the American distance when the foreigners spoke English together. With the exception of the Japanese, Asians and Latin Americans, in general, interact at closer distances than do North Americans or Europeans (Evans, et al., 2000).

De Rivera (1977) used a proxemics-oriented approach to studying words related to emotion and personality. He suggested that when we think about an object or person, we unconsciously decide how to act relative to it and that this decision is at the root of our emotional response. He attempted to understand the emotion-personality link by classifying emotions in terms of specific movements that have important inter-personal implications. Most notably for our purposes, according to his system, we desire closer proximity to objects or persons consider to be positive, and increased distance from objects or persons considered negative. In some cases we wish to be moving, as when we want to approach a loved one, and in other cases we expect the object or person to be moving, as when we want a loved one to approach us.

The desire for inter-personal movement, whether mental or physical, has implications for positive and negative emotional valence, rooted in the survival "instinct." Not only do we move toward the good and away from the bad, but the fact that we are moving toward something, or the belief that we are, facilitates seeing it as good and the fact of moving away from something, or the belief that we are, facilitates seeing it as bad. Moreover, the movement, or perception of movement, need not be of whole body movement. Neumann and Strack (2000), for instance, demonstrated these linkages in a series of fascinating experiments that involved hand movements as well as an impression of whole body movement when no true bodily movement occurred. For the hand movement experiment, participants sat in front of a computer screen on which words were projected. They had to decide as quickly as possible whether the target word connoted something pleasant (e.g., tender) or unpleasant (e.g., lazy). The participants needed to use their dominant hand to press a right-side key in response to a pleasant word and a left-side key in response to an unpleasant word. There were two major experimental conditions – arm flexion and arm extension. Arm flexion was hypothesized to represent one of the body's natural approach systems, since we often flex our arms as we draw something toward us. Conversely, extension was considered to be one of the body's natural avoidance systems, since we often extend our arms as we push something away from us. In the impression of whole body movement experiment, the same basic material and apparatus were used. However, for this study, participants were induced into the visual impression that they either were moving toward or away from the computer screen. The effect was accomplished by projecting a background of concentric circles that were either coming toward the participant, giving him the impression that he was moving forward, or the circles were going away from him, giving the participant the impression that he was moving back from the screen. As Neumann and Strack had predicted, in experiments one and two, pleasant words were identified more rapidly than negative words in both the arm flexion and the perception of body moving toward the screen conditions – the approach conditions – and negative words were identified more rapidly than positive words in both the arm extension and the perception of body moving away from the screen conditions – the avoidance conditions.

Toward-Away, Above-Below, With-Against (TAABWA)

We said earlier that language is a symbolic sensing and moving instrument that promotes survival, allowing us to move figuratively toward the good and away from the bad by enabling us to represent words and ideas that mentally encode something positive or negative. Movement and language are tightly related. For instance, often when people are in intimidating social situations they reduce both their overt physical movement and their conversation, a phenomenon called the "elevator effect," an effect that impacts monkeys, as well as humans (DeWaal, et al., 2000).

Within the context of human culture, language, even more than overt action, provides specifically for inter-personal sensing and moving – for moving our social self and/or the social selves of others. Conversational movement is language movement designed to facilitate our message and/or relationship goals in an inter-personal setting. Regarding messages, much of what we talk about is oriented toward eliciting, obtaining, and giving information in ways that we expect ultimately will facilitate our GBH quest. Regarding relationships, much of what we talk about is oriented toward eliciting, obtaining, and giving social support in ways that we expect ultimately will facilitate our GBH quest. The inter-personal style that we adopt during conversational movements is a critical determinant of our success, and discloses whether we are moving primarily in a way that highlights affiliative, achievement, or power motives.

Through conversation we verbally can move toward or away from our conversational partner – an affiliation-disaffiliation dimension. To move toward in this sense is to relinquish our isolation and/or independence, at least in part, and to adopt a verbal position of greater interdependence with our conversational partner. To move away is to seek increased isolation and/or independence. In addition to moving toward or away (TA) inter-personally, we can move above or below (AB). This directional vector represents relations along an intellectual-achievement dimension. We move above when in conversation we make a remark that explicitly or implicitly suggests an intellectually "superior" attitude (Superior, interestingly is a medical term used to designate an anatomical location **above** a reference point.) to that of our partner. Conversely, we move below when in conversation we make a remark that explicitly or implicitly suggests an intellectually "inferior" attitude. (Inferior is superior's obverse in medical terminology, used to designate an anatomical location **below** a reference point.) A third conversational vector involves a power-relations dimension. Here our comment either represents going with or going against the other (WA) in a way that, respectively, is personally accommodating or confrontational. To go with is to express status equality between conversing partners. To go against is overtly to attack the conversant with whom we speak.

The three directions as expressed above represent, respectively, the conversational equivalents of McClelland's view of the three most fundamental social motivations: the drives to affiliate (TA) with others, to achieve intellectually (AB), and to exert inter-personal power (WA). He considered these motivations to be critically important for individual personality development and for social stability. By assessing an individual's affiliation, achievement, and power motivations, we learn the essence of his social self. McClelland acknowledged that questionnaires could be used which basically asks a person questions to determine the quality and strength of each motivational dimension such as: "Would you rather read a book or go to a party?" Answers to such questions, he felt, might give a reasonably accurate account of the respondent's conscious preferences. However, in McClelland's opinion, direct questions – explicit measures – would not adequately predict the respondent's behaviors. That is, a person who answers a questionnaire item saying that he would go to the party could just as likely choose to read a book when the time came to do so. McClelland believed, and much research supports the belief, that a person's actual behavioral choices are better predicted by implicit measures in which the individual is presented with an open-ended stimulus that allows him to spontaneously react in a way that permits psychological analysis of motivational tendencies. McClelland used ambiguous pictures as stimuli and the individual's verbalized fanciful stories as the "projective" material to analyze, and thus to reveal, personality dynamics of mental health patients. Others have directly compared explicit with implicit measures. Rustad, Small, Jobes, Safer, and Peterson (2003), for example, studied the impact of rock videos having suicidal content with the suicidal thought and attitudes of college students. They found that persons exposed to rock videos with suicidal messages wrote more projective stories with suicidal content than those not so exposed (an implicit measure), but that the two groups did not differ on explicit tests of their affect, attitudes, and perceptions regarding suicide.

Ambiguous pictures presented to patients in a mental health setting and rock videotapes viewed in experimental settings undoubtedly contribute to our understanding the human condition. However, in my opinion, conversation is the ideal implicit, naturalistic measure not only of motivation specifically but of personality and inter-personal relationships generally. As indicated above, by scrutinizing conversation we unobtrusively can observe each speaker's predilection to move toward-away (TA), above-below (AB), or with-against (WA) – giving us their standing, respectively, on the affiliation, achievement, and power dimensions. But we can do much more. To name just a few: Conversation discloses speakers' optimism-pessimism, analogous to their tendency to apprehend the world as good/pleasant/positive as opposed to bad/unpleasant/negative. Conversational material permits us to make such intra-psychic inferences as to whether the speaker is relatively fulfilled or frustrated emotionally and socially, and we also can consider whether the speaker's conversational style is likely to endear or alienate him from his speaking partner. This does not depend merely on the words that conversants use and it is not a mere sterile, academic endeavor. When we scrutinize spontaneous conversations we hear not just the words but also a speaker's prosody, the "music" of discourse, including such elements as the inflection, and rhythm of discourse. Juslin and Laukka (2001) emphasize the importance of such elements, stating that voice cues in general and loudness or talking speed in particular (Planalp, 1998) are among the most central conversational features by which people "…judge the emotional states of others in everyday life." Robert Krauss and his colleagues (2202) show that merely by listening to the voices of speakers without ever seeing them, naïve subjects can estimate the age and height of such speakers almost as well as can naïve observers who see photographs of the same speakers.

Varieties of Conversation

Baseline consciousness provides ideas that whirl about in our minds, pressing for release through conversation. But what kind of conversation shall we have? How are conversations classified? The answer depends on the criteria selected to differentiate the targeted discussions. Should it be based on topic discussed, linguistic structure, or what? Since classification is only a crude tool to promote understanding, we will use an eclectic method, choosing varieties of conversation that will enable us to refine basic premises explored thus far. I have no problem with a somewhat arbitrary classification system, since all classification systems are rather arbitrary. And classification of conversation is especially subjective because conversation categories overlap and conversations are continuously negotiated between conversants in real-time—what initially began as narrative can end as gossip. The classification parameters that I have chosen are drawn both from professional literature and from my own clinical experience.

Let's start by considering Eggins and Slade's conversation subtypes (1997) that include:

Storytelling: narrative, anecdote, exemplum, and recount, all of which share a similar overall discourse structure and a time line of narrative-like clauses. The storytelling subtypes are defined as follows:

> Narrative—presentation that describes an incident of increasing tension/excitement building toward a problem/crisis and then on to resolution.

> Anecdote—defined basically the same as a narrative but the crisis/problem is only reacted to, not resolved.

> Exemplum—presentation oriented more toward advocating a world-view – telling how the world should or should not be—rather than describing an incident.

> Recount—presentation of a series of events in which the narrator is a major player who only indirectly discloses his attitude toward them.

Observation/Comment: text in which factuality is emphasized and followed by a comment.

Opinion: a frank good/bad appraisal, elaboration, or defense of a state of affairs that exists in the world.

Gossip: pejorative appraisal of a person or persons not present during the conversation.

Joke-Telling: straightforward telling of jokes.

The authors studied three hours of conversation during coffee breaks at three different work places and involving three different groups – all-male, all-female, and mixed-gender. Collapsing the data across all groups they found that the percentages of conversation spent in the varieties were: storytelling, 43; observation/ comment, 20; opinion, 17; gossip, 14; and joke-telling, 6. The most common storytelling subtype was anecdote, followed in descending order of frequency by recount, exemplum, and narrative. Eggins and Slade speculated that familiarity and frequency of contact among members that determine which varieties of conversation will be most common within a given group.

The conversation classification scheme emphasized by Goldsmith and Baxter (1996) included Eggins and Slade's gossip and joking, but added "making plans," "catching up," "small talk," and "recapping the day's events." The taxonomy was organized in terms of three dimensions: formal-goal directed, important/deep/ involving, and positive valance. This means that interactants, themselves, perceived conversations as formal versus informal, important versus superficial, and positive versus negative – a clearly personal evaluative scheme. The evaluative significance of a particular conversation, however, would depend, as it always does, on the context in which the talk occurred. In fact, some conversations are by their very nature defined largely in terms of evaluation. "Chit-chat," for instance, is evaluated by our society as informal and superficial, but it could be considered positive or negative by persons engaged in a given chitchat event.

The two systems discussed above support my contention that there are many varieties of conversation with much overlap among them. However, I submit that under ordinary circumstances all of these primarily concern the self and evaluation by the self. In the first place, you can speak only about what has affected your "self" because self-involvement is a necessary prerequisite for encoding experience into a form suitable for vocalizing. If you do not evaluate something as being meaningful, which means meaningful to you, you cannot know enough to converse about it. Second, only when you evaluate something as relevant to your self do you direct enough attentional resources to make it sufficiently memorable to be a topic for later discussion. Third, and most central to our discussion, all conversation relates to the self and to evaluation because all conversation is intended to promote GBH in the person who initiates it.

Recall that persons speak in the mostly unconscious **intention** to feel GBH. From the content side of conversation, any topic that we introduce and anything that we say, no matter how misguided, could be intended to elicit relationship GB/GBH, as is apparent when people make foolish, attention-seeking comments. Similarly, anything that we say can provide us homeostatic benefit H/ GBH by releasing the mental pressure that the thoughts or feelings had exerted on baseline consciousness. In short, any conversation can be driven by a desire to improve relationship and/or to reestablish mental homeostasis. Accordingly, in what follows I will discuss relationship-oriented and homeostatically-oriented strivings specifically only when they have a special significance to the variety of conversation being discussed. I also must acknowledge that the types of GBH that people hope to derive from conversation are as numerous as the individuals who hope for them. The GBH benefits that I suggest are just that – suggestions of potential GBH benefits that may accrue rather than pronouncements of GBH benefits that must accrue. That having been said, let's briefly consider some varieties of conversation mentioned by Eggins and Slade, some mentioned by Goldsmith and Baxter, and some coined by me to illustrate that all involve GBH and the self.

Me-Talk

Much conversation involves a straightforward discussion of what the speaker did or wants to do. This could include Goldsmith and Baxter's making plans, catching up, and recapping the day's events. It's the brief by-the-water-cooler Monday morning talk at work when we relate what we experienced over the weekend or when we speak excitedly about an upcoming vacation. From the message side, me-talk can amount to overt or covert boasting or complaining. Boasting produces GBH when it is done in the hope of raising the speaker's self esteem whereas complaining produces GBH by helping the speaker to more clearly think through conflictual situations, obtain useful advice, or reduce her inner tension with a subsequent return to baseline emotional homeostasis. From the relationship side, me-talk gives the speaker GBH in that it enables him to elicit feelings of empathy or solidarity for him from his conversant partner.

Me-Talk-About-You

This type of conversation concerns the speaker's inquiring about his partner's situation. It often commences with a solicitous question such as, "So how is your tennis coming along?" On the surface, me-talk-about-you is the antithesis of selfish conversation. However, listen for a while and the initiating speaker's GBH needs become apparent. On the message side, he actually may want to tell you about his own tennis prowess and need a subtle entrée into the topic. Here GBH comes to him if he can impress you with his skills and accomplishments. On the relationship side, perhaps the initiating speaker recently was told how narcissistic he is and you are a target for his attempts at self-redemption, a way to show that he does care about others, with GBH deriving from your appreciating his thoughtful inquiry about your progress in tennis.

I recently observed a variation on the me-talk-about-you theme at our local gym. Two young women stood by the check-in desk. Jennifer held an infant in her arms. Morgan gently rocked newborn twins in a coach. Jennifer exuberantly but briefly commented about how "cute" the twins were and then sailed into an extensive, verbose monologue about her own baby.

Checking-In

This is a type of me-talk or me-talk-about-you in which the conversant either is looking to give a "this is what I've been doing" update or is requesting the same from her partner. Message GBH can derive from the conversants' learning each other's strategies for personal life enrichment. Relationship GBH can come from knowing that each has the other readily available to listen when a listener is desired.

Many women are fond of this form of conversation, especially mothers and daughters, and men often are perplexed by it. I have heard men complain that their wives leave a party, having spent hours with their female friend and then call the friend to talk about the party.

As was said in the context of me-talk-about-you, no matter how altruistic the tone of the conversation, checking-in typically is done for the benefit of the initiator of the conversation. For instance, when a mother calls her daughter to find out how dinner was last night, it may be to allay her own fears that the daughter may not be socializing or eating properly.

Reminiscence

Self-centered reminiscing, or personal nostalgia, is a subset of storytelling and primarily an unilateral search for GBH. Werman (1977) emphasizes the centrality of the search per se when he says that personal nostalgia "…leads to an indefinite and indefinable quest – and if an object should appear that seems to correspond to the nostalgic desire, it is promptly rejected; it becomes demythologized; it is not what it promised to be: the subject's projection of what it should be. The subject can only enjoy the search and never the possession." By contrast, conjoint reminiscence, or shared nostalgic conversation between family members or friends, does not lead inevitably to disappointment. Rather, conjoint reminiscence often produces "an air of extravagance and expansiveness" (Kaplan, 1987) that can buoy both conversants. Conjoint reminiscence is ideally suited to provide message and relationship GBH for both persons. By recollecting "good old" times, places, events, and people, each member of the conversant pair has a chance to reactivate pleasant feelings associatively linked to the memory – message GBH. Similarly, by sharing their reveries, they derive relationship GBH by reinforcing their inter-personal bond.

Conjoint reminiscence, of course, involves persons who have a significant history together. It asks, "Remember the time…?" and then progresses to storytelling. The GBH message value comes in part from reliving an emotionally significant event. The initiating speaker has an opportunity to experience the past in a manner far richer than is available when he silently muses about it. In conversing, he says it aloud, acts it out, and witnesses, hopefully, an appreciative reaction from an interested partner. He reconnects with a meaningful part of himself. The speaker reconnects, too, with his partner – a relationship benefit. The reminiscence says, "We are important to one another. We have something worth holding on to. We need this relationship to endure."

No other conversational modality can compare with conjoint reminiscence for allowing both partners to tell a shared story with mutually rich emotional significance. It is the quintessential win-win conversation and this accounts for the special place that conjoint reminiscence holds in our psychic economies; it is, for instance, the factor that makes family and class reunions satisfying. When a reminiscence partner is lost, a piece of our self is lost. There is no one to validate that time at the beach during college break or the day the car ran out of gasoline. Loss of reminiscence partners accounts for some of the emptiness that the elderly face as they attend one funeral after another. They not only have one less partner to talk to, but, as each precious friend and relative pass, the survivor is left with one more constellation of poignant experiences that never again will be consensually validated.

Argument

The word "argument" connotes much of what is considered bad in conversation. Tannen (1998) decried argument in contemporary America, saying "The argument culture urges us to approach the world—and the people in it—in an adversarial frame of mind. It rests on the assumption that opposition is the best way to get anything done. The best way to discuss an idea is to set up a debate; the best way to cover news is to find spokespeople who express the most extreme, polarized view and present them as 'both sides'; the best way to settle disputes is litigation that pits one party against the other; the best way to begin an essay is to attack someone; and the best way to show that you are really thinking is to criticize." Although she spoke principally about public discourse, everyday conversation could hardly escape the influence of an "argument culture." The rampant verbal abuse that tears families asunder is merely one obvious consequence.

On the other hand, in a different venue Tannen (1984), herself, excuses some conversational argument by correctly observing that sometimes argument is nondestructive and perhaps subculturally prescribed. In Jewish relationships, "nonserious" arguments sometimes are regarded as pervasive and salutary (Schiffrin, 1984). And in the Black subculture "talking trash" and "the dozens" can promote group solidarity. Eggins and Slade (1997) suggest that "Confronting reactions are the reactions most likely to engender further talk. Conversation thrives on confrontation and wilts in the face of support."

Argument, therefore, can provide an opportunity for GBH. Among the message benefits is the speaker's chance to feel "good" about developing and exercising her ability to express her views logically, forcefully, and clearly. Even when encountering a powerful counterargument, the speaker might feel "better" if she perceives that she has supported her position more effectively than in the past. Or she could achieve a more comfortable "homeostatic" balance merely by having spoken the information aloud, thus discharging it from her baseline consciousness. In terms of relationship GBH, the arguing person can achieve some satisfaction in having a partner concede a point to her, or to demonstrate respect for her tenacity.

While argument need not be destructive, most often people engage in conversation without argument, hoping amicably to satisfy their needs while permitting their partner to do the same. And they feel distress when arguments are not resolved amicably. Unfulfilling outcomes are especially likely when individuals adopt a zero sum game stance in which their gain must occur at the expense of the other person. As we said previously, the zero sum speaker believes that he will achieve message or relationship GBH only by wrestling it from an unwilling participant. Rather than explain, he argues. An astute observer typically can detect when explanation becomes argument by noting the argumentative speaker's apparent intentions and the ways in which he relates one idea to another (Antaki and Leudar, 1992). This often takes the form of the speaker's making claims, attacking the partner's claims, asking the partner to justify his claims, and then attacking the justifications that were offered (Rips, Brem, and Bailenson, 1999). However, sometimes arguments are less transparent, as when people employ "positively polite strategies" (Brown and Levinson, 1987), responding to their partner's claims with "yes but" responses that attempt to mask inter-personal tensions. But, even in ambiguous situations, the conversations that follow an exchange can give clues to whether an argument had occurred. For instance, persons who had argued tend to discuss fewer subsequent subjects than persons who had not argued (Yoder, 1981). The ways in which intimate conversants respond during conflict also predict the degree of their relationship satisfaction. Alberts and Driscoll (1992), for instance, analyzed couple's complaints and discovered that satisfied ones were more likely to respond to their partner's complaint by ignoring it, changing its focus, downplaying it, or accepting it. By contrast, dissatisfied couples tended to flatly deny the validity of the complaint or to expand the topic and/or the hostility level of the original complaint.

Tannen (1999) recommends that an argument be followed by an apology from the offender and states that women are more inclined to apologize than men are. I'm not going to argue with her, so I will have no need to apologize. I wish only to point out that in the context of conversation I support Eggins and Slade (1997) (both women) who imply that apology is likely to stifle conversation, at least in the short run, since "good manners" dictate that the apologizer not offer elaborate excuses and that the apologee not gloat or retaliate.

To say that one should apologize for arguing is to suggest that offensive, rude behavior should be avoided. Nice people are not rude, so nice people have little need to apologize. But here, as often, we encounter a problem of definition; just as we needed to decide when explanation becomes argument, we need to decide when "innocent" comments become rude. A simple, perhaps circular, criterion would be to consider behavior rude when the receiving person regards it as offensive. In any case, no one wants to be called "rude." People who converse rudely are not "nice." Or are they?

Presuming that indirect requests are more polite than are direct ones, Forgas (1999) investigated the relationship between one's mood and rudeness. By scrutinizing an individual's choice of phrases during the exercise, he discovered an inverse relationship between request politeness and the quality of the requestor's mood. That is, those in negative emotional states were more polite than are those in positive states, and the more difficult and demanding the situational context, the stronger was the affect of mood on the politeness of the request. Thus, one would expect that when individuals feel good and are involved in simple, comfortable conversations, they are more likely to be blunt and direct, and that they are more inclined to be direct with those whom they know best.

All of this discussion underscores the point that explanation and argument, politeness and rudeness, and all elements of conversation must be viewed in the context of the conversational triangle—two conversing persons and their history together. Persons with a conversational history together have a conversational future together because they have learned how to extract GBH from their conversations. We must consider both intra-individual benefits and inter-personal benefits to understand conversation's forms and functions. To ignore either is to invite misunderstanding.

Even ordinarily perceptive persons can be fooled. For her doctoral dissertation, Tannen (1984) analyzed two hours and forty minutes of conversation at her 1978 Thanksgiving dinner in Berkley, California. Of the six conversants, three were born in New York, including Tannen, two born in southern California, and one born in London. In describing the primary objective of her study she said, "I had initially intended this to be a study of the styles of all participants, but the conversation itself made this impossible. It turned out (and this came as a surprise to me when I asked them several months later what they recalled about this Thanksgiving) that the non-New York participants had perceived the conversation as "New York," and they had felt out of their element. Because the New Yorkers present tended to expect shorter pauses between speakers' turns at talk, the non-New Yorkers had a harder time saying something before a faster talker had begun to talk...So, inevitably, this book ended-up as a study of one style, what I call a high-involvement style, which tended to characterize the speakers from New York." In Tannen's opinion, the non-New Yorkers simply could not keep up with the fast-talking, verbose, clipped-sentenced, overlapping linguisitic style of the New Yorkers.

Tannen cannot be faulted for conducting and interpreting her study as she wished. However, there were critically important intra- and inter-individual elements that I feel contributed massively to causing the Thanksgiving conversation to be too restricted for Tannen to achieve her stated objective. In part, it was a matter of the non-New Yorkers having to "fight for" their message and/or relationship GBH on the home turf of two brothers and their life-long friend. But there were other factors, too, that could have contributed to stifling the non-New Yorkers conversational connection. In fact, if I give you just a little more background information, I bet you will see the reasons for yourself. With minimal paraphrasing and reassembling of information by me, this is how Deborah Tannen described the dinner's participants:

Deborah (the author), 33. Heterosexual. Steve's friend since meeting at summer camp at age 14; graduate linguistics student at University of California, Berkeley; lives in Berkeley; born and raised in Brooklyn, New York.

Steve, 33 Gay. The host of the dinner at his home in Berkeley, California; musician and music teacher; born and raised in the Bronx, New York.

Peter, 35 Heterosexual. Steve's brother, a management analyst at a university; born and raised in the Bronx; lives in the East Bay, California.

Sally, 29, Heterosexual. Lived with Steve from 1970 until 1976; musician; now lives in Canada; born and raised in London, England. Canadian. Steve's "partner" for 6 years; had been living apart for 4 years at time of the dinner. At the dinner refers to Steve and Deborah as "a two man team."

David, 29, Gay. Steve's "good friend" for four years, since 1974; artist and sign language interpreter; lives in Berkeley, California; born and raised in Riverside, California.

Chad, 30. Gay. David's friend since they met as university students in 1972; writer for a major film production studio; born and raised in Los Angeles, California. His connection to the dinner group is exclusively through David.

Victor, 39. Gay. David's deaf lover who arrived after the dinner conversation; an engineer. (No other background information is provided.)

Gossip

Of all varieties of conversation, gossip surely gets the most popular attention. Gossip is the "let's me and you talk about her" and "he said she said" talk that everyone both does and condemns. Nicholson (2001) asserts that gossip provides gossipers a thrill that helps to counter boredom in their personal lives. He suggests that the three essential functions of gossip are network facilitating, social influencing, and alliance building and believes that men's gossip tends to be com-petition-oriented and women's, social-inclusion and moral -alignment oriented. The object of gossip, however, often feels excluded and violated. A nation-wide survey of fifth through twelfth grade children found that 66 percent had been the troubled by negative conversation or gossip directed toward them over the previ-ous month (Galinsky & Salmond, 2002). Gossip thus works at cross social pur-poses, enhancing relationships for gossipers and undermining relationships for those who are gossiped about.

Although some men surely gossip, more women are derided for it. Eggins and Slade (1997) did find in their brief sample that "Gossip occurred frequently in the all-women group, not at all in the all-male group, and only minimally in the mixed group." Leaper and Holliday (1995) concluded similarly. They added that negative gossip was more frequent in the all-women group than was positive gos-sip, and that female-female pairs made more comments that spurred further gos-sip. On the "Tendency to Gossip Questionnaire," Israeli women scored significantly higher than did Israeli men (Nevo et al., 1993). Men and women also were found to differ in the gossip-related practice of rumor spreading (Walker, 1991). While both men and women transmitted dread rumors (unpleasant) more than wish (pleasant) rumors, women passed along the dread rumors more frequently. However, conversation differences between men and women are too important to be reduced to the stereotype-oriented question of gossip or rumor. I have no doubt that men and women at times engage in all the conversational varieties stereotypically associated with their opposite gender.

Gossip can provide message GBH. Regarding negative gossip, by getting the "**low**down" on someone, the knowledge we obtain is power that we can turn to our advantage in future dealings. Gossip perhaps is a quintessential device for achieving relationship GBH. By gossiping with you I imply that I can trust you to keep my confidences. You and I are kindred spirits. Both of us are alike, purer in body and mind than the not-quite-so-good fellow of whom we speak so we should we feel one-up from him in self-righteousness. Francine Prose (1999) refers to gossip as an inter-personal "indulgence," as rich and satisfying as choco-late. "It's among the pleasures of being human, of belonging to a species and a community. And it's one of the joys of friendship, that thrill of meeting a pal for lunch and hearing a story so terrific that the world seems, for just a minute, live-lier and brighter connected and sustained by an enormous, thriving, endlessly vital grapevine."

Never-Spoken Conversations

Never-spoken conversations are the converse of gossip. They are for those who lack the courage or opportunity to share their thoughts. These are conversations privately recited but not yet spoken to anyone. They are the "I'd like to give him a piece of my mind" or "I wonder what she would say if I asked her to go out with me" conversations—imaginary conversations we have internally in preparation or in substitution for talking to someone. Never-spoken conversations provide message GBH when they self-instruct and relationship GBH when they self-encourage an individual to successfully deal with his own baseline consciousness issues.

On the face of it, the fact of never-spoken conversations seems innocuous enough, especially when the suppressed conversational content is negative. Certainly, most of us have been advised, "If you can't say something nice, don't say anything at all." But there are circumstances of never-spoken conversation that challenge the advice. At one extreme lies never-spoken conversations regarding grim realities. Physician Jerome Groopman (2002) explains that "More than forty per cent of oncologists withhold a prognosis from a patient if he or she does not ask for it or if the family requests that the patient not be told. A similar number speak in euphemisms, skirting the truth. Today, in most of Europe doctors often do not tell patients that they are dying." At the other extreme are never-spoken conversations of life-affirming significance regarding support and tenderness that, if discussed, could bolster each conversant and their relationship. In some circumstances, never-spoken conversations are never-realized opportunities.

Storytelling

While gossip gets the most press, storytelling deserves top billing. As McAdams (1993) explains, each episode of a story has a setting, characters, initiating event, attempt to attain a goal, a consequence, and a reaction to the consequence—events and characters presented in an integrated and affectively meaningful, goal-oriented way that best approximates real experience. To tell a story is to tell about life as it is lived. No other text comes close in relevance and poignancy; this is why most conversation is storytelling. To tell a story is to "have the floor" and an opportunity to savor relationship GBH by way of self-enhancing inter-personal attention. But while story-telling often seeks relationship GBH, it is equally effective in achieving message GBH, as when telling the story enables the story-teller to use the message to re-experience the thoughts and/or feelings that accompany the narrative.

Our phenomenological awareness of our own personalities is defined in large measure by the self-stories that we tell ourselves and others. Autobiographical stories give coherence to our identities by providing a context that ties together elements of our personal experiences that extend across time and space. Themes that reoccur are themes that exemplify the idiosyncratic self. Peterson (2000) emphasizes the self-serving self in self-stories when he says that, "Everyone engages in an ongoing process of fabricating and revising his or her own personal history. The story each of us tells about ourselves is necessarily ego-centric: Each of us is the central figure in our own narratives each of us takes credit for the good events and eschews responsibility for the bad events. Each of us resists changes in how we think. In sum, the ego maintains itself in the most self-flattering way possible..."

While the ideal self-story is positive and consistent, however, the ideal self-story does not exist. People simply do not have the memory power or resourcefulness to be completely positive and consistent in their stories. Fortunately, to facilitate my social survival, I don't need to tell an ideal self-story. I just need to tell a good-enough self-story, one that, by definition, offers the possibility for GBH at the particular point in time that I tell it. If, I see myself as macho, I'll tell a macho story, but one that includes elements that I consider believable. I certainly won't tell a story about the time that I cried in a movie theatre. This is not to say that we never recall and relate unflattering self-stories. In fact, Wilson and Ross (2001) present research to suggest that people frequently bolster their current self esteem by distancing themselves from their past self. Hence, after describing an incident in which he performed a humanitarian task, the speaker might relate a tale of how self-indulgent he had been years earlier.

Even conversation that is not a story itself assumes story-like qualities. This is because anything mentioned in conversation is part of the holistic, integrated experience of the teller. Whatever is said is part of the *story* of that person's experience in that it connects with his life experience in a longitudinal way – he has noticed it and decided to comment on it because it has a function in the story of his life. Although it is vaguely possible that I would mention a cooking recipe in passing, I ordinarily would not converse at length or introduce the topic of recipes because cooking is not part of my story. But if I do mention a recipe in passing it is because that recipe means something to me at that moment, something significantly connected to who I am at that time, even if it is not usually a significant element of my identity.

You can have all the elements of a story in a nonfiction narrative – such as in straightforwardly explaining how to bake bread—but nonfiction text has limited appeal, because it lacks the essential human interest of affect, continuity, and people that stories have.

When you tell your story, you relive it-the good, the bad, and the ugly. So one motivation to tell your story is to relive the good, cathart the bad so as to feel "better," or to reestablish homeostasis by reaffirming your experience/identity or to relieve the pressure that the deep cognitive processing of the story had sustained. First and foremost, a story relates to your personal identity and, therefore, to how you apprehend the world.

Schank (1990) indirectly acknowledges the GBH-seeking nature of conversation in general and storytelling in particular when he writes, "Conversationalists are looking to tell one of their stories. They are looking to tell a good one, a right one…" Like Peterson, he emphasizes the ruthlessly self-centered nature of conversation by indicating that one can only converse about his own stories, but he frames this primarily in terms of the organization of memory and cognition. To Schank, stories reflect our idiosyncratic labeling and indexing system. Our own stories and those of others provide self-service by reminding us of connections among our mental contents. He goes so far as to say that intelligence itself is the ability to tell the right story at the right time. In his opinion, "Story telling and understanding are functionally the same thing. Conversation is no more than responsive story telling. The process of reminding is what controls understanding and, therefore, conversation." Schank means that my conversational response to you depends exclusively on the self-serving, experience-based associative spheres that light up for me when you tell your story. I will tolerate your story to the extent that it serves my GBH purpose.

Lewis Lapham, Harper Magazine editor and commentator, laments what he sees as today's egocentrically-focused, television-remote-control society in which we "click away" any situation or person who appears different until we find something or someone who is more similar to us. He sees such practices as eroding our society-wide base of common experience that facilitates variegated inter-personal exchange across subgroups and subcultures. He extols the "good old days" wherein fireside chats and network news were all that was available and, therefore, people had similar knowledge that facilitated less self-isolating strivings. In truth, the **desire** to find someone like our self and to tell our own story has always been in the forefront of our GBH search; it merely had been thwarted in the past because then, unlike today, we had less choice in limiting ourselves to our own ruthlessly selfish preferences. People have always been inclined to want to justify the stories that they already believe; today it is just uncommonly easy to do so.

While frankly autobiographical stories obviously reflect personality, all stories are indirectly autobiographical in that story telling broadcasts the speaker's interests and values. To paraphrase the title of a book from the seventies, "real men don't tell stories about quiche."

The autobiographical, personalizing tendency is so strong in our experience of a story that we introject ourselves into the stories that we read. Rall and Harris (2000) note that "Being absorbed in a narrative and 'seeing' the fictional scene as vividly as if one were personally involved in it is an experience familiar to most competent readers. Indeed, it is the picture in one's imagination that often brings about the subjective enjoyment of reading." The authors demonstrate empirically that we literally adopt the perspective of the story's protagonist such that the protagonist becomes the "anchor" from which we judge movement within the story. Both adults and children as young as three years remember movements depicted in a story better when the movements are described from the point of view of the protagonist rather than of someone or something else. This study is especially relevant to us because reading develops as an offshoot of our experiences with conversation. Reading uses the protagonist as an foil for the self because reading, like conversation and all volitional behavior, are organized around the self and its self-story.

Conversation as Self-Talk: Let's Chat, I Need to Tell Myself a Story

To say, as we did, that our phenomenological awareness of our own personalities is defined largely by the stories that we tell is to imply that we listen critically to the stories that we tell others. In short, whenever we converse with someone, we also converse with ourselves.

There are two principal ways to think about talk directed toward the self. Some self-talk, called "private speech," purportedly common in early childhood and consisting mostly of overtly verbalized self-direction, is a process by which young children give themselves the guidance that adults ordinarily do. Prevailing psychological theory posits that this self-directing private speech progressively is "internalized," meaning that it becomes subvocal, or even unconscious, as children become mature problem solvers. (That having been said, Duncan and Cheyne (1999) showed that college students with a mean age of 20 years used private speech, and were aware enough to report it when so instructed. On the other hand, the college students of the study engaged in private speech only when attempting to solve difficult verbal tasks, not when working on easy ones.)

When I say "self–talk," I am not using the aforementioned traditional definition of private speech. Rather, I am using the term broadly to refer to self-talk occurring in the context of common, conventional conversation between two people intent on communicating with each other. I am saying that if conversation is organized around the self and the self story, and if all volitional behavior primarily involves a relentless, expectant search for GBH, then conversation also includes an individual's self-reinforcing attempt to tell a story **to himself** that facilitates his personal GBH. Under ordinary circumstances, conversants prefer to hear themselves deliver good messages and prefer to talk in ways that facilitate a positive self-relationship/positive self-regard. Accordingly, all conversants automatically and unconsciously converse with themselves while conversing with others and always wish to say to others what they, themselves, want to believe or understand. They inadvertently use their conversant partner as a foil for themselves, just as readers use story protagonists for the same purpose.

Conversation is as much self-to-self-talk as it is self-to-other talk. And the self-talk that conversation embodies is critically important in a subjective, affective sense. To cite but one example, as we shall see in our discussion of laughter during conversation, the speaker laughs more often at his own comments than does his listener. The speaker laughs more because he is conversing principally to manage his own thoughts and feelings rather than to manage those of his partner.

If an individual derives benefit from talking to himself, you might wonder whether he would do well to sit alone in his room and have at it! Would a person be his own best conversational partner, since he has unfettered access to his own baseline consciousness, CAMM, and TAMM?

There is no denying that self-talk in the absence of a partner, like classic literature or autobiographical writing, approximates, as well as humanly possible, a fusion of language representation and language communication by giving voice to experienced but virtually ineffable mental experience. But, talk to oneself would be hard to sustain. Such talk would be reabsorbed into the swirling vortex of multi-sensory-motor-visceral baseline consciousness. One would need to expend immense mental energy to maintain a predominately objective focus when overtly vocalizing alone.

By contrast, conversation with others amounts to a well-practiced, automatic ability to transform mental representations into rational, orderly verbal communication. Talking to others makes self-talk more fluid and comprehensible for a number of reasons: First, spoken words distill the essence of a thought, making it less complex. Second, unlike thought elements, spoken phrases are uttered serially, making them easier to follow. Third, semantic and syntactic rules of social language guide us toward some thought elements and away from other competing ones, narrowing our focus. Fourth, our conversant partner gives us a frame of reference, a compass to keep us on track; we try to say only that which is comprehensible and acceptable. And fifth, our partner's responses and his GBH search limits the speed and verbosity of our remarks, preventing us from becoming swept up in our musings. A conversational partner helps one to transform parallel, multi-sensory-motor-visceral mental representations into serial words, phrases, and sentences for shared social communication by requiring conversants to foreground each emergent idea and to keep it sufficiently separated from the din of baseline consciousness. While our mental representations become diluted and anemic when we talk to ourselves as well as when we converse with others, in the latter situation the reconstituted mental representations tend to be more rational processes and more readily applicable to socially adaptive ends.

The speaker is always listening consciously with her two ears and unconsciously with her third ear – the one that Theodore Reik (1948) believed hears the hidden meanings of what we say and do not say when conversing. These three ears, attuned-to-the-self, account for a wide variety of well-recognized conversational facts. Two examples illustrate my point: The cocktail party phenomenon (Moray, 1959) designates the fact that often we can hear someone whisper our name over the clamor of a noisy party when other words spoken more loudly are missed. It is as though we have a personal, automatic radar continually scanning the conversational environment in its own relentless search for spoken self-references. "Coensthetic reception" (Spitz & Cobliner, 1965) describes a personal, automatic self-referential process. In this case, we exhibit an extra-sensory-like awareness of the self-other relationship aspect of conversation. Coensthetic reception is the ability to know intuitively, for instance, that a conversant partner took offense to something that you said, despite the fact that other observing persons present at the time detect no signs of upset from the person that you correctly "feel" was aggrieved. The speaker's listening to herself is analogous to her looking in the mirror – gazing at oneself in a mirror reveals the physical self while listening to oneself in conversation reveals the social-emotional self.

Conversation as self-conversation typically involves talking in ways that encourage personal progress toward one's GBH goals and one's own self story. From the self-reinforcing side of the equation, self-conversation involves the individual's hearing what he is saying in order to reassure and reinforce himself about GBH goals, story formulation, and presentation of self. From the other-reinforcing side, by hearing what he is saying, the individual is better able to converse in ways that make others more likely to dispense message and/or relationship GBH. If I mention to you that I saw our mutual friend Abby, I obviously had an experience with her and thought about it before I mentioned her to you. The experience that I had with her was at least minimally significant, since I remembered. And the thoughts that I had about it were rich in multi-sensory-motor-visceral mental representations that amounted to a nonverbal, largely unconscious private reflection. By mentioning the encounter with Abbey to you, I revive, modify, and enrich some of my personal, relevant multi-sensory-motor-visceral mental representations in ways that are more consciously directed and "explainable" than what I had experienced in my private reflection. In doing so, I can re-experience that which was positive during the actual event of having seen Abby and/or work through, and better resolve, that which was discordant—the former being G/GBH and the latter, B/GBH or H/GBH. When I converse about my experience with Abbey, I avail myself of additional or improved routes to further GBH beyond that which I had already achieved personally and privately before our conversation, since you become a potential GBH satisfier for me.

In the special case of conversing about a previous experience, GBH is possible within the original experience, within private self-reflection about the experience, within social conversation about the experience, and even within subsequent private reflection about the social conversation. A reiterative process is possible such that I can use the conversation that I had with you regarding my experience with Abbey as its own original experience, privately reflect about it, converse with others about it, privately reflect upon the conversation with them about the conversation with you, in an ad infinitum nesting of conversations – all in the relentless expectant search for GBH.

The conversation executor of which we spoke earlier is the intra-personal agency that facilitates self-to-self talk that channels conversation so that an individual can converse in ways that help her to achieve maximal GBH while giving her conversant partner just enough GBH opportunity to keep him engaged. The speaker wants to hear herself say "the right things" as a conversational partner, tell stories and make comments that depict her in ways that promote her self-competence and self-liking, and do so in ways that adhere to mores of social conduct. But, more important, she wants to satisfy raw instinctual gratification, enjoying as much pleasure as possible, even at the expense of others, if necessary. The conversation executor personifies the speaker's ears, especially her third ear, always monitoring what is being said and always attempting to ensure that it does not invalidate or excessively challenge central tenants of her self story, her sense of self competence and self-liking, or her pursuit of raw pleasure.

Special Conversation Issues

The Regulatory Function of Self Talk

Self talk, whether delivered as self-to-self or self-to-other communication, is basic to self management and is not limited to self story telling. Self talk has a hedonic-homeostatic regulatory function when it promotes self-soothing and/or self-control. Regulation of the self involves self talk toward better managing and/or processing one's body, thoughts, emotions, esteem, and experiences. A self-to-self regulatory strategy is apparent, for instance, when an individual reduces his tension via reassuring self statements such as, "Everything's going to be alright" or when he verbally rehearses how to ask his boss for a raise. However, either communication, and virtually any communication, could be expanded into self-to-other conversation.

I use the term "expanded" deliberately to emphasize once more that self-to-other talk always implies self-to-self communication. By expanding self-to-self communication into self-to-other conversation, however, one opens himself up to the promise and peril of the positive and negative influences of the conversant partner.

Consistent with all that we have said to this point, self-to-self and self-to-other self talk seeks satisfying self messages and/or self relationships. That is, whether communicating only to oneself or simultaneously to oneself and to a conversant partner, the individual wants to hear GBH messages and to maintain or enhance a GBH relationship with himself, since to do so is to promote survival, health, and comfort. To be explicit: All self-to-other conversations not only seek message and/or relationship GBH benefits from the conversant partner but also message and/or relationship GBH benefits from the self. Moreover, self regulation is a common, important component of GBH. For instance, when someone recounts to you a relatively bland incident from his day, he quite likely is doing so at least in part to derive self regulatory GBH benefit. Even the very act of conversing with others can be self regulatory. A personal example is instructive. In winter, I began lifting weights and running on a treadmill in our local gym. When I did so, another gym member, Warren, seemed intent on walking on the machine next to me, and he and I would chat. The activity went on for several weeks without fail. Then, one day I came to the gym late and while lifting weights I was accosted by my friend who asked about my tardiness. After I explained, he said, "If it's okay, I'll wait till you're ready to run before I walk. I like you to keep me company. I can't walk too long by myself." Apparently, conversing with me served a self-regulatory function for Warren. In addition to whatever message and/or relationship GBH benefits that he derived from our talks, he used it for homeostatic regulatory purposes, probably both physical and mental.

The Many Routes to GBH

We have said that conversation's primary purpose is to facilitate GBH through message and/or relationship and that when two persons are together it is virtually impossible for them not to communicate. That silence is a communication is clearly illustrated by a situation in which a visitor comes to your home and you sit in the same room together. Imagine how awkward, rude, even bizarre, it would be for the two of you to sit in total silence, ignoring each other. This is because part of the inter-personal and conversational expectation is that we satisfy each other's very basic relationship needs by being at least superficially friendly and minimally interested in each other, and a major way to be so is to engage in at least brief, perfunctory, casual conversation.

That having been said, please recall that while conversation is a most important route to GBH, it is not the only one, or even the preferred one, for all people at all times. Intimate relationships are defined both by the ability to discuss the most personal information and by the freedom to dispense with requisite, perfunctory, casual conversation niceties. Intimates sometimes can sit quietly pursuing their own individual GBH needs without feeling pressure to say or do anything to satisfy basic relationship demands. Accordingly, friends and lovers can enjoy being in each other's presence with minimal chatter while separately working on some satisfying motor activity, even when an observer might conclude that the two were ignoring each other conversationally.

Obviously, then, I unequivocally oppose the position of Eggins and Slade (1997) when they assert: "Thus, we will be arguing that disagreement is essential to the motivation and the maintenance of casual talk." Since I "oppose" their position and they are "arguing" for it, I presume that Eggins and Slade would be eager to have a casual conversation with me! I, on the other hand, would be content to satisfy my relentless search for GBH by directing my energies toward more action-oriented experiments to refine my ideas further.

While conversing, each partner is a being-in-the-real-world, not merely a talking machine. The talking part of conversation is one facet of the total experience. While talking, each partner is responding to BETF, each component of which presses and recedes, like the waves on a beach. She is experiencing her body, seeing sights, hearing conversation and non-conversation-related sounds, thinking thoughts, feeling feelings, and so forth. Some of these BETF elements will be consciously experienced; some will not. Some will be incorporated into the conversation; some will not. But all of the elements are affecting the conversational partners to some extend, if only unconsciously.

From the point of view of volitional behavior, behavior oriented toward the relentless search for GBH, conversation is a subcomponent of action. The GBH search is an organic whole. At any moment in time, GBH may be sought in direct, sensory-motor action. At the next moment, the effort may be via verbal conversation. There is a seamless ebb and flow into and out of direct, sensory-motor action and into and out of conversation. People converse as they visually scan the room, cook, shine shoes, knit, and watch television. It is the total experience of a living person in his real-time environment that determines his baseline consciousness that, in turn, fuels his conversation.

Only when the being-in-the-real-world aspect of the conversing person is acknowledged and investigated will research ever recognize that conversation is part of an individual's unceasing GBH quest. Those who investigate conversation in artificial, laboratory-like situations using contrived scripts will never understand conversation's true essence. Those who do address the conversing person as a relentlessly searching being-in-the-real-world, on the other hand, have an opportunity to access the authentic workings of the human mind and spirit.

The relentlessly searching individual is like a sightseer in an exotic land. He is there to feel good. Toward that end, he wants to see the attractions, handle the artifacts, taste the foods, hear the sounds, and smell the aromas. These sensual pleasures are possible even if our intrepid visitor is unable to communicate verbally with the natives and has to grunt and gesture his way through the foreign landscape. How much richer the experience though, if the visitor can converse with his hosts. Conversation maximizes message-oriented GBH by helping him better know what to see, handle, taste, hear, and smell. Moreover, conversation maximizes relationship-oriented GBH by helping him to exchange thoughts and feeling with the natives.

Laughter

To say that feeling good is the primary conversational goal is to raise the possibility that laughter is an index of conversational success. Should it be? Maybe yes; maybe no.

Obviously, laughter does not require conversation. Researchers have suggested that even rats (Panskepp, 1997), dogs (Simonet, 2001), elephants (Simonet, 1997), and chimpanzees (Matsuzawa, 1998) "laugh" during play activities. Provine (2000), in fact, asserts that laughter is closer to animal calls than to human speech. He, however, did research laughter in conversation. By observing persons in natural settings, such as in malls and restaurants, he found that the speaker in a dyad laughed 79.8 percent of the time and the audience (the person with whom he was speaking) laughed 54.7 percent of the time. That is, the speaker laughed 46 percent more often than did the audience and that gender differences were salient, as revealed in the following chart:

Speaker	Listener	% Speaker Laughter	% Listener Laughter
Male	Male	75.6	60.0
Female	Female	86.0	49.8
Male	Female	66.0	71.0
Female	Male	88.1	38.9

Provine (2000) concluded that women laugh more than men, but that men cause more laughter. Does this mean than men are "funnier" or "wittier" than women? Probably not, for Provine also indicated that the overwhelming majority of laughs, instigated by either gender, occurred coincident with talk that did not seem humorous at all. He hypothesized that laughter is a "within group modulator" that helps to set an emotional tone that facilitates dyadic cohesion. That is, laughter helps people to develop a more comfortable sense of connection with each other – relationship GBH.

Consistent with the notion that all human behavior has both emotional and cognitive features, Wegner (1994) cites Minsky's assertion that laughter often occurs due to an atypical juxtaposition of ideas that surprises us. Laughter in this case amounts to a mental debugging of cognitive errors in that the squealing and screeching of laughter stops our thought processes and allows us to process the novelty of the situation. After we have laughed about something, it ceases to be funny because it no longer is novel; we have debugged the cognitive error that made it funny initially.

So, laughter indicates conversation success if it debugs cognitive errors and, therefore, facilitates mental homeostasis. Laughter also signals beneficial intercourse to the extent to which it supports relationship GBH by making human interaction more relaxing and positive. And, certainly, laughter is a sign of salutary conversation when it occurs coincident with a conversant's achieving message GBH—when he is given information that he believes that he needs. But laughter, in and of itself, is an unreliable measure of GBH success; success only can be determined by knowing whether a conversation has contributed to the conversant's realizing primary or secondary reinforcement as a result of the conversation in which he had participated.

Teasing

As was true of argument and laughter, teasing varies in its functions. At one extreme, teasing is more destructive and mocking; at the other, it is more subdued and intimacy-enhancing. Dacher Keltner and associates. (2001) explain that to qualify as teasing, conversation must include an intentional provocation about something relevant to the "victim" that is communicated along with "playful off-record markers," meaning actions, intonations, or remarks that the tease should not be taken literally. The extent of playful off-record markers is an important metric of the virulence of the teasing; the more markers, the less virulent. For instance, if a teaser laughingly, with rising inflection, and questioning tone, shrieks, "Are you an idiot or what?" the remark carries minimal threat.

Keltner and associates believe that most teasing occurs when the victim has violated a social norm or when teaser and victim engage in inter-personal conflict that they mitigate by teasing rather than by directly assaulting each other. And teasing tends to move down a social power gradient such that persons in authority positions are much more likely to tease a subordinate than vice versa. Affiliation also is relevant to teasing – the more familiar people are with each other, the more likely they will tease. But affiliation is another one of those unreliable criteria, because intimates who engage in inter-personal conflict often are comfortable enough with each other to directly deal with the disturbing issue rather than to tease their way around it. So, once again, we underscore that the analysis of conversation can never be strictly formulaic. Conversation, as all volitional behavior, is driven by a relentless expectant search for GBH that varies as a function of organism in environment.

Negation

Teasing generally is defined as a communication by which playful-off-record markers ostensibly can negate what otherwise would be a hurtful communication. Or can they? Freud (1925) suggests that the unconscious does not accept negatives, that statements of negation are perceived as statements of affirmation. Pennebaker and Stone (2003) provide a related example, saying that interviewees who comment that they are "not happy" tend to have more positive health outcomes than did those who comment that they are "sad." Wegener (1994) contends that negation rarely is complete and, therefore, does not successfully suppress unwanted thoughts.

In attempting to use negation, if I say, "No, I didn't consider saying..." the very statement that I did not consider saying the forbidden thought means that now I have done so. And now that I have said it, and the listener has heard it, the forbidden idea is both irrevocable and more repeatable. I said it, and the statement is forever associated with me. What I intended is largely irrelevant. The effected response displaces the intended one.

To give a rather gross example, one that puts me at grave risk for suffering the same undesirable fate about which I spoke above, if I say to you "Here's an **example** of the affective aspects of negation." and then continue, "I'm **not** going to pick a roach off the wall and eat it!" Even though I said that I am merely giving an **example** and that "I'm **not** going to" do what I say, you heard it just as surely as if I said "I **am** going to pick a roach off the wall and eat it," and you had the very same "yuk!" response that you would have had if I made the "I **am** going to pick a roach off the wall and eat it." remark in seriousness. Even though I made my statement merely as an "example," you heard me say it, and you attach the "gross comment" that I made to your mental representation of me. The attachment probably will stick; you likely will forget that I was giving an example, and only remember how disgusting I was.

What Conversations Tell Us

The Conversational Route

Conversation is initiated as part of our relentless, expectant search for GBH. Some are long, complicated treks; others are brief, simple sojourns. At minimum, conversation can provide H/GBH—catharsis of mental tension by releasing thoughts and/or feeling pressing upon our baseline consciousness. Conversation is **the** primary means for locating and securing many primary and most secondary reinforcers, and **the** essential inter-personal contact medium. Like all volitional behavior, such as overt, direct, volitional action, conversation anticipates and seeks GBH. But, among volitional behaviors, conversation is most extraordinary in the number and variety of routes that it provides.

Survival-wise, language is preeminent over conversation, but language without conversation would be emotionally bankrupt, since it is conversation, more than anything else, that keeps us vitally connected with each other. Conversation without stories would be insufficient, because it would lack the reality-based drama and holism that confer intra-personal continuity to the events of an individual life, and inter-personal continuity of individuals to each other. Conversation drives human beings because it gives expression to cognitively and/or emotionally powerful elements of baseline consciousness that relate to common, fundamental GBH desires shared between people.

Because we consciously and/or unconsciously converse to achieve GBH, conversation discloses an individual's expectations and values. Each conversant partner presents as an unexplored territory. You may be attracted to the exterior terrain, her surface beauty and allure, to the riches that you presume lie hidden below the surface, or both. Your conversant partner talks to you because he sees you as a potential GBH source – message and/or relationship. In the first case, you have valuable knowledge, and in the second you, yourself, have some qualities or resources that he covets. While message and relationship goals can shift and overlap, they have been at the heart of conversation since its inception.

166

The Road to Message GBH

Conversation can lead us to GBH through messages. The very words and ideas of messages, themselves, can be positive, connoting GBH, and uplifting our thoughts and/or feelings. By conversing with someone I can discover message information that ultimately leads me to eat the best meals, see the best sights, reflect on the best thoughts, and experience the best emotions. Conversation also enables me to experience before-the fact GBH, as when I excitedly discuss my upcoming vacation itinerary with someone. Conversely, speaking with my partner provides me after-the–fact GBH when, after returning from vacation, I vividly re-experience past pleasures by talking about them about my adventure. Finally, the message dimension of conversation facilitates GBH in that it provides a release of obsessive thoughts. In this case, the H/GBH is reduction in mental pressure, which can include emotional catharsis, as when after a visit to a doctor's office I talk with someone about a health problem that was discovered.

All people instinctively know that knowledge leads to message GBH and that the easiest route to knowledge often is through other people, rather than struggling to discover knowledge completely on one's own. This is why children incessantly ask adults questions and why adults seek all manner of professional advice. The conversational transmission of knowledge is one of man's greatest advantages over other members of the animal kingdom. It enables us to accumulate and disseminate information of exact relevance and timing to make GBH more probable. Because this information in conversation is on-line and of the proper timing and relevance, we can apply it most directly without taxing our memory or ability to generalize. Moreover, the message value of information from conversation is value-added rather than raw information because the knowledgeable person with whom you speak already has processed the information, has distilled its essence, and has identified its targets.

The Road to Relationship GBH

Conversation as relationship-GBH enhancer is no less valuable than conversation as message-GBH dispenser. Conversation is one of the safest, most efficient vehicles for attaining relationship GBH, because it permits us to move TAABWA with reduced ego depletion, without overt action, and without all-or none responsibility. In fact, graded conversation is fantastically adaptive in that it offers GBH with minimal risk. Through graded conversation, our inter-personal movement can be incremental. I can test out your reaction to my indirect assertion, dependency, and other GBH sub-goals and then, guided by your response, ratchet my comments up or down accordingly. I even can act as though I had been joking all along and laugh aloud when you respond unfavorably to conversational elements, meaning in ways that do not further my GBH; in doing so, I disavow conversation responsibility in a face-saving way.

Through conversation as relationship-enhancer, we choose conversational partners that we expect will help us physically and/or mentally to feel good, better than we currently feel, or, at least, more homeostatically balanced. This expectation rarely is fully conscious nor is the fact that the message and/or relationship will lead us to the GBH that we seek. Of all the reinforcement accessible through conversation, secondary reinforcement of our sense of self is paramount. While conversation can enhance the likelihood that we obtain some primary reinforcers, like food, or some secondary reinforcers, like money, many primary and secondary reinforcers also are obtainable through direct, overt, physical action. But conversation is uniquely social and uniquely tied to social reinforcement by way of social approval. Social approval virtually requires conversation as its primary transmission vehicle. The stronger an individual's need for social approval, the more dependent he is on conversation. For many such persons, self esteem rises and falls largely in response to approbations or criticisms from others regarding domain-specific areas of life experience (Crocker & Wolfe, 2001). For instance, a person may need others to tell him that he is thoughtful and caring. That same person may be motivated to avoid thinking and talking about achievement-oriented issues wherein he feels inferior. Even a person whose self esteem is more achievement-oriented than social approval-oriented may be inclined toward conversation because achievement usually requires the self to be contrasted with persons having lesser success in the relevant achievement area.

GBH benefits from relationship features of conversation are extremely powerful. First and foremost, the relationship dimension helps satisfy our primate need for contact and support. Conversation is the glue that holds social relationships together. One literally cannot become a human being without conversation. The social self emerges through an iterative process of talk and feedback in which we both define ourselves to others and are defined by them. Conversation enables us to maintain close proximity without risking direct physical contact. It permits us to express our affection, commitment, and dependability to another person and they to us while still maintaining a comfortable social distance. The simultaneous need for affiliation and independence is an inherent, if perplexing, feature of human behavior, whose satisfaction is absolutely essential in order for us to maintain our lives physically and emotionally. It can be explained at least in part by referring to the central role of our sense of self where all GBH resides: a self that is physical and mental, conscious and unconscious; a self that wants both to be autonomous and cared for. The self lives via an unceasing flow between these two poles: too much autonomy and it yearns for succor; too much succor and it wants autonomy.

Traveling Partners

To converse frequently with someone is to make her an essential part of your life, with all the power and privileges appertaining. If someone told you that she is "best friends" with a nearby neighbor, and then added that, unfortunately, she and the friend have not spoken to each other in over a year, you would seriously doubt their friendship. By quantitatively estimating the frequency and length of your conversations with others, you derive a measure of your GBH dependency on them. The more often you initiate conversation or accept their initiating it, the more GBH-dependent on them you are. This does not necessarily mean that you overtly enjoy the discussions. Some conversations, although superficially casual and voluntary, are subtly coerced either internally or externally. You might feel compelled by guilt to telephone your parents regularly or by fear to chat with your boss at the lunch table. In such cases, H/GBH amounts to a diminution of your baseline apprehension concerning those relationships.

Subtly coerced conversations exemplify the "sunk cost" effect (Arkes and Ayton, 1999) in which the more that people have invested their resources in another person or situation, the more they continue to invest. It is a matter of feeling that one must hold on in order to justify having "spent" so much. In this case, you continue to engage in conversations in the relentless, expectant search for GB/GBH that never has been adequately forthcoming, and settle instead for the H/GBH of familiar interaction and discourse.

Relationship mutuality is a root factor underlying the dynamics of conversation in that participants assume the role of both speaker and listener, moving automatically and smoothly in and out of each role. The amount of time spent in either capacity is unconsciously negotiated on-line during conversation, but the participants' implicit expectations about the speaker-listener balance must be met in order for the discussion to continue. Many psychologists, such as Pasupathi (2001), describe conversation as a "co-construction" and suggest that what speakers present and retain is profoundly influenced by the specific listener with whom he speaks. Hupet, Chantraine, and Nef (1993) propose that "...when speakers make a definite reference, they try to establish with their partners the mutual belief that their partners have understood the reference before letting the conversation go on. They establish the belief through an acceptance process that is initiated by the speaker but carried through by both speaker and interlocutor." Speakers regularly incorporate and expand their conversant partner's comments into their own verbalizations in order to maintain topic coherence (Bodamer & Gardner, 2002).

As I demonstrated earlier in the example of my nursing station discussion with a coworker, what is mentioned in recounting an experience when speaking to one person is not necessarily what is mentioned when recounting the same experience to another. Moreover, the quality and effectiveness of speaking and listening varies according to the behavior of both participants. Bavelas, Coates, and Johnson (2000) found that distracted listeners make fewer specific responses, and that speakers with distracted listeners tell their stories less well and produce circumlocutions and/or abrupt or choppy endings.

I agree with Pinker (2000) who says that our ability to converse enabled our species to thrive while other protohumans, no less physically capable than we, passed into extinction. If this drive toward conversation had not developed and remained constant, homo-sapiens would not be here today to discuss the issue. I disagree with Zeldin (2000) who, taking a macro-cultural view of conversation, asserts that conversations vary by age epoch, their content depending on the prevailing ethos of the day. Although the vocabularies obviously have differed, to my way of thinking, the underlying essence of the casual conversations of Dark Age peasants, Renaissance priests, and 21ˢᵗ Century physicians have not been materially different from the casual conversations of everyday people of every age, because conversations occur to facilitate satisfaction of the most fundamental needs and desires of life itself.

Indiveme in Conversation

Conversation is a total experience of body and mind, thought and feeling that occurs at a particular moment in time within particular veridical and presumed environments. It is partly conscious and partly unconscious. Each conversation is unique because each person's thoughts and feelings are indivemes that exist as single elements of the complex whole that makes up an integrated physical and mental individual. Since no two people truly share the same integrated thought or feeling, no two conversations can be the same. On the other hand, conversation themes and trends do emerge that reflect the enduring physical and mental GBH needs and desires of individuals and of conversant partners and these themes and trends offer valuable insights into the psychologies of people-in-conversation.

Earlier we considered the progression "from mentation to remark" in which we bring our CAMM and baseline consciousness to a conversation setting that includes our conversational partner. This confluence of CAMM, baseline consciousness, setting, and partner comprises a "zone of maximal conversation consistency" wherein previous conversations are most likely to predict subsequent conversations. Consistency is possible because these conversations satisfy demands of the organism-in-environment such that each individual not only brings to the conversation an intra-personal, mental predisposition toward specific ideas, but he also is provided with the extra-personal cues of physical setting and conversational partner that were present during past similar discussions.

It is important to emphasize that consistency need not be present in the literal words of a conversation, or even in basic denotations expressed. Rather, the consistency is a relative consistency of affective valence that sometimes is confined mostly to the conversation's connotations.

Affective consistency is possible in the valence (good versus bad), intensity (strong versus weak), and balance (the proportion of good versus bad and strong versus weak content) of affective content. Valence, intensity, and balance, in turn, are revealed in at least three ways: First, affective consistency usually is present within the personality of the conversant. Although fluctuations obviously occur, an individual tends toward either a predominantly positive or predominantly negative view of self and non-self, predisposing him toward a preponderance of positively-valenced or negatively-valenced remarks. This trait, or dispositional, optimism or pessimism is one of the most researched aspects of affective consistency, comprising a dimension that is informative and reliable (Scheier & Carver, 1987). Second, certain conversational content is marked by our language and/or culture as affectively positive or negative. It is possible, but difficult, for instance, to recount an event of genocide in which positive remarks predominate. Certain conversational content clearly is biased either toward affectively positive or negative regularities. Third, as we have emphasized, conversants tend to exhibit affective regularities related to context, with the context including all that exists outside of the self, and, especially, the aspect of context that is the conversational partner. Two buddies at a funeral of their mutual friend would be inclined to speak fondly of him, regardless of his foibles.

My Synergistext™ analysis system targets conversation to determine intra-individual affective valence consistency. We expect fair affective valence consistency when an individual discusses a topic with anyone at any time due to trait-oriented affective consistencies related to optimism-pessimism features of his own personality. We expect strong affective valence consistency when two persons discuss a topic that language and/or culture have affectively marked. And we expect the strongest affective valence consistency concerning topics that two intimates have discussed many times and that language and/or culture have affectively marked.

When the basics of conversational topics have been worked through in the past with this same conversational partner, each conversant's indivemes have been reshaped in a way that is contextualized for the target conversation, and readily elicited by it. Yet, despite a shared conversational co-construction, when we converse, we contribute our thoughts and feelings and respond to the thoughts and feelings of our conversational partner in a way that is uniquely our own. Every contribution from oneself and from the other is an indiveme—sifted through the filter of one's life story and incorporated into it. That which cannot be incorporated will be misunderstood, rejected, and forgotten.

As was said regarding emotion, conversation is a matter of moving and being moved. We deliberately, but usually unconsciously, move toward a GBH goal despite occasionally being temporarily jostled and sidetracked from the goal by GBH efforts of our partner. Each person wants to make the conjoint conversation-story in his own image, but each has an intuitive awareness that he can only approximate his personal goal, and then if he allows his partner to do the same.

The Diagnostic Value of Wording

Indivemes never are directly expressed, since no communication mechanism exists to do so. When it comes to conversation, as the Bee Gees sang, "It's only words and words are all I have…" But, while imperfect, words have been sufficient to enable humans to talk their way from caves to classical literature. Wording reveals the familiarity conversants have with a topic and with a partner. Words' detail, directness/indirectness, and affective valence all reveal a conversant's relationship with his partner relative to a topic (Holtgraves, 1997).

Part of the magic of words is that they permit ideas to be expressed with limitless shades of meaning. On a day when the thermometer reads fifteen degrees Fahrenheit, for instance, I could comment to you that the weather is frigid, brutal, terrible, invigorating, refreshing, or wonderful. The adjective that I choose will tell as much about me as about the day. I am similarly self-disclosing if when speaking with you about my lunchtime experience, I refer to having eaten with somebody, a coworker, a colleague, a woman, Jen, Jennifer, Mrs. Smith, sweetie pie, or the witch. The person with whom I had lunch is represented in my mind as an amalgam of multi-sensory-motor-visceral impressions and their associations. To converse with you about her, I must summon up the relevant CAMM and TAMM, culling out those that best describe my thoughts. The CAMM and TAMM modules then need to be sifted through the CASS and TASS appropriate to the topic and to our relationship. Only then am I ready to fashion a phrase suitable for our conversation. What ultimately is said reflects the dynamics of my self and my beliefs about what is proper to say to you at this time and place. So my choice of words discloses my self and my relationship with you (Wiener & Mehrabian, 1968). If I refer to my lunch partner as "sweetie pie" or "the witch," I reveal my passion about her and my comfort in speaking frankly to you. If I call her "somebody" or a "coworker," I reveal minimal emotion about her and/or about her as she impacts my relationship with you.

While I am acknowledging the power of words, please note that I do not advocate a micro analytic look at isolated word meanings. The meaning of any communication is powerfully influenced by its intra- and inter-personal matrix – meaning does not inhere in the words; meaning lies in conversing people and their context. It is not the words but the underlying thoughts and feelings that matter most. For instance, if I am walking down the street and I begin talking about how hungry I am, the meaning is at least partly determined by the person with whom I am talking, by my implicit message to that person, and by my expectation of their response to my remark. If I say I'm hungry to my wife, I may be reminding her that she forgot to cook my favorite meal last night as she had planned to do. If I say I am hungry to my colleague at a staff meeting, I may be hinting that it's time to adjourn for lunch.

Analyzing Conversation

If language is a second level sensory-motor system employed in our relentless, expectant search for GBH, then conversation is its primary instrument. Conversation facilitates message GBH by helping us discover and secure information that leads to primary reinforcement, such as food and shelter, and secondary reinforcement, such as money and diplomas; it facilitates relationship GBH by allowing us to interact with others in ways that create and sustain important social affiliations.

Because it is so central to our GBH success and so ubiquitous in our lives, conversation is a unique portal into our minds and personalities. By looking at conversations we can discover whether there is a conversational style, similar to a personality style, that defines each of us.

Pennebaker and King (1999) asked a similar question, but they used written, rather than spoken language, to research the answer, scrutinizing daily diaries of substance abuse inpatients, daily writing assignments of college students, and journal abstracts of psychology professors. The language samples were compared with psychological test results, subjects' self reports, and health-markers. The researchers concluded that:

> "Taken together, the data demonstrate that the ways people express themselves in words are remarkably reliable across time and situations. The dimensions of language that are reliable are impressively diverse as well. From the use of highly specific articles to general emotional language, both positive and negative emotion words, use of large words, and even verb tense are stable across individuals.…Use of negative emotions in language may serve as a good example. People who are consistently harsh in their comments on friends, the weather, and their use of time will use a high rate of negative emotion words. Even if they claim that they are not angry or upset, their use of negative emotion words may (or may not) betray an underlying sense of distress. Indeed, it is interesting that use of negative emotion words was significantly correlated with both alcohol and tobacco use, whereas self-reports of neuroticism (basically a measure of trait anxiety) were uncorrelated with these behaviors."

Pennebaker and King's comment about self-report of neuroticism not being correlated with behaviors is reminiscent of our previous discussion of the difference between explicit and implicit measures of personality. As you may recall, McClelland (1985) and I believe that explicit measures, such as self reports, are adequate to assess what people would prefer to do, but not what they actually do, while implicit measures, such as Pennebaker's and the Synergistext™ system that I am proposing, are better predictors of people's actual behaviors. The research of Egloff and associates (2002) supports the power of implicit over explicit measures relative to public speaking and anxiety. They note: "Whereas the explicit test showed modest relations within only 1 measure of cardiovascular reactivity, the implicit test predicted heart rate and blood pressure reactivity during preparation and delivery of the speech."

Conversation as Emergently Organized

Implicit measures predict conversation best because conversation is mostly an unconscious, emergent, action-oriented process. Unlike a basketball game that has organizers whose job is to plan and execute a strategy, a typical conversation has no one who consciously organizes its content and route, but an organization does emerge. Similar emergent processes have been said to govern the development of other complex interacting systems, as diverse as an ant colony and a city (Johnson, 2001). Although specific features of emergence are just beginning to be investigated, and their precise nature is elusive, Greenberg, Partridge, Weiss, and Haraway (1999) explain that the emergent process is a property of an entire system that is not present in any single element of the system, but which arises from novel arrangements of the system's parts. They offer as analogy the fact that a water molecule "emerges" when two oxygen atoms and one hydrogen atom are catalyzed by a spark of energy. Ackerman (2001) makes the emergence of the water molecule even more relevant and personal to human experience when she says:

> "Imagine the task. Take two hydrogen atoms and a single oxygen atom and make them into a molecule shaped like a V. Make the angle between the arms 104 degrees and the distances between the atoms—the dashes in H-0-H—precisely .095718 nanometer. Make the molecule conservative and self-loving by giving it an odd electrical asymmetry, clustering the electrons near the oxygen atom, allowing one molecule to bond easily with another so that rivers, lakes, and oceans hold together, so that water remains sweep liquid at room temperature when it should be gas, so that my metabolism, the basic

business of my bodily living, does not bring on a temperature that would set my bones afire."

Ester Thelen (1995) unflinchingly unites the sciences of emergence and psychology, asserting "All behavior is always an emergent property of a confluence of factors." And she specially identifies emergence as necessary for mental phenomena when she says, "As Linda Smith and I have written (Thelen & Smith, 1994), higher order mental activities, including categorization, concept formation, and language, must arise in a self-organized manner from recurrent, real time activities…"

Because humans are so intensely social, the "confluence of factors" that catalyze emergent processes often have inter-personal relationships as a critical ingredient. For example, many middle-class Americans could awaken any weekday morning and literally go anywhere in the world. Purely from the point of view of possibilities, we would be hard-pressed to predict the theoretical destination of such Americans. But, from the point of view of practicalities, we easily could predict the average middle-class American's morning destination merely by observing him over a few days or few weeks, since most of them head automatically to work. Imagine now two spouses from a rural environment who have only one car and who work for the same employer located in the next town. Our ability to predict their weekday destination is even greater than our ability to predict either one separately, since each spouse's options are reduced due to having to accommodate to the needs of the other. To have a partner whom you try to satisfy is to restrict your own choices. Having a partner makes you and him/her more behaviorally consistent.

Self-induced-constraints, partner-induced-constraints, and their interaction are powerful factors that emergently organize conversation, and other conjoint volitional behaviors, and make them predictable. Conversation involves more than mere co-construction. To use our earlier metaphors, conversation is both shaped and restricted by the joint influences of the conversational path and conversational triangle that funnel us toward some discussions and away from others.

Consider the funneling-like effect to result from an emergent process that increasingly limits what will be discussed in the following way: First, the individual constrains himself to the subset of GBH goals that are important to him at any given moment in time. Second, he restricts himself to particular message and/or relationship features of those goals. Third, the individual confines his search to message and/or relationship objectives that he believes are potentially attainable with his current partner. And fourth, he pursues only those goals that his current partner is willing and able to accept here and now. In graphic form, the process is:

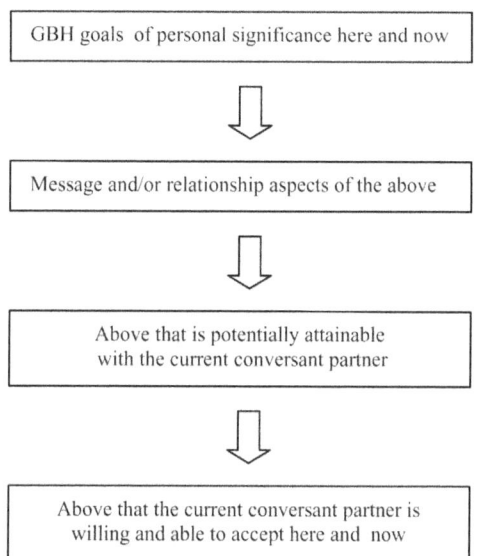

GBH goals of personal significance here and now

Message and/or relationship aspects of the above

Above that is potentially attainable with the current conversant partner

Above that the current conversant partner is willing and able to accept here and now

Most important, all four of these steps usually need to be synchronized between the two conversant partners, because conversation toward GBH is most likely to be mutually pursued and continued when it maximizes GBH opportunities for both partners. Although conversations theoretically can go anywhere, conversations between intimates tend to follow more or less predictable routes. While the words vary, the cognitive-affective-interactive processes remain fairly consistent.

Each individual's conversation executor determines what each individual will say and what each will hear the other say. To harken back to our discussion of wording, what is said is not mere words, nor even mere memes. We speak in indivemes, communicating an approximation of our ideas that have idiosyncratic cognitive-affective-interactive significance which is time- and context-dependent. The more conversant partners' indivemes overlap, the more their conversations are mutually understandable. To converse, then, is to share indivemes as fully as possible, despite the fact that, by definition, no two people ever hold the exact same indivemes.

While much more research must be done to validate my hypotheses, I suggest that when partners converse over time, cognitive-affective-interactive patterns spontaneously develop, because each person has been willing and able to satisfy certain enduring GBH needs of his own and/or of the partner, and unable or unwilling to pursue others. Merely by pursuing his own GBH needs vis-à-vis a given partner regarding a given subject each person has tended to follow a more or less predictable conversational route. Each conversant has unconsciously traveled a route to enhance his own GBH while enhancing, or at least not obstructing, the partner's route. In so doing, a repeated subject-specific conversation between two intimates will have produced a relatively consistent cognitive-affective-interactive topographic profile, with coherent content and a coherent structure that has arisen naturally. By interpreting the conversation profile, we gain valuable insight into the psychologies of each person separately and of the dyad that they comprise.

Sometimes when discussing the same topic, a conversational partner might repeat verbatim some comments that he had made previously. However, verbatim repetition is not necessary to support my hypothesis. The essential element is the affective valence (AV) – either positive affect or negative affect—that obtains. AV is much more likely to endure from conversation to conversation than are the specific words used during previous discussions. Moreover, an individual's AV is more likely to persist across conversational partners when the same topic is discussed than would the specific words employed to express the AV. For example, when talking to a best friend about a co-worker, one might refer to the co-worker as "an idiot;" whereas, when discussing the co-worker with one's wife the co-worker is referred to as "ignorant," with one's mother as "frustrating," or with one's minister as "needy." While the words are quite different, the AV is unequivocally negative. The AV of conversation reveals critically important information about the speaker and to the listener because people are influenced by the underlying affective meaning of interaction to a vastly greater extent than they are by the surface wording.

Synergistext™

Some early science fiction movies depicted aliens who transmitted thoughts to each other without speaking. This surely would be the ultimate conversation. The communicators would know their counterpart's GBH needs, message and relationship, and could adjust their responses accordingly. Deception would be unnecessary and impossible. We literally would know where our partner's "head is" in terms of baseline consciousness.

But, alas, no human has ever directly experienced another's thought. Even the most mindful person often is unaware of what she, **herself**, thinks and why she thinks any given thought. We all have had the experience of making a comment and then wondering, "Where did that come from?"

Being unable to read minds, people have scrutinized the comments of others to try to discern what they are thinking and why—that which people say has been the primary focus. Psychologists and educators, politicians and clergymen, salespeople and judges, among others, have specialized in this art, and thousands of book and articles have been published trying to perfect it.

Since elusive unconscious processes lie at the root of language both as internal representation and as communication, non-scientific analysis of conversational remarks is doomed to failure. However, people do employ some widely shared, consciously controlled communication processes that can be reliably explored. The conscious processes enable us to volitionally and deliberately structure conversation in ways that promote our own needs and listeners' understandings. When assessed scientifically with the proper instrument and method, the consciously-controlled communication processes can be dissected to reveal underlying unconscious strivings that prompt and sustain conversational synergy.

"Synergy" emerges when two or more elements flow together such that their combined power is increased beyond a simple summing of their previous individual powers. And "text" describes discourse, in our case, spoken discourse. **Synergistext™**, my method for assembling conversation profiles, presumes the coming together of two lines of conversational input in a way that has the potential for enhancing the well being of the communicating dyad better than either partner could do independently. The enhancement is accomplished by each person's better understanding her own individual conversational needs, the conversational needs of her partner, and their joint conversational needs.

But why waste our time on casual conversation that seems so unconsciously determined and so capricious? Why not analyze a more conscious, serious, scripted version of conversation such as the highly pragmatic business conversation that is direct and no-nonsense? For example, the conversation between a salesperson and customer might be instructive, since it is very time efficient, affording succinct exchange of relatively dispassionate information that can result in GBH for each communicator. By analyzing such conversations, couldn't we learn some very valuable information about how people communicate?

There is no doubt that highly pragmatic conversation provides valuable insights into communication. But highly pragmatic conversation is poorly suited for revealing personal, fundamental GBH strivings and strategies, because highly pragmatic conversation typically is motivated principally by non-inter-personal, nonaffective goals that militate against authentic expression of self. By contrast, because it is so much less scripted and so much more unconsciously and egocentrically focused, casual conversation is the quintessential device for realizing GBH through liberating our authentic selves. More than any other human activity, casual conversation reveals the deeper parts of our inner selves and our true interpersonal strivings. Casual conversation puts people, their most basic needs, desires, apprehensions, and relationships at the forefront of discourse. For instance, to be blunt about it, in a casual conversation, one might readily say, "Oh, one minute. I'll be right back. I have to throw-up." Few people are "authentic" enough to say that during a business discussion.

Overview of Synergistext™ Rationale

Synergistext™ regards conversation as two streams that flow into one. Each conversant contributes her part, each expects to realize GBH, and the contributions and expectations of each co-mingle to give every conversation its unique character. The entire emergent process occurs so automatically that conversational meaning and understanding have been described as a co-construction that results in a "relational unconscious" wherein partners powerfully influence the "generation, awareness, and expression" of the other's unconscious experience (Zeddies, 2000). This relational unconscious affords people the opportunity to understand each other in ways that can not be articulated verbally, in ways that permit what Ickes and his colleagues (Ickes, Stinson, Bissonnette, & Garcia, 1990) call "accurate empathy" comprised of

> "a) a skill, ability, or facility (b) to understand, apprehend, infer, interpret (c) with accuracy (d) the private, covert, subjective (e) phenomenological reality, mental experience, thoughts and feelings (f) of some other person(s). In a social interaction context, empathic accuracy can be defined more simply as the degree to which one interactant is able to accurately infer the specific content of another interactant's thoughts and feelings. Although there are a number of different aspects of empathic accuracy that one might choose to study, the two aspects we regard as most important are content accuracy and valence accuracy. *Content accuracy* refers to the degree to which one interactant's description of the inferred content of an interaction partner's thoughts or feelings matches the actual content of the specific thoughts or feelings reported by the partner. *Valence accuracy* refers to the degree to which one interactant's inferences about the emotional tone (positive, neutral, negative) of an interac-

tion partner's thoughts or feelings match the actual valence of the specific thoughts and feelings reported by the partner."

Synergistext™ targets both the personal and relational conscious and unconscious to provide intra-individual, and inter-individual information that discloses valuable features of the psychology of the individual, of the conversational dyad, and of the dyad's interactions around particular topics. Synergistext™ allows us to glimpse and respond to accurate empathy that occurs between two conversants who may not even be conscious of its presence.

At the intra-individual level, we see, among other things, the individual's choice of topics, phraseology, and emotional tone. We observe not only that individuals tend to speak to the same people about the similar things, but that they talk to them in similar ways—with similar emphasis, affect, participation, contribution, and so forth.

At the dyadic level, we see the depth, breadth, and affective valence of interaction, whether the conversants share the same ideas and affects, and the extent to which they move above, below, toward, away, with, or against each other. As noted earlier, we find that conversation is most predictable at the zone of maximal conversation consistency, the intersection of person-topic-setting wherein, relatively speaking, the same persons discuss the same issue under the same environmental circumstances. This is true because each person brings to the event the same topic-specific chronically accessible memory modules (CAMM) stimulated by the same inter-personal and environmental cues.

At the topic level, we see how the conversants present themselves, consciously and/or unconsciously, concerning the issue at hand. Given what we have said about holism and the artificiality of separating human experience, it is not surprising to realize that some elements of the conversation cannot be neatly pidginholed into a particular conversational analysis category. For instance, when a conversant does not speak about a particular aspect of a given issue, it could be due, among other things, to intra-individual predisposition, dyadic aversion, or absence of sufficient content regarding the subject.

The Synergistext™ profile is able to disclose baseline consciousness, how we and others view ourselves, our inter-personal movement, optimism-pessimism, positive-negative affect, our reinforcers, what we talk about, when we talk, what subjects we discuss, our affective tone, taboos vs. foci, and the types of conversation we have with particular people. It can illustrate the inherent self-organization of conversation.

Synergistic analysis offers some basic, general insights for virtually all conversations. We, for instance, should be able to discern the overall emotional tone of any conversation. But, because conversation is fluid and multidetermined, neither Synergistext™ nor any analysis ever will completely satisfy our desire for consistency, clarity, and closure. Some conversations will provide greater insights in some areas than in others. We will more fully understand the inter-personal movements of some conversations than of others because of the idiosyncrasies of some conversants and their partners. By acknowledging the protean nature of conversation and analyzing conversation as it is, rather than how we wish it to be, we are better able to efficiently focus our resources on what is available in any particular conversation.

To accept a conversation as it is, is to accept the inevitability of co-construction and of the relational unconscious. Synergistext™ analyzes the total conversation, each conversant, and each conversant relative to each other. Among other things, it reveals the proportion of time that each person speaks, the contour of speaking turns, the affective quality of each statement, and its relationship to statements that precede and follow it. Data depicting the time line and affective valence of conversation is especially valuable. To cite but one example, Jacob and Johnson (2001) find that the sequential-affective flow of conversation in families with a depressed member predicts problems generally and depression in the children specifically. Positivity suppression, the tendency for one member to follow another member's positive comments with non-positive ones, differentiates families from each other. Families with a depressed father tend to demonstrate the positivity suppression effect, while those with a depressed mother tend not to.

Conversational Unit of Analysis

In order to analyze conversation, we need to define the unit of conversational expression to be observed. Should we analyze words, sentences, or something else?

In some cases, a word clearly does express one or more ideas. If I lock my keys in the car and screech, "Damn!" I may be thinking, "Oh, not again. I did this last month. This is going to cost me $90. I'm going to be late for work. I feel like a moron." If you were standing next to me, you would not know the specifics of my internal ruminations, but you would know the gist of my thought content. Sometimes, a phrase is a legitimate unit of mental expression. "No way!" expresses one's general position concerning an issue. On other occasions, an independent clause like – "I am very pleased" – lucidly communicates a more specific notion.

Any verbal expression, then, from a single word (or even less) to a complex, compound sentence can represent a single idea, or multiple ideas. However, we must accept that no conversation analytic system will disclose multi-sensory-motor-visceral thoughts, only attenuated thoughts as expressed in conversational ideas, meaning thoughts that have been filtered through the "from mentation to conversation" funnel. If Synergistext™ is to interpret these attenuated thoughts to illuminate the psychologies of the conversants and of their conversations, we must conduct our analysis at every major level of expression.

Chafe (1987) argues convincingly that most conversations consist of verbalizations in which one item of information is produced after another by way of intonation units which he defines as a sequence of approximately five or six words... "mbined under a single, coherent intonation contour, usually preceded by a pause."that lasts about two seconds. Altmann (1997) cites research indicating that each conversational pause circumscribes a "chunk" of utterance best described as a clause. For practical purposes, then, there is good reason to believe that we converse primarily in closely-spaced phrases and/or clauses rather than in full grammatical sentences.

My Synergistext™ experience does support Chafe's general views that phrase-level intonation units predominate in most conversations, but, as emphasized earlier, we need to be able to analyze whatever conversation that people produce. I have found that a significant amount of conversation can be filled with stammer-like and sub-phrase comments. To ignore or discount this information is to miss valuable data that reveal important insights into what is happening with the speakers and with their discussion. Synergistext™, therefore, does record and score stammers and subphrases to the extent that it is possible.

The Analytic Process

At first glance, it may seem odd to parse conversation in a way that gives ahs, and broken phrases credit as scoreable conversation. Intuition suggests that only a full comprehensible phrase should be counted. Yet, a moment's reflection is all that is needed to appreciate the rationale.

For one thing, think of it this way: The speaking person is controlling the time dimension and the content of conversation. This is true no matter how much or little sense he makes in the process. His status as speaker defines the partner as listener for as long as the listener allows it, for as long as the speaker commands the conversational floor. The stammering, "broken-speeched" person **is** communicating. Even if the content is pure gibberish, the "gibberishing" speaker is communicating his confusion, anxiety, brain injury, or whatever else lies behind his incomprehensibility. Remember, conversation is not equivalent to content, but rather to the use of volitional speech in the expectant search for GBH. The stammering person can be just as expectantly searching as can the smooth elocutionist. We score conversation to determine the effect that we believe a speaker is having on himself and on the listener, and that effect eventually will be disclosed by the speaker's and listener's initiatives and responses to whatever clear or broken communication that has occurred.

For another thing, ahs and other dysfluencies may have a significance all their own. Christenfeld and Creager (1996) suggested that ums, ers, and ahs may represent a speaker's excessive self-consciousness about what he is saying. This explanation is similar to that offered to explain "choking" when performing a competitive sport, such as when golfing (Beilock and Carr, 2001); it is a matter of experiencing disruption of volitional action by self-consciously trying to control an activity that ideally is automatized to the point that it flows without deliberate direction to each subroutine of the complex act. That disruption of these two dissimilar behaviors – speaking and golfing – occurs under similar circumstances illustrates once more Willingham's (1998) dual mode principle which explains how conversation, as a volitional, primarily unconsciously directed activity of speaking and listening, is governed by many of the same rules that govern the relentless, expectant search for GBH through overt, primarily unconsciously directed, motor action.

What is the point of analyzing conversation? If you want to understand personality or to predict someone's behavior, why not have her fill out a self-report questionnaire?

Winkielman, Knauper, and Swartz (1998) explain that self-reports are problematic, especially when one assesses emotion-oriented issues. They note that self-report questions of emotional significance have inherent ambiguity, are powerfully affected by the reference period that the subject uses in answering them, are confounded by concurrent versus retrospective features of self-reporting, and the interpretations of the self-reports lead to different corrective recommendations based upon the self-reports. Most important for our purposes, Winkielman and associates note that the "conversational process" used by investigators to explain self-report to the subjects, themselves, biases their self-report results because "…research participants are cooperative communicators who do their best to provide the information (they think) the researcher is asking for. Unfortunately, what kind of information that may be is often insufficiently specified, and participants have to draw on contextual features of the research conversation to disambiguate the meaning of the questions asked or the nature of the task presented to them."

Okay then, to understand personality or to predict someone's behavior, how about giving the subject a psychological test?

There are a thousand reasons to prefer natural conversation to a test. To name a few: First, conversation is real life. With a test, the tester always must question whether the behavior as expressed on the test is similar to and/or relevant to the behavior as enacted in reality. To give merely one example, the value of results provided by the internationally famous Rorschach Test, or "inkblot test," formally released in 1942, are still being hotly debated (Garb, et al., 2001). Second, tests are intrusive and contrived. Many people are reluctant to be tested, feeling manipulated or dehumanized by it. The mere fact of being tested can significantly change the behavior being targeted. Third, if the results of the analysis are intended to improve conversation, by using conversation, itself, rather than a test, one can better plan reparative recommendations by understanding the initial behaviors that prompted them. Finally, Synergistext™ assessment ideally is performed across time, not just as a one-shot endeavor. It, therefore, has a built-in means for determining how enduring and representative the targeted conversational behavior is and so maximize the prediction that flows from the analysis.

Biesanz, West, and Graziano (1998) emphasize that the over-time consistency of an individual's behavior is critical for us to predict the behavior of persons with whom we interact in our day-to-day lives. They say that most tests merely giving an individual's "average" behavior, rather than her "consistent" behavior. For example, imagine that Jan and Fran each earned $120,000 this past year. Jan earned a $10,000 every month and Fran earned the following monthly sums: $15,477, $7,363, $5,403, $3,489, $2,479, $4,367, $8,094, $4,325, $15,672, $4,266, $4,4530, $4,535. Which salary scenario offers the better opportunity for accurate monthly prediction?

While we will never find behavioral consistency anywhere near equivalent to the monthly earning consistency of Jan, we need to come as close as we can. We do so by sampling the individual's behavior over time in as stable an environment as possible, and, in the case of conversation, "stable environment" more than anything else means stability of conversational partner. Thus, we ideally analyze conversation between two persons over time to best understand each person and their relationship together.

Synergistext™ *Analyses*

The relentless, expectant, overt action-oriented GBH search of a primordial hunter is obvious. We see him pursue his prey over hill and dale in the hope that he will secure a meal. He trudges onward with a single-minded purpose despite fatigue, rugged terrain, vermin, and inclement weather. When obstacles arise, he surmounts them and resumes the pursuit.

In conversation, the relentless, expectant GBH search is less transparent. Mental GBH associated with conversation can be especially subtle, subjective – even arbitrary. Where is conversational GBH?

To find GBH, we need to regard conversation both as a general encounter and as a series of specific encounters. Beginning at the most general level, think about conversant participation as an individual's willingness to commit herself to an interaction with another person with all of its opportunities, demands, and risks. She engages because she sees the possibility of GBH message and/or relationship. But to achieve her goals, she needs to introduce and explore self-relevant areas in a way that keeps the conversant partner sufficiently satisfied that he will maintain an adequately cooperative demeanor throughout the encounter. She also must follow many social conversation-structuring conventions. For instance, only one individual can speak at a time and the information communicated should be relevant, concise, and nonredundant (Grice, 1975). At this general level, the conversant can extract message or relationship GBH from the encounter as a whole. However, conversation proceeds from topic to topic. At this specific level, too, each topic presents message and relationship GBH opportunities. For instance, to have the speaking floor in and of itself can have GBH value, since having the floor enables one to set one's own agenda powered by the BETF issues salient for his life story at any given moment in time.

Like the primordial hunter, the conversant pursues her partner over vast expanses of verbiage in the hope that she will secure her GBH goals. She talks on with a single-minded purpose, tolerating interruption, misunderstanding, and diversion. When obstacles arise, she surmounts them and resumes the pursuit.

If people could have achieved all of their GBH desires via grunts and calls, humans never would have developed refined language skills. Conversation, especially, has been the linchpin of social interaction, and a link to relationship repair. Acknowledging this is trite but true. What is not so obvious is that each relationship partner, consciously or unconsciously, uses conversation primarily to realize his/her own ends. The fact that much of conversation is unconsciously determined means that one cannot merely ask the conversants to explain their needs and tensions; we need a scientifically-based analytic system to look through the epidermis of conversation and get to its heart. Heyman (2001) recognizes these realities when he says:

> "Couple communication is the common pathway to relationship dysfunction across theories, therapies, therapists, and clients. All theories and therapies emphasize the role of communication (see Jacobson & Gurman, 1995) and both therapists (Geiss & O'Leary, 1981) and couples (e.g., Storaasli & Markman, 1990) rate communication as the top problem area. However, every clinician knows two things about couples' complaints about communication. First, such presenting problems tell us everything and nothing at all. Communication is the common pathway **for getting what you want** in relationships (*emphasis added*)…Second, couples' reports of their difficulties, although useful in understanding their own conceptualizations of their distress (e.g., Buehlman, Gottman, & Katz, 1992), may not provide the information necessary to construct useful case conceptualizations and treatment plans. Partners' reports are subject to attributional biases (see Bradbury & Fincham, 1990) and selective attention. A particularly common form, sentiment override (Weiss, 1980), involves distressed individuals attending almost exclusively to their partner's negative behaviors and interpreting even neutral or positive behavior through a negative filter (cf Fincham, Garnier, Gano-Phillips, & Osborne, 1995). Therefore, outsiders' observations can add very useful, nonredundant information to that gleaned from self-reports."

To discover useful, nonredundant, conscious, and unconscious conversation patterns, a Synergistext™ evaluation ideally assesses the same dyad on several occasions. In this way, conversational consistencies emerge that empower conversants to better understand and improve themselves. Data relevant to each person and to their discussions are presented as texts, graphs, and charts. Some basic questions and issues addressed are:

1. What needs are being pursued? (Maslow)

2. What material seems to be emerging from baseline consciousness?(BETF, CAMM, TAMM)

3. What are the targets of the GBH searches? (messages and relationships)

4. How relentless and expectant are the searches? (percentage of conversation and topic dominance)

5. What level of specificity and topics are disclosed? (CASS, TASS)

6. What are the directions of inter-personal movements? (TAABWA)

7. What conversation categories are disclosed? (e.g., story, gossip)

8. What are the conversants' affective valences? (affective valence direction percentages)

9. What are the conversants' affective concordances? (affective agreement percentages)

10. What is the affective conversational topography? (chronographic profile)

Listening to a conversation without an analytic plan is little more than voyeurism. We need Synergistext™ to make sense of the overwhelming mass of information contained in even brief discussions, and we must narrow our focus to make this manageable. Since Synergistext™ emphasizes affective and personality-based features of conversation, the analytic raw data is heavily weighted in that direction.

With the data in hand, we construct as comprehensive a profile as we can. Acknowledging once more that the content of conversations is so variable that no profile will be complete, I add that incompleteness is not a problem per se. In fact, whatever is or is not available in a given conversation is, itself, significant in disclosing both the uniqueness and the personalities of the conversants, the dyad, and the conversation.

While a clinical Synergistext™ analysis contains considerable quantitative information useful to a mental health professional, that data would be rather tedious and burdensome in the context of this book. Accordingly, in the conversation examples here, we report only the most essential quantitative information, and, instead, elaborate on the qualitative.

Synergistext™ Evaluation Profile

The moment of truth has arrived in which the fantasy of theory confronts the reality of actual conversations: How much validity of the Synergistext™ theory is self-evident in the data presented here? How much is apparent with only minimal explanation? How much is supported only by my detailed explanation? How much of the theory is at odds with the evidence from the conversations? How much of the theory is unaddressed by the particular conversations presented here? You can decide for yourself.

My emphasis on the importance of context and of stories as structuring experience demands that I begin by setting the stage and describing the participants. The conversations transcripted below were conducted via telephone. Three of the four occurred on the same day – Saturday – and the final one, on the next morning.

All the conversants are related. Mom, age 80, married to Fred, is the biological mother of Mara, age 50 and married to John, Robin, age 43 and married to Rick, and Lara, age 57, widowed. Hana, the daughter of Mara, is the mother of a five month old son, and is married to Eugene. The conversations are presented in chronological order. Mara called Hana, then Robin. Subsequently, Mara was called by Mom, and then by Lara. It also is important contextually to know that nine months prior to the conversations Fred's brother, Bill, died; six months prior, Fred's sister-in-law, Fran, died; and one month prior Fred's dog, Bridget, died. The history of the conversants and of their topics are important because both strongly determine what is and is not discussed: the conversational triangle has a context that includes people, times, and places.

Of the many recorded conversations available to me, I chose these because they occurred in close temporal proximity to each other; they involved intimates who literally have had lifelong acquaintance with one another; they all were effected through the same medium – telephone—and they all revolved primarily around the same mundane subject – concern about parents and selection of a pet – that could affect virtually any of us. To test out some of the Synergistext™ assumptions about conversational consistency, I focus on Mara, since she is the primary link in this conversational chain.

Aside from minimal revisions necessary to safeguard the autonomy of the speakers, the transcripts are uncensored, illustrating conversation in its most pedestrian, authentic form. Most speech imperfections and misstatements have been transcribed, and punctuation is minimal in order to simulate the choppiness of the discussions. Accordingly, while the conversations can be a bit tedious to read, they afford one an opportunity to analyze real, detailed discourse of every-day people. Those interested in the fine details of conversation analysis should read all the dialogues in their entirety, so that the subsequent analyses will be maximally informative. Others might choose to skim or even skip the dialogues, and still profit from reading the analyses.

Quantitative and Qualitative Results

Let's begin by considering all the conversation data of all conversants taken together, since this helps us to get a feel for the depth and range of the discussions. In the interest of conserving space, stats refers to statistical data; conv one designates the first dialogue, conv two, the second, and so forth; avg indicates the arithmetic average; and sd is the standard deviation or average variability. When space is at a premium, speakers are abbreviated as follows: ma=Mara, ha=Hana, rb=Robin, mm=Mom, and la=Lara.

Individual Conversations Stats	conv one		conv two		conv three		conv four			
	ma	ha	ma	rb	ma	mm	ma	la	avg	sd
Affective comments	31	5	50	22	69	21	120	40	44.75	33.82
Affective % over all comments	0.17	0.17	0.16	0.17	0.19	0.13	0.21	0.1	0.167	0.024
Total negative comments	12	3	27	16	22	15	61	27	22.88	16.24
% negative of total affective	0.39	0.6	0.54	0.73	0.32	0.71	0.51	0.7	0.559	0.14
Total positive comments	19	2	23	6	47	6	59	13	21.88	19.35
% positive of total affective	0.61	0.4	0.46	0.27	0.68	0.29	0.49	0.3	0.441	0.14
Total number of comments	181	30	309	128	358	163	579	294	255.3	158.4
% of conversation domination	0.86	0.14	0.71	0.29	0.69	0.31	0.66	0.3	0.5	0.241

All Conversations Stats	conv one	conv two	conv three	conv four	avg	sd
Positive %	0.1	0.07	0.1	0.08	0.088	0.014
Negative %	0.07	0.1	0.07	0.1	0.085	0.014
Affective %	0.17	0.16	0.17	0.18	0.173	0.007
Neutrality %	0.83	0.84	0.83	0.82	0.827	0.007

Because an important feature of Synergistext™ is the extent of consistency of an individual's conversational style, we gain valuable insights by inspecting the data from Mara across all four of her conversations. However, please note, as we have said continually, conversation is not unilaterally determined. Conversation is co-constructed. Mara's data are as they are because of her interactions with the specific persons with whom she spoke. Had she spoken with other persons, at least some of her data would have been different to some significant degree. That having been said, a gross, quantitative overview of the aggregated conversations of Mara is as follows:

| Conversation Partner | Hana | Robin | Mom | Lara | | |
Conversant used for this table's stats	Mara	Mara	Mara	Mara	avg	sd
Affective comments	31	50	69	120	67.5	33.2
Affective % over all comments	0.17	0.16	0.19	0.21	0.18	0.02
Total negative comments	12	27	22	61	30.5	18.4
% negative of total affective	0.39	0.54	0.32	0.51	0.44	0.09
Total positive comments	19	23	47	59	37	16.6
% positive of total affective	0.61	0.46	0.68	0.49	0.56	0.09
Total number of comments	181	309	358	579	357	144
% of conversation domination	0.86	0.71	0.69	0.66	0.73	0.08

While all of the numbers above are simple averages or standard deviations, they can be intimidating to persons averse to mathematics. You can choose to scrutinize the numbers or to ignore them, since I verbally will describe the results right now, using slightly more precise numbers than the ones listed above.

Considering all four conversations and all five conversants from an affective point of view, we see that on average the conversations' contents are .827 affectively neutral and, therefore, .173 affectively charged. Clearly, most of the information is being communicated in a dispassionate manner. The affectively positive content averages .0875 of the total conversations and the affectively negative content averages .0852 – extraordinarily balanced affective content. These are "mature" conversations conducted by mature persons, rather than ones involving overly emotional content or overly emotional people. The extent of perfect affective agreement—the correspondence between the affective charge of a given remark and of the remark that the listener makes immediately after having heard the first remark – is a strong .925. To explain this statistic: if during a conversation I make ten affectively negative remarks and you respond immediately with an affectively negative remark each time, the extent of perfect affective agreement would be 1.0. If during a conversation, I make ten affectively negative remarks and you respond immediately with an affectively negative remark five out of the ten times, the extent of perfect affective agreement would be .50, and so forth. The conversations being analyzed here, like most conversations of significant duration, have a high degree of affective agreement. Most people in conversation are biased toward overt expressions of agreement rather than of disagreement.

The chart above presents some interesting facts concerning Mara: Although two of the conversations were initiated by her and two by her family members, Mara dominates all four in terms of the total number of comments made. She also has the greatest number of affective comments in all but one conversation, and in all conversations she makes more affectively positive and less affectively negative comments than does her conversant partner. Each successive conversation is longer than the preceding one, and each succeeding partner makes a higher percentage of comments. Having told Robin that she anticipated that Lara would have a negative affective response to getting Zoey, it is not surprising that Mara's affective agreement proportion is lowest during her discussion with Lara. Interestingly, Lara's percent of agreement with Mara is no less than had been the percent of the other conversants agreement with Mara. Finally, three of the tapes document that Mara's conversant partner initiated the end of each conversation. The Mara-Lara conversation also was ended by Lara, but this is not documented because the conversation concluded after the tape ran-out.

Where is Mara's relentless, expectant search for GBH? For one thing, her baseline consciousness is consumed with concern for her parents, especially for her father. Witness the repeated, emotionally-valenced remarks that she makes about him in every conversation. By talking with others about this, she achieves an improved state of H/GBH by discharging the tension associated with her concern. Second, the conversations are pleas for family support about having decided to get her parents a dog. Mara clearly is worried about whether the dog will be appropriate for them. This is a search for relationship G/GBH in that Mara hopes to have others agree with what she has done, and to have her own sense of self-confidence reinforced. Additionally, by talking with the others, Mara has elicited some message G/GBH, informational advice about how to improve the chances of successfully introducing the dog into the parents' home. For instance, Lara indirectly suggested that Mara should check to be sure a strong leash is available for securing Zoey outside the house.

Now let's look at each individual conversation and see what we can learn about the speaking partners. We will begin with Mara and Hana and then move on to Mara's discussions, in turn, with Robin, Mom, and Lara.

The Zoey Conversations

Mara and Hana

Mara: You tell them the kind of dog you want
        and they go through a list
        And she goes
        Well here's one that came in last week
        It's a woman that needs to get rid of three dogs
        And
        Da you tell them what kind of dog
        And she goes
        One's a Lahasa
        One's a Poodle
        One's a, you know
        So
        She gave me her name
        Um
        So I called her
        I think I woke her up
        Um
        She's
        recently divorced
        She's starting her own business
        Sounds like Cory's mother.
        She lives near
        um
        You take the
        202 north before Southtown
        There's an exit for Paoli-Chesterbrook

Hana: Uhuh

Mara: You come off there and
         It's…it's in a, a townhouse down around this shopping
         center or something

Hana: Uhuh

Mara: And
         She has
         One dog is 8
         One dog is 5
         And the other one is a terrier that she said she wouldn't
         match up because it's not a little foo foo thing
         And
         They're precious dogs
         They love ta
         go fa in the car
         They love ta
         Go for a walk
         And she said they
         are just adorable
         And ah

Hana: She's getting rid of them

Mara: Because she's not home anymore.

Hana: Oh

Mara: And she can't have them in the townhouse

Hana: Oh

Mara: So
         And she said I'll cry like a baby
         I said well
         Trust me
         that this dog will live like a human
         And you could visit it any time (Laugh) you wanted to
         And plus
         And I'm going there tomorrow at 12:00
         So before I hung up and she said
         And if n
         If

	this doesn't work out I'll take em back
	So there was a good sign
Hana:	Yeah
Mara:	She said but I you know So I call Mom
Hana:	You want the Poodle
Mara:	Yeah Any one I don't
Hana:	I think it would be hard for a dog that old ta Readjust
Mara:	I asked her that And she said no They're kind of independent dogs It's not like they Travel around together You know She said no They don't One doesn't follow the other around er She said that's funny they don't all sleep together or anything (Laugh) She said you know they're kind of independent Um So I called Mom And I told her She goes well don't get the old one (Laugh) That was the first thing she said Don't get the 8 year old one
Hana:	Which is the Poodle
Mara:	Ah la has I don't know

I don't know
It,... its
Either
Oh, and I said to the girl
We've never had boy dogs
And I said
I was always grown up
Told that
you know
They pee on the corners of beds and stuff
She goes
these dogs
do not mess in the house (Laugh)

Hana: Yeah

Mara: And she said no they don't
The one
that she's thinking of
I think
Zoey
Um
Just lays on her back for you to pet her

Hana: Umhm

Mara: And ah
So Mom said
When I called her and told her
She was real quiet and she goes well don't get the older one
And I said, well Mom
I'm gonna get
She
The woman kept saying well
You know
I just want you to see the dogs because you'll know right away
which one you can see him with

Hana: Umhm

Mara:	So I'm going tomorrow at 12:00 and she said you know you can take him and I said how do I I don't even know Do I pay you? And she goes no She goes the thing with St. Fran She goes I don't know anything about I'm not even going to call them Saying you're gonna take one She said um We'll just work it out with us But she said my understanding Somebody gave me the number because Unlike the SPCA these dogs will not be put to sleep
Hana:	Right
Mara:	You know you just find families for them
Hana:	So its free?
Mara:	Yeah Yeah So Mom said Dad's really scaring her He said to her last night did Bridget die last night?
Hana:	God!
Mara:	Yeah So He's just very depressed
Hana:	Did she tell him?
Mara:	No I just got off the phone with her

	I just hung up
	I said Mom I'm going to get it tomorrow
	And if I like one
	I'm
	Gonna get it
	And then well see what he does
Hana:	Yeah
Mara:	I mean
	Even if he says no
	I think
	He's gotta see it
Hana:	Yeah
Mara:	So
	And I said to the woman you can go see him (Laugh)
Hana:	(Laugh)
Mara:	(Laugh)
	She goes oh
	That would be good
	So
	Alright
	What do you think?
	Do you think I'm wrong?
	(Laugh)
Hana:	No
	It's a good idea
Mara:	Dad's laughing at me
	I'm excited
	I'll keep one
	But Mom was funny
	Don't get the older one
Hana:	Yeah
	Why?
Mara:	I guess cause they don't
	She doesn't want to go through another dog dying

Hana:	Oh—Mom (to her husband) Eugene just got off the exerciser So I'm going to feed Justin And then go down and do it myself
Mara:	Alright Oh I wish I was going today (Laugh) Alright Do you want a dog?
Hana:	No
Mara:	(Laugh) Alright See ya
Hana:	Bye

Synergistext™ Analysis

Mara's conversation with Hana is extraordinarily one-sided. The proportion of time that Mara talks is far greater than in any other conversation reported here, and the conversation is far shorter. Much of Mara's GBH probably is powered by an H/GBH need to externalize the contents of her baseline consciousness. There is little obvious GBH that Hana derives from this talk. She probably realizes some relationship GBH, remaining on the telephone line more to support her mother than anything else. This demonstrates the tug-of-war phenomenon that we discussed earlier – that each participant must exert just enough tension on the conversational rope to maintain adequate discourse equilibrium. Not even their strong relationship can sustain this lopsided discussion, however. Accordingly, Hana lets go of the telephone line relatively quickly, ending their brief talk.

For her part, Mara is bursting with anticipation and excitement. Much of what she says is mental preparation for getting the dog and a recounting of what had already transpired regarding it. She rehearses where to go, what to say, and generally how to proceed with this endeavor. Mara tells a self-story that depicts her as a dutiful daughter who is rescuing her father from infirmity or death. She at times indirectly and at times directly solicits encouragement that getting the dog is a good idea. Given her several remarks to that effect, Mara is intent on explaining that these candidate pooches are "good dogs" that the "lady" must surrender, not that she is "getting rid of." Similarly, many times she states that the dog can be returned to its owner if "things" don't work out. Given her tone in discussing that fact, this "out" is important to Mara.

Mara introduces environmental factors (E/BETF) into the discussion in the form of her husband, John, conscious that he is listening and implying that he is evaluating her and her plan. Hana also uses environment factors (E/BETF), in the form of her husband, Eugene, to break off the conversation. In light of Mara's previous reference to her husband, John, Hana might be employing mirroring, seizing upon the possibility of using someone or something external to the mother-daughter relationship as an excuse for exiting.

Our next conversation is of Mara and Robin:

Mara and Robin

Robin:	Hello
Mara:	I found them a dog
Robin:	Get the hell out of here!
Mara:	Unuh
Robin:	I cant bel… Rick just said to me today Just Here's a Jack Russell terrier Robin, just go out and buy him a dog
Mara:	Yeah well they're hyper Um
Robin:	Rick it's Mara (to husband) The one I never thought would bend She goes I found him a dog What the hell I cannot believe it
Mara:	Wait till you hear it
Robin:	Oh god
Mara:	Um One of the girls I work with

told me about this humane society
It's called St. Francis
It's in
near the Southtown Mall
and,
She said my cousin was saying something about it
It's small animals
So when I got home yesterday
It was Gina on the
She goes, here's the number of St. Francis
Well I called last night
They weren't there
It said we're open at nine
So I called at nine
and they
I said I
I, I know nothing about your organization
All these dogs are barkin' and
She said well we
we have
no dog
Cause I said
you know
I went through this story
briefly
And she said well we don't ha
Let me look through the list
And she goes well here's a woman that just called
A week ago
It was funny
On the 20th
which was my birthday
She has a dog
3 dogs that she needs to get rid of and
two of them are
One's a Lahasa
and one's a
Shitzu mix or something

On the 20th

because I said I want a little daw
a little furry dog
And she goes they're two furry dogs
So
She gave me her name is Jane
So I got off the phone
Its like 9:30
I said to John should I call her?
He goes yeah
Well
I woke her up
And I said
You know
I understand
I don't know if you got rid of your dogs
And I say
I started telling her the story
And she goes
I have
two little furry dogs
She goes
the third one is a terrier that I won't
You know
It doesn't sound like the kind you're looking for
She said I have
Kippy is eight or nine
and
Or Zoey is
four

Robin: Uhuh

Mara: And she said
Oh my god
They both sound like exactly what
your father needs
These dogs
just want to be petted
They love to ride in the car

	They
	Are just precious
	And
	I said do they
	You know we've never had boy dogs
	Do they pee?
	She said
Robin:	Oh, they're both
	They're boys
Mara:	Yeah
	and she said no they do not
	They're tr
	They're completely trained
	And she said
	I just got divorced
	I had to move from a big house
	That I had a yard for them
	Into a townhouse
	I opened my own business
	I'm not going to be home
	I have to travel
	And I just cant keep them
	And she said
	It breaks my heart
	She said I am devastated but
	Um
	I don't have a choice
	You know
	I've had a life style change
	So I sa
	Um
	Well, I'm going there tomorrow at 12:00
	And she said
	I, I don't want to tell you what one to take
	Because you have
	You'll have to see
	And she said

	Before we hung up She said I'll take the dog back, if it doesn't work And So I thought that that I like that
Robin:	Yeah
Mara:	And she said um I said well my parents live in Prospect You could visit the dog (Laugh) And I said if I take one of theses dogs
Robin:	She lives in Elmwood?
Mara:	Yeah
Robin:	Yeah
Mara:	I said if I take one of these dogs Your dog will live like a human being You know I said this dog would be spoiled to death And she said, Oh that makes me feel so good
Robin:	Yeah
Mara:	And ma So I told Mommy I said let me tell ya So I went through the whole thing She goes well don't get the older one
Robin:	Yeah That's the first thing I thought too
Mara:	Get the four or five year old
Robin:	Yeah

Mara: And ah
        I said Mom even if he says no
        I think we should get it
        And show it to him
        I said

Robin: I wouldn't even
        I think we should do what we did last time
        Knock, ring the doorbell
        And hide (Laugh)

Mara: Well, she's going to tell him
        Um, going tomorrow at noon
        And she said
        She said he
        She said he's really worrying me
        He said to her last night
        Did Bridget die last night?
        So
        I said to the woman
        I think the man
        is deteriorating

Robin: Yeah

Mara: And I said
        he needs something
        She said
        Let me tell ya
        Either one of these dogs would be perfect
        And I said, Will they walk without a lease?
        She goes
        She said they love to walk
        But I would put them on a leash

Robin: Yeah
        And that would be fine

Mara: Lara
        Last night Lara called
        And I said I

	you know I'm trying to call around She says no They don't need a dog They could trip
Robin:	Rick and I have been talking about it and he goes let's go get him one
Mara:	Yeah
Robin:	And I mean he really feels
Mara:	But I, I But I kept thinking they couldn't do a a puppy
Robin:	Yeah No I wanted to go We have a humane society over here
Mara:	Yeah
Robin:	And I said Well let me you know think about it Let's give it another week
Mara:	Does this sound good?
Robin:	Yeah You know what Mara Let's face facts He's not going anywhere
Mara:	No
Robin:	He and Mommy are not movin'
Mara:	Well Until something happens

Robin:	Yeah
Mara:	To one of them
Robin:	Yeah
Mara:	But I'm just afraid he's going to die
Robin:	Yeah I am too
Mara:	You know
Robin:	I was talking to May I said I said, May can people die of a broken heart? Like She goes yeah They just give up
Mara:	Oh yeah He has Cause remember I told you about the snow I don't give a shit what it does
Robin:	Yeah
Mara:	And Just the tone of his voice was like I just I am so excited She sounded so nice And she said I'm She goes, This is perfect I cou I couldn't a I said to John could we take one? (Laugh)) So I gave her my name and number

	I said if any
	You know
	If something comes up you can't make it tomorrow
	But I'll be there tomorrow at 12:00
Robin:	So
	Are you then gonna get the dog?
Mara:	Yeah
Robin:	Ok
	Can we plan to meet at Mommy's or something?
Mara:	Yeah
Robin:	Because I'd like to go over
	Maybe Lara wants to
	Oh Lara's
Mara:	Lara's going' to the shore
	Yeah I was gonna call her
	She's goin' to the shore
Robin:	Tomorra
	But I
	You know maybe
	You know
Mara:	Well, we're goin' down
	for dinner
Robin:	You're moochin' dinner off them?
Mara:	No, no, no
	Wednesday
Robin:	Oh yeah
Mara:	Right?
	Well, I'm not keeping it till Wednesday
	I'll just pick it up and go
Robin:	Yeah
	Happy anniversary
Mara:	(Laugh) Yeah

Robin:	We're here
Mara:	But I just I didn't wanna I thought I'd run it by Mommy I said Mom don't And she didn't say no
Robin:	Yeah I
Mara:	She just said Don't take the older one
Robin:	I think she's worried sick
Mara:	Yeah
Robin:	Too
Mara:	I said Mommy even if he says no Say well We'll see what he looks like Oh I don't know Do you think they'll be that upset that it's a boy? Are boys too gross?
Robin:	No I don't think so
Mara:	Yeah
Robin:	I mean they can be They can but not little dogs
Mara:	Yeah
Robin:	You know
Mara:	Zoey
Robin:	That's a girl's name
Mara:	I know That's what I thought too

	I think she said one was Kippy And I thought she said I know she said Zoey was the four year old.
Robin:	Yeah
Mara:	And she said he's laying right now up against my
Robin:	Hold on a minute Yeah Rick said they're fine
Mara:	(Laugh)
Robin:	(Laugh) He had a He had a Poodle and he said, "Nasty little bastard." (Laugh)
Mara:	Yeah No she didn't say these are nasty at all She said as a matter of fact
Robin:	Nasty poor thing (to Rick) It's a Lahasa Apse
Mara:	I don It's some furry combination
Robin:	(to Rick) Furry, icky dog that I hate
Mara:	(Laugh)
Robin:	Mara I hate those dogs
Robin:	Yeah I hate the I hate em
Mara:	Well He needs a lapdog
Robin:	Yeah Yeah he needs something

	I think And what does John say?
Mara:	Oh yeah
Robin:	He agrees
Mara:	Yeah I'm surprised
Robin:	I think he needs
Mara:	John just kept sayin You know what I was sayin About a puppy
Robin:	Yeah
Mara:	I didn't wanna get a puppy
Robin:	Oh, I agree That's why I wanted to go to the SPCA And in my mind I was goin' to take Daddy out there
Mara:	Well, then the only thing with an SPCA People take it there because they don't really care about their dogs and if they're put to sleep, they're put to sleep
Robin:	Yeah
Mara:	Where this humane society? They want to find a home for their dogs
Robin:	Yeah
Mara:	You know I just liked it when she said I'll take him back
Robin:	Yeah
Mara:	If he If he You know But I

	The dog is not going to be that sad
	long
	Because Daddy's goin' be ah
Robin:	Yeah
Mara:	(Laugh) It certainly will get attention
Robin:	I know
Mara:	So
Robin:	I think he needs it
	I think he has no reason to live
Mara:	Umhm
Robin:	You know what I mean
	I'm really
	He's just so depressed
	What did Schmidt the quack give him?
Mara:	Zantax
	What Aunt Kate was on
	I said Mom
	He should not drink on that
Robin:	She said
	because I was sayin to May
	this quack
	gave him something
	I said Xanax
	or Zantac
	She said well one of them's a stomach medicine
Mara:	It
	Right
Robin:	And she said then the other one
	She said I don't know why he's on that
	She said that's like a
	Sleeping, a sedative
Mara:	Right
	Right

But it can
John is Zantec
an antidepression too?
(John: No, it's for your stomach)
Oh, Zantec is for your stomach
Xanax
(John: Xanax has antidepressant qualities)
Has anti
It's primarily an antianxiety
but it
It does have antidepressant
But I don't think its doin' a damn thing

Robin: Yeah
I gotta go
We
We're goin' to some rodeo
Show

Mara: Goin' to some what?

Robin: Rodeo

Mara: Oh, at the Civic Center

Robin: Yeah

Mara: Oh good

Robin: The boy scouts

Mara: Alright

Robin: We have to leave in a half an hour
I'm mad

Mara: Okay
Um

Robin: Anything else exciting?

Mara: No
Are you doing anything tomorra?

Robin: No

Mara:	Oh, you have Paula's party, right?
Robin:	Tonight
Mara:	Okay
Robin:	It's tonight; its not tomorra I might ride down
Mara:	Well, I'll probably be there about two
Robin:	Yeah
Mara:	So just for ya to budget your time Lara will be mad at us but Oh well
Robin:	For us to give it to him No Well she's so against it I'm like Lara I To me I mean I'm a dog person and that's what Daddy is you know
Mara:	Mmhm
Robin:	And that's
Mara:	And I wanted John I'll tell you real quick On the internet it said people who have asthma and cats All the health problems you can get and I said to John, Pull that up I'm interested So I told her She goes

	My problems are not my cats And I said what if they were? Well, I wouldn't get rid of them I said I know that But I don't think you should replace them When they die
Robin:	Right
Mara:	So Because I don't agree with her I think it's her problems
Robin:	Oh I think that's sure It is
Mara:	And her cat-lovin' kids don't even agree
Robin:	And they Went and got cats Hurt Derek
Mara:	Yep
Robin:	Exactly Oh, I talked to Hellene last night
Mara:	Wait a minute Did you see Tommy boy?
Robin:	No
Mara:	Okay You saw Talking to who
Robin:	You see Tommy boy, Rick? Tommy boy was that Chris Farley, I think? I think Did you like it? He, Rick said it was okay It was funny
Mara:	Okay

Robin: I wouldn't rent it
          Um
          I talked to Hellene last night
          She said that
          Sue and Mike Ruler are getting married
          Sue Tremmel

Mara: Uhu

Robin: Remember?
          They're getting married

Mara: Wow

Robin: (Laugh)
          Get outta here!

Mara: Hu

Robin: Probably going back together for the third time
          in twenty-one years

Mara: That's funny

Robin: Yeah
          So
          Alright
          I gotta jump in the shower

Mara: Alright
          Talk to you later

Robin: So I'll
          Around twoish you say

Mara: Yeah
          Unless
          If I hear from her
          I'll call ya right away
          But
          She sounded like she was goin' be home

Robin: Alrighty

Mara: Bye

Robin:	Bye- bye
Robin:	Hello
Mara:	I found them a dog
Robin:	Get the hell out of here!
Mara:	Unuh
Robin:	I cant bel…
	Rick
	just said to me today
	Just
	Here's a Jack Russell terrier
	Robin, just go out and buy him a dog
Mara:	Yeah well they're hyper
	Um
Robin:	Rick it's Mara: (to husband)
	The one I never thought would bend
	She goes I found him a dog
	What the hell I cannot believe it
Mara:	Wait till you hear it
Robin:	Oh god
Mara:	Um
	One of the girls I work with
	told me about this humane society
	It's called St. Francis
	It's in
	near the Southtown Mall
	and,
	She said my cousin was saying something about it
	It's small animals
	So when I got home yesterday
	It was Gina on the
	She goes, here's the number of St. Francis
	Well I called last night
	They weren't there
	It said we're open at nine

So I called at nine
and they
I said I
I, I know nothing about your organization
All these dogs are barkin' and
She said well we
we have
no dog
Cause I said
you know
I went through this story
briefly
And she said well we don't ha
Let me look through the list
And she goes well here's a woman that just called
A week ago
It was funny
On the 20th
which was my birthday
She has a dog
3 dogs that she needs to get rid of and
two of them are
One's a Lahasa
and one's a
Shitzu mix or something
because I said I want a little daw
a little furry dog
And she goes they're two furry dogs
So
She gave me her name is Jane
So I got off the phone
Its like 9:30
I said to John should I call her?
He goes yeah
Well
I woke her up
And I said
You know

I understand
I don't know if you got rid of your dogs
And I say
I started telling her the story
And she goes
I have
two little furry dogs
She goes
the third one is a terrier that I won't
You know
It doesn't sound like the kind you're looking for
She said I have
Kippy is eight or nine
and
Or Zoey is
four

Robin: Uhuh

Mara: And she said
Oh my god
They both sound like exactly what
your father needs
These dogs
just want to be petted
They love to ride in the car
They
Are just precious
And
I said do they
You know we've never had boy dogs
Do they pee?
She said

Robin: Oh, they're both
They're boys

Mara: Yeah
and she said no they do not
They're tr

They're completely trained
And she said
I just got divorced
I had to move from a big house
That I had a yard for them
Into a townhouse
I opened my own business
I'm not going to be home
I have to travel
And I just cant keep them
And she said
It breaks my heart
She said I am devastated but
Um
I don't have a choice
You know
I've had a life style change
So I sa
Um
Well, I'm going there tomorrow at 12:00
And she said
I, I don't want to tell you what one to take
Because you have
You'll have to see
And she said
Before we hung up
She said
I'll take the dog back,
if it doesn't work
And
So I thought that that
I like that

Robin: Yeah

Mara: And she said um
                I said well my parents live in Prospect
                You could visit the dog (Laugh)

	And I said if I take one of theses dogs
Robin:	She lives in Elmwood?
Mara:	Yeah
Robin:	Yeah
Mara:	I said if I take one of these dogs Your dog will live like a human being You know I said this dog would be spoiled to death And she said, Oh that makes me feel so good
Robin:	Yeah
Mara:	And ma So I told Mommy I said let me tell ya So I went through the whole thing She goes well don't get the older one
Robin:	Yeah That's the first thing I thought too
Mara:	Get the four or five year old
Robin:	Yeah
Mara:	And ah I said Mom even if he says no I think we should get it And show it to him I said
Robin:	I wouldn't even I think we should do what we did last time Knock, ring the doorbell And hide (Laugh)
Mara:	Well, she's going to tell him Um, going tomorrow at noon

	And she said She said he She said he's really worrying me He said to her last night Did Bridget die last night? So I said to the woman I think the man is deteriorating
Robin:	Yeah
Mara:	And I said he needs something She said Let me tell ya Either one of these dogs would be perfect And I said, Will they walk without a lease? She goes She said they love to walk But I would put them on a leash
Robin:	Yeah And that would be fine
Mara:	Lara Last night Lara called And I said I you know I'm trying to call around She says no They don't need a dog They could trip
Robin:	Rick and I have been talking about it and he goes let's go get him one
Mara:	Yeah
Robin:	And I mean he really feels

Mara:	But I, I But I kept thinking they couldn't do a a puppy
Robin:	Yeah No I wanted to go We have a humane society over here
Mara:	Yeah
Robin:	And I said Well let me you know think about it Let's give it another week
Mara:	Does this sound good?
Robin:	Yeah You know what Mara Let's face facts He's not going anywhere
Mara:	No
Robin:	He and Mommy are not movin'
Mara:	Well Until something happens
Robin:	Yeah
Mara:	To one of them
Robin:	Yeah
Mara:	But I'm just afraid he's going to die
Robin:	Yeah I am too
Mara:	You know
Robin:	I was talking to May I said

	I said, May can people die of a broken heart? Like She goes yeah They just give up
Mara:	Oh yeah He has Cause remember I told you about the snow I don't give a shit what it does
Robin:	Yeah
Mara:	And Just the tone of his voice was like I just I am so excited She sounded so nice And she said I'm She goes, This is perfect I cou I couldn't a I said to John could we take one? (Laugh)) So I gave her my name and number I said if any You know If something comes up you can't make it tomorrow But I'll be there tomorrow at 12:00
Robin:	So Are you then gonna get the dog?
Mara:	Yeah
Robin:	Ok Can we plan to meet at Mommy's or something?
Mara:	Yeah

Robin:	Because I'd like to go over Maybe Lara wants to Oh Lara's
Mara:	Lara's going' to the shore Yeah I was gonna call her She's goin' to the shore
Robin:	Tomorra But I You know maybe You know
Mara:	Well, we're goin' down for dinner
Robin:	You're moochin' dinner off them?
Mara:	No, no, no Wednesday
Robin:	Oh yeah
Mara:	Right? Well, I'm not keeping it till Wednesday I'll just pick it up and go
Robin:	Yeah Happy anniversary
Mara:	(Laugh) Yeah
Robin:	We're here
Mara:	But I just I didn't wanna I thought I'd run it by Mommy I said Mom don't And she didn't say no
Robin:	Yeah I
Mara:	She just said Don't take the older one
Robin:	I think she's worried sick

Mara:	Yeah
Robin:	Too
Mara:	I said Mommy even if he says no Say well We'll see what he looks like Oh I don't know Do you think they'll be that upset that it's a boy? Are boys too gross?
Robin:	No I don't think so
Mara:	Yeah
Robin:	I mean they can be They can but not little dogs
Mara:	Yeah
Robin:	You know
Mara:	Zoey
Robin:	That's a girl's name
Mara:	I know That's what I thought too I think she said one was Kippy And I thought she said I know she said Zoey was the four year old.
Robin:	Yeah
Mara:	And she said he's laying right now up against my
Robin:	Hold on a minute Yeah Rick said they're fine
Mara:	(Laugh)

Robin:	(Laugh)
	He had a
	He had a Poodle and he said, "Nasty little bastard."
	(Laugh)
Mara:	Yeah
	No she didn't say these are nasty at all
	She said as a matter of fact
Robin:	Nasty poor thing
	(to Rick) It's a Lahasa Apse
Mara:	I don
	It's some
	furry combination
Robin:	(to Rick) Furry, icky dog that I hate
Mara:	(Laugh)
Robin:	Mara
	I hate those dogs
Robin:	Yeah
	I hate the
	I hate em
Mara:	Well
	He needs a lapdog
Robin:	Yeah
	Yeah he needs something
	I think
	And what does John say?
Mara:	Oh yeah
Robin:	He agrees
Mara:	Yeah
	I'm surprised
Robin:	I think he needs
Mara:	John just kept sayin
	You know

	what I was sayin About a puppy
Robin:	Yeah
Mara:	I didn't wanna get a puppy
Robin:	Oh, I agree That's why I wanted to go to the SPCA And in my mind I was goin' to take Daddy out there
Mara:	Well, then the only thing with an SPCA People take it there because they don't really care about their dogs and if they're put to sleep, they're put to sleep
Robin:	Yeah
Mara:	Where this humane society? They want to find a home for their dogs
Robin:	Yeah
Mara:	You know I just liked it when she said I'll take him back
Robin:	Yeah
Mara:	If he If he You know But I The dog is not going to be that sad long Because Daddy's goin' be ah
Robin:	Yeah
Mara:	(Laugh) It certainly will get attention
Robin:	I know
Mara:	So
Robin:	I think he needs it I think he has no reason to live

Mara:	Umhm
Robin:	You know what I mean I'm really He's just so depressed What did Schmidt the quack give him?
Mara:	Zantax What Aunt Kate was on I said Mom He should not drink on that
Robin:	She said because I was sayin to May this quack gave him something I said Xanax or Zantac She said well one of them's a stomach medicine
Mara:	It Right
Robin:	And she said then the other one She said I don't know why he's on that She said that's like a Sleeping, a sedative
Mara:	Right Right But it can John is Zantec an antidepression too? (John: No, it's for your stomach) Oh, Zantec is for your stomach Xanax (John: Xanax has antidepressant qualities) Has anti It's primarily an antianxiety but it

	It does have antidepressant But I don't think its doin' a damn thing
Robin:	Yeah I gotta go We We're goin' to some rodeo Show
Mara:	Goin' to some what?
Robin:	Rodeo
Mara:	Oh, at the Civic Center
Robin:	Yeah
Mara:	Oh good
Robin:	The boy scouts
Mara:	Alright
Robin:	We have to leave in a half an hour I'm mad
Mara:	Okay Um
Robin:	Anything else exciting?
Mara:	No Are you doing anything tomorra?
Robin:	No
Mara:	Oh, you have Paula's party, right?
Robin:	Tonight
Mara:	Okay
Robin:	It's tonight; its not tomorra I might ride down
Mara:	Well, I'll probably be there about two
Robin:	Yeah

Mara: So just for ya
                to budget your time
                Lara will be mad at us but
                Oh well

Robin: For us to give it to him
                No
                Well she's so against it
                I'm like Lara
                I
                To me
                I mean I'm a dog person
                and that's what Daddy is
                you know

Mara: Mmhm

Robin: And that's

Mara: And I wanted John
                I'll tell you real quick
                On the internet it said
                people who have asthma
                and
                cats
                All the health problems you can get
                and I said to John,
                Pull that up
                I'm interested
                So I told her
                She goes
                My problems are not my cats
                And I said what if they were?
                Well, I wouldn't get rid of them
                I said I know that
                But I don't think you should replace them
                When they die

Robin: Right

Mara:	So Because I don't agree with her I think it's her problems
Robin:	Oh I think that's sure It is
Mara:	And her cat-lovin' kids don't even agree
Robin:	And they Went and got cats Hurt Derek
Mara:	Yep
Robin:	Exactly Oh, I talked to Hellene last night
Mara:	Wait a minute Did you see Tommy boy?
Robin:	No
Mara:	Okay You saw Talking to who
Robin:	You see Tommy boy, Rick? Tommy boy was that Chris Farley, I think? I think Did you like it? He, Rick said it was okay It was funny
Mara:	Okay
Robin:	I wouldn't rent it Um I talked to Hellene last night She said that Sue and Mike Ruler are getting married Sue Tremmel
Mara:	Uhu

Robin:	Remember? They're getting married
Mara:	Wow
Robin:	(Laugh) Get outta here!
Mara:	Hu
Robin:	Probably going back together for the third time in twenty-one years
Mara:	That's funny
Robin:	Yeah So Alright I gotta jump in the shower
Mara:	Alright Talk to you later
Robin:	So I'll Around twoish you say
Mara:	Yeah Unless If I hear from her I'll call ya right away But She sounded like she was goin' be home
Robin:	Alrighty
Mara:	Bye
Robin:	Bye- bye

Synergistext™ Analysis

Much of the basic content of the conversation with Robin is either identical or very similar to that which occurred with Hana, but the sequence varies, probably due in large part to differences between Mara's relationship with Hana versus Robin – daughter versus sister. This is true from the outset.

The conversation with Robin begins with a tone of subdued but obvious sibling rivalry. Robin seems to feel that her idea about getting the father a dog was preempted by her older sister. Mara attempts to neutralize Robin's threatened initiative toward a Jack Russell Terrier by deprecating to them as "hyper." Given Robin's excitable initial response to the conversation, Mara's quick use of the term "hyper" also may reflect her unconscious feeling about Robin's emotional reaction. To bolster her one-down position, Robin immediately looks for environmental help (E/BETF) by first referring to and then directly speaking to her husband.

Mara proceeds in a manner showing she continues mentally to prepare for getting the dog, to rehearse the process, and to attempt to elicit support for the endeavor. H/GBH still is being served. As had occurred with Hana, Mara mentions that the candidate dogs are "boys." Their maleness with its implications for unruliness and messiness clearly causes Mara some concern. She wants to be reassured that male dogs are okay.

Robin does not want to be left out of helping her father, so she indicates her desire to be present when he is given the dog. She mentally rehearses the scene, imaging how they could place the dog at the door and ring the bell – a suggestion that further supports the likelihood that she is in a sibling-oriented, child-like state of mind concerning the dog, her sister, and her father. The comment also leads one to assume that Robin derives G/GBH from the conversation by way of anticipating positive emotions flowing from the presentation of the dog to him.

Mara changes the subject, voicing concern about their father's mental deterioration and how the dog could help mitigate it. In imagining the dog, she thinks about how it needs to be leashed which makes her recall Lara's previous warning that the dog could cause Fred to fall. Mara is implicitly asking for support but Robin's baseline consciousness is somewhere else; hearing about Lara, Robin is back to thoughts suggesting sibling rivalry, about how she could have been the one to get Fred a dog. Mara needs to ask explicitly for Robin's support, support against the expected criticism from Lara – another sibling rivalry/power issue. It is not until Mara says, "But I'm just afraid he's going to die" that Robin's GBH needs resonate with Mara's. At that point Robin recalls a previous conversation with her friend, May, a registered nurse, about the possibility of Fred's death. The issue also has been circulating through Robin's baseline consciousness and she engages the subject of his potential death, presumably realizing some modicum of H/GBH relief in the process.

This brief discussion of death is cathartic enough to free Mara's mental energy sufficiently so that she can return to her rescue fantasy. She lightheartedly imagines getting the dog for her father. That talk, in turn, brings Robin back to wanting to be one of the rescuers and that mild sibling rivalry theme makes her think about the third leg of this sibling triangle – Lara. Mara reminds Robin that Lara is heading for the seashore and Robin soon returns to her rivalry with Mara asking "Are you moochin dinner off them?' meaning their parents. They then both entertain the mutually G/GBH satisfying thought of presenting the dog to Fred and Mom, laughing about it.

Soon Mara again expresses uncertainty about getting a male dog; the issue has cycled back through her baseline conscious and presses for homeostatic release. Mention of the dog appears to have spiked Robin's sibling rivalry and she disparages the Lahasa Apse, just as Mara earlier had disparaged the Jack Russell Terrier. Perhaps feeling vulnerable, Robin looks to environmental support (E/BETF) for her position– to her husband, Rick, and even to Mara's husband, John, who she suspected would be opposed to the dog-getting plan.

In her stirred-up emotional state, it is now Robin who mentions the possibility of her father's death. His doctor is scapegoated, perhaps in part an unconsciously determined way to deflect attention from the sibling rivalry issues. However, as had occurred earlier in this conversation with Mara, the thought of death also prompts Robin to recall again the earlier conversation that she had with her friend, May, about the possibility of Fred's death and about what needs to be done to help him. The issue has continued to circulate through Robin's baseline consciousness and, once again, to engage the issue presumably is to realize H/GBH relief.

The next sequence illustrates the fact that everyone continually is at least subliminally aware of E/BETF, for Mara asks John to answer the medication question that Robin posed. Robin had referred to her outside expert – May – and Mara wants to use hers – John. The conversational tug of war proceeds.

The brief Mara-Robin verbal disengagement coincident with bringing John into the discussion is opening enough for Robin to end the conversation. Robin mentions, "I'm mad," presumably about going to the rodeo. Unconsciously reacting to her own excited state, she asks Mara, "Anything else exciting?" Here we see illustrated the self-serving bias of conversation that was mentioned as ME-TALK-ABOUT-YOU. Robin is not really interested in hearing an exciting story from Mara; she is interested in telling her own "exciting" story that concerns her previous conversation with Hellene that mentioned the engagement of Sue and Mike Ruler. But before launching into that topic, Mara and Robin unite against their big sister Lara, marginalizing her as a "cat person" and resolving to give their father, a "dog person," his life-sustaining pet. Agreement here further reinforces their collaborative, sisterly relationship.

The conversation ends with both Mara and Robin having accomplished what each individual wanted: Mara – rehearsal for getting the dog and recruitment of support for giving it to the parents – and Robin – being included in rescuing her father, and what they both conjointly and unconsciously wanted – to resolve their implicit sibling rivalry over being the ideal daughter.

The following is the conversation of Mara and Mom:

Mara and Mom

Mom:	Did you see about Secluded Harbor?
Mara:	No
Mom:	It was on
Mara:	Get out We watched it up to the weather and then I turn it (Laugh)
Mom:	Then it came on after that
Mara:	Ohh What did they say?
Mom:	It was just They showed that bridge goin' across
Mara:	Yeah we saw that
Mom:	Then you know had been harmed And then it showed the ocean road And then it showed them tryan ta push dirt back into the beach
Mara:	Yeah I saw
Mom:	Sand rather
Mara:	Yeah the only

Mom:	You probably saw the
Mara:	Yeah I didn't see the ocean road but I After the weather I said ah they're not goin' to say any- more
Mom:	Yeah
Mara:	Cause they I saw the things of the week It showed The Shore bu
Mom:	Uhu
Mara:	Well the sun's comin out
Mom:	Yeah A little bit
Mara:	Where you goin'?
Mom:	Down the market
Mara:	Yeah What did he have to say? Was he mad?
Mom:	No He said I don't know whether I'm ready or not
Mara:	Well
Mom:	And I said well She'll take it back Well what do you think? I said it's up to you I'm worried about him I don't You know anything's fine with me
Mara:	Yeah
Mom:	With or without

Mara:	I don't think we have anything to lose
Mom:	No But eh It Is the four year five year old, a Lapsa
Mara:	Yeah I, I forget They're both Lahasa Or Shitzu Or Poodle Mix Cockapoh Something
Mom:	Uhu They're little
Mara:	Yeah Uhu They're both (Laugh) John's laughing They're both something I'm confused on which one's a Cockapooh and which one's a Lahasa
Mom:	Uhu
Mara:	So But she sa And I don't even know what color they are
Mom:	Yeah
Mara:	Or the 4 year old one is
Mom:	Uhu
Mara:	I don't know But she said he's a big baby The four year old

Mom:	Yeah
Mara:	He just wants to be held and You know He just is ah You know Very Well she said both of them are very affectionate But she did say the four year old was a big baby I said well he's used to babies
Mom:	Well yeah But Bridget was very aristocratic I mean she didn't like a cuddler
Mara:	Oh this one is I
Mom:	You know you'd try to put your arm around her and boy she'd get down
Mara:	Yeah No this one
Mom:	Down
Mara:	This one wants to lay right up on your lap
Mom:	Uhu
Mara:	And I think he likes that
Mom:	Oh yeah
Mara:	He likes to pet And the little one the Well she said they both like ta Walk and they love to go for a ride But she said

	the younger one
	Loves
	the car
	Absolutely loves to go out
	But I said
	you know
	She said I had a ha
	When I had my house
	I had a big fenced-in yard and I would just put them
	out back
	But she said now that I don't I
	I walk them on leashes
	And I said do they walk good
	she said oh yeah
	She said they love to walk
	But I wouldn't put them outside without anything
Mom:	No
Mara:	Cause they're used to a fence
Mom:	We still have Sam's leash out front
Mara:	Yeah
	But she seemed
	She said
	they don't chew
	They don't mess
	And ah
	I told her
	I said well if
	You know they do end up takin it
	You could stop and see them (Laugh)
	I said they live in Prospect Park (Laugh)
	Because she said
	it just breaks my heart
Mom:	Where does she live?
Mara:	In um
	I go off the

	Before the Valley Ridge Shopping Center I go 202 North like I'm going to the Southtown Mall
Mom:	Oh yeah
Mara:	and I get off at 252
Mom:	Uhu
Mara:	And she lives at ah some town houses along there So she said my lifestyle has changed and I I just can't have them anymore So she didn't go into it She just said that So I said to John that St. Francis he was the one With the animals right?
Mom:	Oh yeah Yeah
Mara:	Well I said to her I I have no idea how this organization works You know Do I pay you? She said absolutely not This is between us and if it works that's wonderful and if it doesn't I'll take them back and she said I went with them because

I don't want them put to sleep
and
and
really
if you love your dogs
that's what you want

Mom: Oh yeah

Mara: You just want a
and I said
well
this dog will live like a king
trust me
and she you know
She just said
that would
she said I couldn't ask for anything more
that's exactly what I want
so I said well it would work out for everybody
(Laugh) if it does

Mom: Yeah

Mara: If it does
so
He didn't seem mad though?

Mom: No
No he just said I don't know if I'm ready or not
then when he came back down again
and I went over it again where the woman was and that
Robin was ca
I just tried to call Robin
There was no answer

Mara: She was goin' to the rodeo

Mom: Oh, today they're gone

Mara: Yeah

Mom: Oh, I thought it was tomorrow

Mara:	No
Mom:	And then I I Lara called and I told her She said well don't tell him I said I can't keep that
Mara:	No Was Lara mad?
Mom:	No
Mara:	Cause she said to me
Mom:	Oh no no no She said I don't think (Laugh) I don't think that you should get a puppy because you're liable to trip over it
Mara:	Yeah
Mom:	Daddy said, What in the hell do they think we are?
Mara:	Well that was Lara saying that Lara said it could race down the steps She just didn't want you having a real hyper dog
Mom:	She said I almost ah trip over the cat
Mara:	Yeah
Mom:	Which is true I know that But da
Mara:	Oh, she said these dogs sleep all day I mean they're not Puppies
Mom:	Yeah I mean that's what I say I mean could we go out to lunch

Mara: She
               Well she has her own business
               I think that's why she's getting rid of it
               because
               she's not home

Mom: Unhu

Mara: Cause I said
               do you think the dog's going to be too upset
               separating from the others?
               She said no they're all very independent
               It's not like
               They follow each other around
               Or anything
               She said no I don't think that's going to be a problem
               And she said
               they're
               They're used to being
               Now she
               She said something about
               Kids dressing them up in doll clothes all the time
               (Laugh)

Mom: God

Mara: She just said they're
               they're very docile (Laugh) dogs (Laugh)

Mom: Uhu

Mara: She said they're very
               Friendly and
               You know
               Good-natured
               Cause I said I
               you know
               We've never had boys
               and she said oh
               these dogs have never
               Messed

	or any
	you know
	They don't do that
	So
	I think she would have told me if she can't go out
	(Laugh)
Mom:	Yeah
Mara:	I mean she's
	She's a ya
	single woman
	I doubt if she's
	And she was going out today
	Cause I said you know
	Oh and she said when
	I said when can I come
	She said oh
	You know I want you to see them
	Because I think you'll know right away which one
Mom:	Oh yeah
Mara:	But ah
	She said I want you to
	You know could you come tomorra at 11:00?
	I said that's fine
	So I gave her my name and number
Mom:	Uhu
Mara:	Sigh
	She called on the 20th (Laugh)
	To the
	Humane society or whatever this place is
Mom:	How about that!
Mara:	Yeah
	And she said
	it just breaks my heart
	She said I'm goin' be a mess
	So

I said well we'll certainly let you know
how they're
how he's doin' and
You know
She'll take him back
I mean
I don't think we have anything to lose

Mom: No

Mara: And I think it
it's a good
It could be the best of both worlds
You're going to get a dog that's trained
And its either a Cockapooh or Lahasa mix

Mom: Yeah
Yeah

Mara: But she said but they're both le
You know
She said you know I can pick them both up
They're not heavy dogs
And I said about 15 pounds
she said yeah probably
So that's probably between
Bridget and Corky was

Mom: Yeah
Well Corky was a nice dog

Mara: Yeah

Mom: That's what Daddy said
He's got
I said I hope you wouldn't mind walkin' the dog on a
leash
He said, "No, that wouldn't bother me."
He said I could
We still have Sam's leash
He said

               we could put the dog out front on that
               every now and then

Mara: Yeah
               Yeah

Mom: Early in the morning when you're not dressed

Mara: Right
               Did he sound interested at all?

Mom: a little bit

Mara: Spart, yeah

Mom: I said you're not doin' Bridget a disservice
               Not grieving

Mara: No

Mom: The only thing he said I (bell sound)
               we kind of
               we hoped we could go down to
               St. Michael's
               but that's just to get away
               you still have to come home

Mara: Right

Mom: And ah
               he could call St. Michael's
               maybe they'll take a dog

Mara: Yeah

Mom: You know
               It's not as though they're the ritziest place in the world

Mara: Yeah
               well
               we'll see
               I mean it might
               You might not

Mom: It might not work out
You might look at the dog and figure no we don't want
it

Mara: Umhum

Mom: You know
So don't
take it
You know

Mara: No, I'm not
she
That's what she said
She said I
It sounds perfect to me
But she said I want you ta
come look at them

Mom: Uhu

Mara: But
She didn't ev
She wasn't even
Telling me about the terrier
She said from what you're telling me
It sounds like
he
wants a little
Shaggy dog
And I said well I think so

Mom: Yeah

Mara: So

Mom: Is the terrier older?

Mara: She didn't say

Mom: Oh

Mara: She didn't tell
She didn't even talk about that one

Mom:	Yeah
Mara:	Zoey and Kippy (Laugh) were the ones she was talking about
Mom:	Yeah
Mara:	So She just she they They're very sweet dogs
Mom:	Okeedokee
Mara:	But I think the eight year old You know I'd rather go for the The younger one
Mom:	Oh yeah definitely
Mara:	(Clear throat) So (Sigh) Alright Um
Mom:	Okay
Mara:	That's what um Robin said Oh Somebody said you should have made it a surprise I said well At this point I don't think we need surprises (Laugh)
Mom:	No no no
Mara:	So Do you have any food? or biscuits or anything left or just
Mom:	We gave everything away to Robin
Mara:	(Laugh)

Mom: Which is fine

Mara: Well, I'll ask her what he eats
            I mean he might like wet dog food
            I mean I don't know

Mom: Yeah

Mara: So we'll,
            I'll ask her what he likes to eat

Mom: We can get stuff; it doesn't matter

Mara: Hah?

Mom: We can get stuff
            I even gave Bridget's bowl to Robin and his little blanket

Mara: Did you have a regular leash?

Mom: Ah
            Yeah, we have one in the kitchen I think.

Mara: Do you still have it?

Mom: Yeah I think so
            around the door

Mara: Yeah

Mom: Maybe she's got one

Mara: Yeah
            maybe she'll give me one

Mom: Yeah

Mara: But she said
            they both love to walk
            And I said well they don't pull
            Because I don't want him walkin'
            Draggin'

Mom: Yeah

Mara: She said oh no
            They love to walk

	So
	And love to go in the car (Laugh)
Mom:	Yeah (Laugh)
Mara:	She was funny
	She said these da
	Either one of them
	She said would be perfect
	(Clear throat)
	So
	She said right now the one's leaning up against my back
	She must have been in bed
	She said it sounded like I woke her up
Mom:	Yeah
	Did they give you her number?
Mara:	Yeah
Mom:	Yeah
Mara:	They gave me two numbers
	They gave me a number of a guy who had some kind of a Poodle mix
Mom:	Uhuh
Mara:	But
	She had three dogs and I just happened to call
	Now I didn't call the guy yet
	Do you want me to call him too?
Mom:	No
Mara:	Or just wait and see if this one
Mom:	No well just wait
Mara:	Yeah
	You goin' out to lunch?
Mom:	Yeah probably
Mara:	Did he cry again this morning?

Mom:	Umah, filled up
Mara:	Yeah Did he ask the name?
Mom:	I told him Zoey
Mara:	Um
Mom:	I don't now why that name's familiar to me
Mara:	(Laugh) I always thought it was a girl's name
Mom:	Yeah He's a fruit cake
Mara:	Yeah So I don't even know what color
Mom:	Yeah Well Okay then
Mara:	Alright Talk to you later
Mom:	Bye- bye
Mara:	Bye- bye

Synergistext™ Analysis

This conversation begins out of character for Mara and Mom who usually start by checking-in-like questioning of what the other is doing or has done. This atypicality of the talk betrays its underlying tension.

Mom's banal opening about the weather goes nowhere, and Mara returns to their tried and true "Where you goin?" – a subject that proves even less fruitful than the weather.

Without using any referent to indicate what she is speaking about, Mara asks, "What did he say?" and Mom knows precisely what is on Mara's mind, because it is precisely what is on Mom's mind – what to do about getting Fred a dog. Here we see a clear example of concordance of the contents of baseline consciousness between two conversants who are intimately familiar with and connected with each other.

Mara is uncertain about the answers to many of Mom's questions about the candidate dogs. She tries to lighten the mood by referring to E/BETF, stating that her husband, John, is laughing about her remarks. Mara's relentless expectant search is for H/GBH, for a lessening of her anxiety about Mom's accepting the dog. Mom also seems to be looking for the H/GBH that would come from resolving her apprehension about the implications of letting him into the home. She seems to want a dog that will be as close to a stuffed animal as possible – one that won't be too cuddly and one that won't disrupt her current lifestyle. Yet, Mom tries to make it sound as though she is "fine" with the dog; it is only that her husband might not be.

Mara's conversational input is virtual salesmanship, attempting to market Zoey as a "good dog." She repeatedly tries to reassure Mom, especially about the fact that the dog can be returned to its owner, if necessary.

Just as she tried to distance herself from the dog issue by starting to converse about the weather, Mom attempts to change the subject by introducing Robin into it. The reference to Robin might have begun as a slip of the tongue, since it appears that the context favored saying "Mara," and Mom is notorious for substituting one daughter's name for the other. In any case, she seizes the opportunity to speak first about Robin and then Lara. The reference to Lara is especially noteworthy, since she represents the outspoken, unapologetic voice against getting Zoey, and mentioning her gives Mom a way to voice dissenting issues without taking responsibility for them, just as she did about her husband's possibly not being "ready" for another dog.

The threat of dissent causes Mara to launch into another round of dog salesmanship in which Mom is mostly silent. Mara inadvertently strikes a responsive cord in Mom when she describes Zoey as being like Bridget, Fred's former dog, and Corky, a dog that Mara had; both of whom Mom liked. Mom apparently realizes B/GBH in equating the new dog with these old, familiar ones. She, however, then betrays her own reservations by saying that she had "hoped" to go to St. Michael's, a quaint tourist spot, and to other places, first implying that Zoey could interfere with such trips and then proposing a solution. Mom is conflicted, both desiring and fearing commitment to Mara's scheme. Her remark "okeedoekee" is one she usually interjects to signal the end of a conversation. Mom wants to avoid this unsettling discussion and its implicit pressure on her. Mara initially accedes to the signal by signaling back with her own end-of-the-conversation marker, "so" followed by a sigh and then "alright" and "um." Mom utters another remark to show her intention of ending the discussion—"Okay."

But Mara is not satisfied enough to end yet. She has not achieved a sufficient level of message or relationship GBH. She is as unsettled, or more unsettled, now than she was when the conversation began. Mara needs to press on in order to achieve some modicum of relief. She goes outside the Mara-Mom dyad, reintroducing Robin as a support, just as Mom did when she felt stymied in the conversational impasse with Mara.

The strategy buys Mara time to lobby anew for Zoey. She gets concrete about dog biscuits, bowls, and leashes, implying that the dog will be coming, so Mom better get ready for it. Mara's use of light-heartedness and positive affect terms increases. She laughs. She uses such words as "likes," "love," "funny," and "perfect" in her talk about the dog and his activities. Not until near the end of the conversation are any more negative issues mentioned and the comment is extremely brief, being Mom's remark that Fred "filled up" with tears that morning. The dysphoric topic is glossed over immediately, and the conversation ends on a fairly light-hearted note when Mom refers to the dog as "a fruit cake" because his name seems feminine.

Our final chat involves Mara and Lara

Mara and Lara

Mara:	Hello
Lara:	It's me
Mara:	Yeah
Lara:	Uhhn
Mara:	Have you (Laugh) talked to her
Lara:	Oh several times
Mara:	She seems happy
Lara:	I'm sure She'll hate it by Oh Wednesday
Mara:	Do you think?

Lara:	I'm sure Ah they I don't think they're gonna take it in the car with them
Mara:	No Cause he sits right on your lap
Lara:	Yeah that's what she said They took him today but he kept trying to get on Daddy's lap
Mara:	Yeah
Lara:	I can see him wrapping the car around a pole
Mara:	Yeah
Lara:	Then I'd have to break your legs
Mara:	She It was weird When I talked to you Friday the girl at work left a message on my machine about this St. Francis place And I called Saturday And that's And I talked to that woman and called Mommy and told her and she goes I said and she'll take it back
Lara:	Umhm
Mara:	She said alright I said Mom it's entirely up to you I don't know what to do

	She said well If she'll take it back (Laugh)
Lara:	(Laugh)
Mara:	He is Adorable
Lara:	Is he?
Mara:	He is so cute I, I think he really did good for his first day don't you?
Lara:	Oh yeah
Mara:	I mean
Lara:	She said he slept with them last night
Mara:	(Laugh) I know And she said he's very calm comin down the steps Like The whole way home I was petrified I said to John If I get What do I do if I get in the car and the dog starts growling at me or something?
Lara:	Yeah
Mara:	I mean I was nervous
Lara:	Yeah
Mara:	And eh But he Jumped right on my lap And sat there And looking out the window And I thought Well

	And I had my arm around him
	Like
	to hold him so he would
	I didn't know if he was goin' ta jump
Lara:	Yeah
Mara:	I mean I didn't know this dog from Adam
	But I had my hand like under his chest
	He wasn't
	he wasn't
	one bit nervous
Lara:	Ha
Mara:	Like his heart wasn't beatin' fast
Lara:	How come she didn't want to keep him?
Mara:	She just got divorced
	She ju
	moved into
	A small townhouse
Lara:	Oh
Mara:	And
	She, she opened her own business
	She said
	It's just not fair
	I've had a whole lifestyle change
Lara:	Yeah
Mara:	And I can't
	I can't keep them anymore
	She said I had a big house
	I had a yard
	And she said it's just not fair to them
Lara:	Yeah
Mara:	And the little boy
	When I came in he goes
	You gonna take Zoe?

Lara: Ah

Mara: And I said
             Ah, I think so
             I mean he didn't want me to take that one
             The other one was ah
             I mean you
             And I kept saying to Mommy
             They have a nine year old
             She goes oh I don't want that one

Lara: Yah (Laugh)

Mara: She wanted no parts of that dog
             But you could tell he was older

Lara: Yeah

Mara: But this one's been fixed
             He is just cu
             He is like silver
             Did Mommy tell you what he looks like?

Lara: She said it looks like my cat

Mara: (Laugh) He's like silvery
             and he has black ears
             And like a black snout
             And
             His bottom teeth stick out

Lara: What kind a
             What kind of dog?

Mara: Peekapoo

Lara: Oh, okay

Mara: And he's got like long fur on his tail
             But I wish
             I mean we went in there
             Of course he sniffed all over the place

Lara: Yeah

Mara:	And ah ran upstairs And down And then I And then a couple minutes later I said to Dad, Why don't you walk him? Ah I got tears in my eyes watchin' She gave me a red He had a red collar on So she gave me a red leash
Lara:	Yeah
Mara:	And Dad took au And he walks really good Like he doesn't pull
Lara:	Oh good
Mara:	I mean ah And the girl when I talked to her Satur Saturday Friday No wait Saturday She sounded so nice
Lara:	Yeah
Mara:	You know when I was telling her about Mommy and Daddy And I said I'm afraid my Dad's gonna Die
Lara:	Yeah
Mara:	If he doesn't And I really I talked to John about it

	and I said
	They're not goin' any where
Lara:	Yeah
Mara:	And
	I think this was so much better than a puppy
Lara:	Oh god yeah
	I didn't want a puppy
Mara:	No
Lara:	This one?
Mara:	No
	And she
	But I
	What are we going to do?
Lara:	I know I know
Mara:	But he is sweet
	And and the woman said
	you can leave that dog all day
Lara:	She said
	Mommy
	Mommy said he kept sayin'
	pettin' him sayin
	You're a nice dog
	but you're not Brigitte
Mara:	I know
Lara:	Did he cry?
Mara:	Nope
Lara:	No
Mara:	Well
	He filled up
	when I was leavin'
	He went out to the kitchen to get a soda
	And he comes walkin' back in

	And the dog was following him out to the kitchen
Lara:	Yeah
Mara:	And then back And he goes Well I'm gonna tell you one thing right now And he was sayin' it so we could hear He goes You're not Bridget Or somethin' like that And his lip started quiverin' I said Dad he's not askin' to be Bridget He just wants some at You know Wants you to pet him And he's sittin' there looking at Daddy
Lara:	Ah, heh
Mara:	And I said he just needs a friend So jer I think Daddy feels disloyal He's gonna be tough commin' around
Lara:	Oh yeah
Mara:	But I asked Mommy I said, Was he any better today? Well she can't talk in front of him She goes yeah, yeah
Lara:	Yeah
Mara:	But she said I think its good for me too Well you know

And I said Mom I was worried about you letting him
out
She said
I brought the chain in the house

Lara: Yeah

Mara: And ya
When Robin and I were going out yesterday
I was at the front door
I said
Stay
I opened the door
He didn't come any where near (Laugh)
Commin' out

Lara: Yeah

Mara: Like he's not hyper
He

Lara: Did the woman say that he was ah
He listened to commands er

Mara: She just said
he's a very easygoing dog
She said
I'll be shocked if you call me
if they don't want him
She said he ran away
Her son took him out two years ago and lost him
Er
Took him off the chain or whatever
That's what I said to Daddy
You have to keep him on a leash

Lara: Yeah

Mara: And ah
Because not many dogs
walk
like Bridget did and not run after things

Lara:	Oh I know
Mara:	And um He He ran away and she didn't find him for a couple days And the people who found him loved him And he was perfectly content there (Laugh) Cause I said do you think he's goin' to miss the other dogs? She said, No they're all independent She said It's not even like they
Lara:	Yeah
Mara:	Pal around together
Lara:	Hum
Mara:	So And she said He's a big baby He just wants He She said if you lay on the couch he's right up beside ya
Lara:	Yeah Welp
Mara:	So he seems much more affectionate Then Bridget ever was
Lara:	Yeah
Mara:	How did she sound tonight?
Lara:	She sounded fine I talked to her around dinner time
Mara:	Uhu How'd she?

Lara: And I told her
           You te
           I said
           When you
           If you're makin' dinner
           I said tell Daddy you want him to either make the pota-
           toes
           or make
           set the table
           or put

Mara: I know
           She's cookin' now, isn't she?

Lara: Yeah
           I think so, yeah

Mara: Yeah
           John

Lara: And I said because he'll get up and do whatever you ask

Mara: Well I told her that too
           He seems terrible to me

Lara: Yeah I know

Mara: He asked me
           Ten times
           What the dog's name was
           I mean
           His memory
           Is awful

Lara: I know

Mara: He's like
           In a fog

Lara: Mommy said a couple times that he thinks Bridget died
           yesterday

Mara: I know
           He

Lara: Which is why he kept crying I think

Mara: Yeah

Lara: Ye

Mara: Well I

Lara: Like it wasn't passin'

Mara: Yeah
            Yeah, I don't know whether he's had a stroke
            I don't know what the heck wrong with him
            He's just not doin' good
            I don't think

Lara: Un um

Mara: He
            It just doesn't seem like him anymore

Lara: No

Mara: So

Lara: She's doin' more and more I'm sure

Mara: Yeah

Lara: But

Mara: So

Lara: You know
            You can't
            It's gonna be
            It's goin' be awful
            because we're goin' have make a decision
            I know were goin' get a phone call

Mara: Umhm

Lara: And

Mara: And that was
            That's what I thought too
            I thought
            you know

	I mean He could die next month I mean Changes could happen You might as well make him happy now If we can
Lara:	Yeah
Mara:	This might not work He might not get ever get over Bridget
Lara:	Yeah
Mara:	But It's makin' him walk around the block (Laugh)
Lara:	Yeah And I said You know In another couple months it will be daylight savings time
Mara:	Yeah
Lara:	And maybe hell take a walk at night
Mara:	Yeah And sit with him out front
Lara:	Yeah
Mara:	I don't know
Lara:	Mommy said that he took off with the eh That chain alright that they have?
Mara:	Yeah
Lara:	It's strong enough and all?
Mara:	Ah Out front?

Lara:	Yeah
Mara:	I ha I didn't check it but I don't think they like rust out (Laugh) I Ill look at it again
Lara:	She said he went flyin' across the lawn after the boy sit- tin' on the curb barkin'
Mara:	oh
Lara:	Scared the crap out of him
Mara:	(Laugh)
Lara:	Not out of Mommy but out of the boys
Mara:	Oh Yeah
Mara:	I was thinking too I thought Oh my god when the weather gets a little nicer and that woman walks Miko, Bridget's boyfriend
Mara:	Uhuh
Lara:	Daddy goin' have a stroke you know
Mara:	Oh she doesn't He's been looking for her
Lara:	I'm sure
Mara:	He's been looking for her to tell her
Lara:	I know So at least now he'll have somebody else
Mara:	Mhm

Lara: To introduce

Mara: Yeah Mr. Spark saw him
                 he said
                 Oh, he looks just like the other one (Laugh)
                 He's bigger
                 than Bridget

Lara: Is he?

Mara: Yeah
                 I mean he
                 He doesn't weh
                 I
                 He still weighs under twenty pounds
                 I mean he's nothing to pick up

Lara: Yeah

Mara: But he's taller
                 But he
                 is as cute as anything

Lara: Well

Mara: So
                 I
                 It
                 it just was so weird
                 how it happened

Lara: Yeah

Mara: I said to John
                 You probably couldn't do that again
                 if I tried

Lara: Right

Mara: I mean
                 it was just completely
                 a fluke

Lara: Yeah

Mara:	And um you know I thought well should I go and get it I thought no I'm goin' tell her And see what she says
Lara:	Yeah
Mara:	And she said Yeah, well get the younger one Don't get the older one I don't want to outlive another dog
Lara:	Yeah
Mara:	(Laugh) So
Lara:	Haha
Mara:	Who knows But I'm surprised at her Oh he was Did she tell ya I was putting on my slippers and he was sittin' on the bed waggin' his tail at me?
Lara:	Yeah
Mara:	And then when she went up to get dressed He came up the steps and laid on the lounge chair While she was getting dressed
Lara:	Yeah
Mara:	So it's company for I said at least they have something else to talk about
Lara:	Yeah
Mara:	And last night I called her and she was They were laughin' He was getting that Robin bought him that braided rope because

	Snickers likes it It's this
Lara:	Oh right
Mara:	Like a yarn He was throwing it all around the living room
Lara:	Uhu
Mara:	Now this is a dog that just came yesterday
Lara:	Yeah
Mara:	But I said to ma
Lara:	Is Bridge's toys gone?
Mara:	Yeah they got rid of them
Lara:	Oh good
Mara:	But I said well you're not used to havin' a young dog I said Bridget really didn't feel good for the last couple years
Lara:	Right
Mara:	With her coughin' This dog is younger and he's healthy
Lara:	Yeah
Mara:	So I said you're gonna have to throw
Lara:	Did somebody get the records?
Mara:	Yeah Well the woman told me she'd get them together She said he had all his shots and he's fixed
Lara:	Right

Mara:	But you can te he doesn't have testicles or anything (Laugh)
Lara:	(Laugh)
Mara:	I mean you can hardly tell that he's a boy
Lara:	Yeah
Mara:	Because he is all furry But of course And we were (Laugh) Daddy goes lift his damn leg every two seconds
Lara:	(Laugh)
Mara:	So
Lara:	Maybe it's better it is a male You know
Mara:	Oh I don't know I, I just Oh, and Daddy said about that About Bridget You're not Bridget I said Oh, I can remember you saying that about Mitzi To Bridget
Lara:	Yeah
Mara:	And I said And he didn't say anything
Lara:	Yeah
Mara:	But he was never goin' love another dog besides Mitzi

Lara: Yeah
                Mitzi who?

Mara: Yeah
                But I
                I mean I don't think he'll ever feel
                About this dog
                Like

Lara: No

Mara: Bridget
                But

Lara: No

Mara: Just because
                His memory isn't good either (Laugh)

Lara: God

Mara: So
                You go tomorrow?

Lara: It scares me
                Er ah
                Him drivin'

Mara: Oh god
                me too

Lara: M mm Mmm Mmm

Mara: If his mind is that bad
                he can't be that quick with thinking

Lara: No
                not payin' attention

Mara: No
                He's
                he's in a fog
                I know
                And I don't know why they have to go to the market

	every damn day I mean it's absolutely ridiculous
Lara:	I know Habit
Mara:	Yeah
Lara:	Ah
Mara:	Um What time you go tomorrow?
Lara:	Nine
Mara:	You takin off all day?
Lara:	No No It's not goin' take that long
Mara:	Oh
Lara:	An electrocardiogram I'll just a
Mara:	Then you go Wednesday
Lara:	Thurs
Mara:	Thursday
Lara:	Thursday Yeah Now were supposed have nasty weather
Mara:	Oh, shit that's right
Lara:	Umhm Cause Mommy said if it's really bad we'll cancelled dinner going out till next week
Mara:	Alright
Lara:	So

Mara:	Oh I forgot all about I mean I didn't forget about goin' out but I didn't put two and two together
Lara:	What Bad weather and goin'
Lara:	(Laugh) yeah
Mara:	Yeah I forgot that it was Wednesday it was goin' to be bad
Lara:	Yeah That's what they said
Mara:	Yeah
Lara:	Tomorrow night
Mara:	Well It could be just rain
Lara:	Yeah But even if it is rainin hard
Mara:	Yeah Alright
Lara:	Why don't we just ah Because if They said that the temperature was gonna drop
Mara:	Umhm
Lara:	Cause Weather you know
Mara:	We could get out and then it could get bad
Lara:	Yeah right Right
Mara:	Alright

Lara:	That's what I mean So what we'll do is ah Make a decision like about two o'clock
Mara:	Ok
Lara:	On Wednesday You know you call Mommy from where you are And then Ill call her around 2:00, 2:30
Mara:	Ok
Lara:	And we'll decide then And then Robin can just check in
Mara:	Alright That's a good idea
Lara:	You know But we'll wait till at least two
Mara:	And we're not You didn't get them anything
Lara:	No
Mara:	We're just ah, ah
Lara:	I sent them a card today
Mara:	Yeah
Lara:	And eh No She keeps sayin' No, you get us this You get us
Mara:	Well I thought what can we get them?
Lara:	We can't

Mara: You know
         Send them balloons or plant

Lara: Did the dog cost anything?

Mara: Nothin
         I said to the woman
         Do I
         give you money?
         She goes, "No"
         She said so don't call St Francis
         It's just between us
         And she said
         I'm just glad he's goin' to a good home
         I said
         This dog will live like a king
         Trust me
         And I said to Dad
         Don't give him chicken
         Dad

Lara: Yeah

Mara: He should get used to dry dog food
         She told me he loves canned dog food

Lara: Yeah

Mara: Now she
         they
         She fed him twice a day
         but they're not
         They're only gonna feed him at night
         I told Mommy
         I said give him a little this morning
         But she didn't (Laugh)

Lara: Yeah

Mara: So
         But
         Oh well
         Time will tell if were did the right thing (Laugh)

Lara:	Yeah Well what you gonna do?
Mara:	Yeah Well I just I mean he just was not getting better
Lara:	Yeah I know I was I haven't seen him but
Mara:	Oh
Lara:	You know I've ja He answered the phone the one time and he sounded awful
Mara:	Oh did he
Lara:	Yeah I mean he just Said here she He didn't want to talk
Mara:	Yeah Well It's funny I said to him Couple days ago I said oh whacha you do today Oh we Wa, Mommy went to Kohl's and then we went to Bennigan's Now he knew that
Lara:	Yeah
Mara:	It, It's so weird
Lara:	I know

Mara:	John showed me a whole article on ah dementia from depression and it sounded like him
Lara:	Really?
Mara:	Cause all this started when Uncle Bill died
Lara:	Yes it did it started after him more so
Mara:	So
Lara:	More so with unc I mean it was a little bit
Mara:	Yeah
Lara:	But not much
Mara:	No
Lara:	And it just went down hill
Mara:	Umhm
Lara:	And ah And of course Mommy doesn't help with that because she would constantly say Oh We're watchin' the game and Daddy always used to call Uncle Bill
Mara:	Oh I know I know Well I told her she finally had to shut up about Daddy getting his tickets takin' Bridget
Lara:	Yeah
Mara:	(Laugh)

Lara:	I mean start a new routine
Mara:	Well that's what I said And really it is safer not to take the dog in the car
Lara:	Yeah Yeah
Mara:	They don't have to take it out
Lara:	No
Mara:	So I mean he's not going to be Bridget (Laugh)
Lara:	No
Mara:	So I just wanted to have him ta have something to pet
Lara:	Yeah
Mara:	And to walk
Lara:	Yeah, yeah
Mara:	And ta feed and have something to do
Lara:	Yeah
Mara:	Yeah Mommy was telling me she was makin' the potatoes tonight and the pork chop

	and (Sigh)
Lara:	Yeah
Mara:	Well She should sit and say well can you do the dishes
Lara:	Yeah Yeah cause if she says it to him he'll wi he will
Mara:	Why I told her that
Lara:	
Lara:	I know But then she won't have anything to bitch about
Mara:	Well that's true What did she say anything to you about makin' dinner?
Lara:	No Unun No She, she'll, she'll Only She'll say something if I ask
Mara:	Umhm
Lara:	But she won't volunteer
Mara:	No She covers
Lara:	Yeah And Ah Now she said Say if the weather's bad well just cancel so I just said we'll

	We'll see See how it is
Mara:	Yeah
Lara:	And eh If it is nasty I think it will be better if we did wait
Mara:	Oh Yeah
Lara:	Yeah end of the week
Mara:	Yeah I was listening to the weather all day thinking oh Wednesday night (Laugh)
Lara:	(Laugh) Yeah
Mara:	Great
Lara:	Yeah cause they still don't know if it's goin' change over
Mara:	Yeah But like you said even if it's pourin' I hate to drive
Lara:	If it's goin' rain I hate drivin' in the rain
Mara:	95 and Yeah
Lara:	Yeah and you have further to go than I we do
Mara:	Yeah
Lara:	So it's It's probably
Mara:	Well Robin's drive's no better

Lara:	She's only about ten minutes past me
Mara:	Yeah So (Sigh)
Lara:	You know we'll call Call her around two and I'll tell her tell her tomorrow and we'll make a decision then
Mara:	Okay

Synergistext™ Analysis

This conversation between Mara and Lara is the only conversation of the four that occurred after Zoey was delivered to Fred. It is interesting to note that Mara still provides an abbreviated historical version of the details, contained in the previous conversations, explaining how she discovered the dog, but here she focuses on a post hoc justification of what she had done, presumably in anticipation of at least some criticism from Lara.

Mara begins this talk with a nervous laugh and tries to channel the conversation in a positive direction, saying that Mom "seems happy." Lara counters with the negative prediction that "She'll hate it by Wednesday," betraying her own irritability about the dog and confirming Mara's expectations of her. Lara vents more directly and intensely when she says that she would "have to" break Mara's legs if the dog causes their father to have an automobile accident.

Mara deftly side-steps the threat and returns to her justification for getting the dog and her experience of bringing him home. This unconsciously-determined strategy works, for soon Lara adopts a more benign emotional tone, and even describes Zoey as looking like Lara's own cat. The confrontation with Lara resolved, Mara is open to expressing the other emotions swirling within her baseline consciousness – mostly fear and the hope of saving her father. She refers to how her eyes filled with tears as she watched him walk the dog; she says that she told the dog's original owner, "I'm afraid my dad's gonna die."

Despite the more constructive tone, Mara is not satisfied and continues to try to win Lara over to her side. She inadvertently makes Robin's comment her own when she remarks, "They're not going anywhere." This is meant to defuse the potential argument that the presence of the dog reduces the chance that the parents will sell their home and move into an apartment as the three daughters had recommended. The fact that Mara incorporated Robin's phrase into her current conversation shows that it had resonated with Mara at the time Robin said it – that it satisfied both Robin's and Mara's GBH strivings when they were speaking together. Mara also comments that Zoey, a mature dog, is "much better than a puppy," also likely to be an unconsciously determined remark that came from Mom who said that she was quoting Lara.

Mara and Lara become analytic of their father's initial response to Zoey. In commenting about his reaction to the new dog, Mara states "I think daddy feels disloyal" to his dead dog, Bridget, if he expresses liking for Zoey. The notion of disloyalty came to Mara from Mom, but chances are strong that Mara is not aware of that source when she makes the remark. In taking one comment from Robin, two from Mom, and using them as her own, Mara illustrates mirroring and the fact that conversations with others affect our own individual thoughts and feelings in ways that are automatic and unconscious.

After Mara spends some more time selling Lara on Zoe's virtues, the topic switches to Mom and Fred as a couple – their shortcomings and ways to address them. This demonstrates a positive evolution of the conversation regarding Mara and Lara. At this point in their discussion, both of them likely derive H/GBH from the lessening of their competitive tensions and G/GBH or B/GBH from speaking as a unified team. The change is especially salutary given Lara's "break your legs" remark early on.

The conversation proceeds in a way to suggest that both Mara and Lara are feeling more optimistic about having brought Zoey into the parents' home. The anxiety-arousing feature of the new situation is being adequately worked through within and between them.

But Mara's preoccupation with Zoe's gender remains. She has not yet come to grips with having a male dog. She uses the conversation to talk to herself, to reassure herself by laughingly saying, "He doesn't have any testicles or anything...I mean you can hardly tell he's a boy."

The thought that her father is in rapid decline prompts Mara to recall that Lara is to have an EKG, and her comment about it supports the view that B/BETF exerts press on Mara's baseline consciousness, seeking an outlet via conversation. For Lara, however, the EKG is not open for extended discussion. Perhaps the thought is too anxiety arousing to be dwelled upon. In any case, she changes the subject to an upcoming family-of -origin dinner in which all three sisters and the parents will celebrate Fred and Mom's anniversary. For a brief period they discuss the where and when of dinner and mention anniversary presents, but Mara derives little GBH from this and she returns to *her* story – the thoughts prepotent in her baseline consciousness – about Zoey and Fred.

Mara and Lara recycle their fears about the father's mental deterioration, and, as they had previously, they intellectualize about it, presumably to help them control their feelings of helplessness regarding him. They also use this occasion to place some blame on their mother for reminding the father of having lost his brother and dog. By doing so, Mara and Lara achieve some conjoint B/GBH, since they now have a mutual target to vent their frustration, and perhaps to influence, in order to improve their father's chances. That hypothesis is supported by the section of the transcript which shows that soon after attributing blame to Mom. Mara and Lara offer their solutions to making Fred more animated and involved in day-to-day living.

In the end, blaming Mom does not sit well with Mara and Lara, so they change the subject back to the emotionally safe topics of the upcoming anniversary dinner, traveling to it, and even the prototypic safe topic – the weather.

By the end of the conversation, Mara and Lara have achieved GBH about the continuing integrity of their relationship, their collaboration to help Fred and Mom, and the concrete issue of the dog. Mara is reassured that Lara will not be an obstructionist about the dog, and Lara is satisfied that her issues have been addressed and respected. Sibling rivalry instigated by this event has subsided, and the sibling balance has been adequately restored, at least for the time being.

Enhancing GBH for Conversant Partners

The Zoey conversations demonstrate that Synergistext™ analysis of conversations provides valuable insights into the personalities and relationships of conversants. But you need not conduct a lengthy, formal analysis to benefit from insights contain in this book. You can deduce your own insights merely by applying a few elementary Synergistext™ principles.

Many applications are implicit in all that we have discussed. In this section, I will make some explicit, explaining how you can better understand and structure what you receive from and contribute to your conversations. And whatever I say about you, obviously, also is applicable to your conversant partner.

Strategy for Informal Synergistext™ Analysis

To organize your analysis, first listen to the **music**. What is the sound quality of the conversation? For instance, is it light or heavy, quick or slow? Next, listen for the **melodies**. Does the pace change? When? How? In what way does each performer contribute to the composition? What is the tone of the final notes?

Listen to the **lyrics**. Is this mostly a positive or negative song? Does it focus on past, present, or future? What topics are initiated or conjointly developed? What topics are avoided or dismissed? Is this a ballad, a battle, or something else? What is the song's **refrains**? Can you find ideas that reoccur in this song and between this and other songs sung by the performers?

Finally, think about the **setting** and the **performers**. Where is the interaction occurring and when? Who are the performers? Who initiates which topics? What are their individual histories and their history together?

Having applied our informal strategy to grasp the overall structure of your conversation—music, melodies, lyrics, refrains, setting, and performers—you now are ready to consider some other essential issues to which we now turn.

285

Survive and Thrive

Realize that conversation is a mechanism that evolved to promote surviving and thriving, so that you can better accept and cope with its self-centeredness. Do not be ashamed to use talk to attain GBH, since the relentless, expectant search for GBH is at the heart of the conversation process, but don't lose sight of the fact that your chances for realizing your self-centered GBH usually are increased by facilitating your partner' s realizing his.

Determine as best you can how much of what you seek is message GBH and how much is relationship GBH. If message GBH is primary, be guided in your conversation by answers to questions such as:

> "Am I primarily trying to get or to give a message?"

> "Does the person with whom I am speaking really possess valid information that I seek?"

> "Is there someone else accessible to me who knows it better?"

> "Am I willingly to consider information he might give me that is at odds with my expectations?"

If relationship GBH is primary, another set of questions is appropriate, among them:

> "How do I expect to benefit from this relationship?"

> "Is conversation an effective vehicle for developing or strengthening our inter-personal bond?

> "How can I identify and exploit topics of mutual interest in order to afford us mutual GBH satisfactions?"

> "In which veridical and/or presumed environments should we converse to facilitate building our relationship?"

Affective Valence

Conversation enables us to learn about our predominant affective valences (AV). By listening with our third ear we can note how often we use negatively-valenced terms and how often we use positive ones. Positive conversations should be sought, but there is nothing inherently wrong with using affectively negative words. In fact, Labouvie-Vief and Medler (2002) believe that when negative affect is used to promote reality-based understanding of the complexity of experience, it contributes to one's ability self-regulate emotions of all valences.

Some conversations virtually demand that we speak negatively. For example, when describing death and destruction, it would be disingenuous and perhaps a sign of personal psychopathology not to do so. But persons who consistently speak in negative terms are persons who drag themselves and their partners down emotionally. In conversation you can talk about anything. To speak negatively, you must avoid positive features of experience and selectively attend to the unpleasant. Those biased toward excessively negative conversations need to ask why they choose to speak so.

Evaluation Words: Elevating and Discounting

Earlier we said that the overwhelming majority of words have good-bad connotations regularly associated with them and that, by contrast, evaluation words have affective valance as part of their denotative structure as well. The latter feature makes evaluation words especially revealing during conversation analysis. The affective valence of denotative evaluative words virtually leaps out at us as though the speaker were announcing, "Pay attention to what I'm saying. This is important to me!"

Because all evaluation words have a bipolar opposite, when a conversant uses a positive word, she is elevating it, discounting the corresponding negative word, and vice versa. When she says, "I had a great day" she also is saying, "I did not have a bad day." (This presumes of course that she is sincere and not speaking ironically.) To say that the day has been "great" is to focus on some feature or features that support such an appellation – elevating those aspects of experience – and ignoring some feature or features that contradict it – discounting those aspects.

When positive evaluation words are used sincerely, we have reason to suspect that the conversant's mental representations at this point are positive – to return to our previous analogy, that her green associative spheres are lighting up. And when negative evaluation words are used sincerely, that her red spheres are illuminated. One incident of such communication does not enable us to know whether the spheres regularly light up this way – CAMM – or whether this is merely a time-limited illumination – TAMM, or whether the communication is likely to occur often – CASS—or infrequently – TASS.

For example, at the end of an afternoon visit, when escorting Beth and her spouse Jake to the door, Sue and Steve show them their new, obviously expensive, bedroom furniture that Steve had selected. Sue asks what Beth and Jake will be doing the rest of the night and Beth replies, "Nothing much, I made some soup Thursday; we'll have the leftovers tonight." Sue nonchalantly says that she and Steve will be going out to dinner at Steve's favorite restaurant, an upscale place downtown. Beth then jokes, "I should have married Steve. He has good taste."

Having chosen to evaluate Steve as having "good taste," Beth places him at the pinnacle of the desirable mate pyramid, discounting his other characteristics, including the fact that he is intolerably narcissistic, drinks to excess, and has a hair-trigger temper. By her statement, Beth also implies that Jake is an inferior mate. At the level of mental representation, the Steve container is flooded with bright green lights and Jake's, with bright red ones. At the level of communication, Beth's remark is a thinly veiled flirtation to Steve and a slap in the face to Jake. We will need to observe Beth over time to determine the CAMM, TAMM, CASS, or TASS nature of her mental representations and communications regarding this matter. But we need no further comments from Beth to infer some likely conclusions: She is jealous of Sue, values fine furniture and restaurant dining, and resents Jake's failure to provide them.

Mindlessness and Mindfulness

In conversation you can expect to talk mostly in a mindless way, since most people operate like that most of the time. By being aware of your mindless versus mindful conversation contributions though, you gain valuable insights into your own psychodynamics. People converse mindlessly, in an automatic mode, when they are relatively comfortable with their conversant partner and have their guard down. If you find yourself excessively measuring what you say, you do not trust your partner to accept your authentic self. This could be his problem if he is overly harsh or brusque, or it could be your problem if you are overly self-critical. In either case, your chances of realizing relationship GBH are severely compromised. Mindfulness has its place as well. By being mindful, you can counter a personal predilection toward narrow, stereotyped, or otherwise rigid thinking. A mindful attitude also makes deliberate, healthful meta-communication more possible.

CAMM, TAMM, and Baseline Consciousness

When you speak with others you have an opportunity to observe what topics come to mind. In so doing, you glimpse you CAMM, TAMM, and baseline consciousness. When you find yourself referring to a subject repeatedly, you know that it often is pressing on your baseline consciousness. Look to see in which BETF area the idea resides, since this will disclose issues important to you at any given moment in time. When you determine that it is a specific body, environment, thought, or feeling issue, you are empowered to do something about it, especially if the issue is a reoccurring one. Similarly, when you find yourself talking about a topic that you ordinarily do not talk about, you can look to see what in the current situation, in you, or your partner is prompting this novel expression.

CASS and TASS

When you discuss something out of character for you, you probably do so because you are experiencing a TASS change that ordinarily is short-lived. Try to determine why you temporarily have altered your standards, since this can reveal valuable insights into your personality.

On the other hand, the changed speaking standards may not be temporary and fleeting, but rather may offer the promise of a more enduring alteration in your conversational style – a new CASS standard. Perhaps after speaking about a formerly forbidden or otherwise avoided topic, you find that the anticipated untoward consequence did not occur. If you come to that realization, you have an opportunity to grow in your conversational repertoire, at least regarding the person with whom you are speaking. Even conversing on a new topic once presents an opportunity for enduring self-growth and inter-personal expansion.

Templates and Fingerprints

The only way to be mindful enough to profit from speaking on an atypical topic is for you to be aware of your conversational templates. You may be surprised to learn how repetitive your topics are, either with one individual partner or across many partners. As we had said regarding negatively-valenced terminology, it is not necessarily "bad" to be template-like in your conversations, although, by definition, it is constraining. Template discussions have been co-constructed by you and your partner for a reason or reasons. But those reasons may no longer be valid. Perhaps you and a friend never mention spouses because when the two of you met you were married and she recently divorced, so you unconsciously chose to eliminate talk of spouses from your conversation repertoire. Circumstances change, however. You now may have been friends for several years. She could be remarried, dating, or less sensitive about spouse-oriented talk. Templates can be revised or replaced. Your conversations can become more spontaneous, free-wheeling, and fingerprint-like.

Control

Cast a discerning eye upon the persons with whom you converse. Why do you talk to them? How often? Do you feel better or worse afterward? Remember that H/GBH is a powerful trigger for conversation. H/GBH exerts its power by making us believe that we need to talk to this person if we are to be in "balance" and so quiet our baseline consciousness references to him or her. Many of us at times have thought or commented, "I wouldn't talk to her at all, if she weren't my cousin." Such comments speak volumes about our conversational preferences.

Do you converse with a person and find that talking with him brings you down? To speak with him is to give him control over you. The more you talk to him, the more control he has. As we mentioned earlier, such persons can "infect" you with their negativism in ways that are virtually undetectable by you. By becoming aware that your talking to him is motivated by feelings of guilt and responsibility, you can structure yourself to eliminate the toxic conversations, or to limit them to the absolute minimum necessary to maintain your H/GBH integrity concerning the relationship in question.

TAABWA

Conversations provide valuable insight into your TAABWA movement. Be cognizant how often you speak in ways that show a desire to affiliate with the other, to demonstrate your intellect relative to him, or to exert your power over him. If you are overloaded on one of these big three dimensions, try to understand why. Perhaps you converse with virtually everyone that way, in which case TAABWA reveals an enduring personality trait. Perhaps you are excessive on one of the dimensions because of factors specific to this person at this time, in which case TAABWA reveals a temporary personality state that will pass. Maybe there is a "sociological" explanation in that you are "above" him on the social ladder and both you and he are playing culturally prescribed roles. In all of these cases, to be knowledgeable of conversational movement is to be aware of the most powerful inter-personal motivations of yourself and of your inter-personal partners and to be empowered to keep TAABWA within more manageable limits for you and for them.

My Story

The narratives of conversation are the narratives of your life. You choose to introduce topics and you choose to enthusiastically discuss topics introduced by your conversant partner that are important to your life story. You choose not to introduce topics and you choose not to enthusiastically discuss certain topics introduced by your conversant partner that are not important to your life story. I can not emphasize strongly enough that conversation always includes self-talk, and that self-talk very often is **the** psychologically most important element of our discourse.

Listen to the topics that you introduce and the emphasis that you place upon them. I bet that you will hear many templates conversations – many repetitive themes. As advised earlier, listen not only to the words; listen to the music. Is it light or heavy, quick or slow? What is its affective valence (AV)? Does the music or attitude change when your conversant partner changes? Who are the characters in the stories? Are they richly described or skeletally portrayed. In the first instance, they are essential to you; in the second they are just means to your end. While themes of life stories are as numerous as the people who establish them, McAdams (2001) suggests that some common ones center upon: care, love, affirmation, connection, friendship, competence, achievement, status, victory, loss, responsibility, faith, and integration. Which life story themes are most representative of you?

Conversation Varieties

Some people are forever directly telling you about their experiences. Some people directly disclose little. Some talk incessantly about the past. Others mostly speak of their future. Even though stories comprise the bulk of most conversations, since everyone talks to herself while talking to others, the classes of conversation that you embrace reveal your what you want to hear and your personality characteristics.

Considered at the surface level of language, some distinctions are more obvious than others. Me-talk is unabashedly and blatantly self-centered. Gossip is clearly focused on others. Persons who converse predominantly via me-talk have little interest in exploring people outside themselves. Persons who converse predominately via gossip have little interest in overtly disclosing themselves.

If your conversation is filled with observation and comment, you likely are grounded solidly in reality. If it is characterized by extensive opinion, you are inclined to give your overt, good-bad appraisal of the world as you see it or how you believe it should be. If you tell many jokes, the tone and direction of your banter will be markedly different than that of someone who does not.

While all stories have the same general discourse structure and time line, the subtype that you favor also is noteworthy. Full-fledged narratives depict an incident of excitement building to crisis followed by resolution. Those strong in narrative production are storytellers in the traditional sense and must have at least some elementary dramatic flair. An anecdote is essentially a narrative characterized by reaction to crisis that is not resolved; persons favoring this type story are ones able to tolerate lack of closure. Exemplums advocate a world-view. Persons inclined toward a "preachy" approach to situations are likely to embrace this story style. Those who recount give a good presentation of connected events but little disclosure of his attitude toward them. If this is your preferred story-telling strategy, you probably have a good working memory but need to maintain interpersonal distance from your conversant partner.

Talk the Talk, Walk the Walk

As repeatedly emphasized, conversation is one of the best means for looking into people's hearts and minds. But, conversation is a subtype of volitional behavior, and volitional behavior includes nonverbal action. Both conversation and action proceed as part of the expectant, relentless search for GBH. The best way to know yourself and others is to scrutinize that which you and they say and do. By comparing what people say with what they do, we learn to appreciate how each volitional verbal behavior and action behavior either complements or undermines the other. We all have known people who refer to themselves as "sports nuts." They know all there is to know about their area of athletic interest, yet many of these people are sedentary to the maximum. They talk a good game, but never play one. Their sport's action is all mental. The essence of what people are can be found at the intersection of what they say and what they do. Is the "sports nut" more athletic than the person who runs two miles per day, three days per week, but who knows nothing about professional teams?

The extent of inter-personal interaction also exemplifies the relevance of the overt action versus talk dichotomy. Gratch (2002), Tannen (1990), and many others have suggested that women talk about relationships more often and in greater detail than men do. But, despite occasional protestations to the contrary, men live in the same world as women do, and are subject to inter-personal pleasures and pains as much as women are. We need to look at male and female actions, as well as words, in order to know what is important to them. Neither the language of actions nor of words can be taken at face value. Men may act out their desires and needs more often; women may talk out their desires and needs more often, but, in the end, both actions and words seek GBH. There are times when actions are more effective, important, and revealing, and times when the same is true of words. It is absurd to say that men cannot talk about feelings. Feelings are not talk; feelings are feelings. Just because some men can't or won't **directly talk** about their feelings doesn't mean that they are not **mentally representing them, experiencing them, and communicating them**. Whether conscious of feelings or not, men do have a multi-sensory-motor-visceral awareness of them, and they are affected by them.

293

Don't believe for a minute that Synergistext™, or any analytic system, gives the whole story of message or relationship. GBH is the route to striving, surviving, and thriving. And GBH is sought through action, as well as words. Modern humans, as opposed to our early human ancestors, have refined and rarefied language so that we value it and focus on it as though it were able to **represent** and **communicate** all that we experience. But neither is true. Representations and communications are far more than conversations, far more than words of any sophistication. Conversation and words are epiphenomena that, although profoundly valuable, are not the be all and end all of existence. To know self, other, self with other, and subject, look at actions, words, conversations, and each relative to the other.

To learn more about the theory and practice of Synergistext™ or about having your conversations analyzed, please connect to synergistext@aol.com.

Appendix A

The following is an untested, but scientifically plausible, hypothesis regarding the phylogenetic development of conversation:

From Chattering to Conversing

A pre-human foraging on the ground hears a charging lion, feels the ground shaking, and sees a tawny blur advancing toward him. The pre-human scurries up a tree. As he recovers there, the multi-sensory-motor-visceral representations of the chase linger in his body and mind, amounting to his "thinking" about the chase—the thoughts being interoceptive elements related to the scene in the form of mentally baring fangs, tensing legs muscles as if running, feeling his pounding heart, hearing the snarling predator, snorting, hyperventilating, and so forth. If he overtly, physically acts out his own aforementioned interoceptive experience and/or the exteroceptive experience of the behavior of the lion, or any combination of both, this externalization of the internal mental experience of the pre-human amounts to an observable discharge of baseline consciousness, affording homeostatic release of tension.

Another pre-human might see the first one acting out the chase scene and, having observed the incident, the second "knows" what the first is "talking about." The second pre-human could imitate the first, acting and chattering in ways similar to the first, or doing his own variation of that which he saw during the chase. If the second's actions and chatter are more accurate or convincing than that of the first, the first pre-human might imitate the second's version of the chase, rather than persisting with his own initial version.

Thus, "language" that was internal, private representation becomes conversation that is external, social communication, and communication skills are transferred from one group member to another. In time, the troop's best "talkers" could achieve high status, becoming language-meme-creating leaders that other members imitate. Thus, a social language, based on shared interoceptive-exteroceptive experience, evolves that is employed by all.

Appendix B

The following is an untested, but scientifically plausible, hypothesis regarding the ontogenetic development of conversation:

Ontogenetic Change from Private to Social Conversation

1. Mental life begins inside the head in the form of multi-sensory-motor-visceral internal representations.

2. First receptive and then expressive language develops inside the head as sounds emitted by others and by the self are associated with one's own one's own multi-sensory-motor-visceral awarenesses, one's own internal representations, and the social sights and sounds of others. Regarding the latter, the fact that one's own internal multi-sensory-motor-visceral awarenesses and one's own internal representations are repeatedly associated with the sounds (verbalizations) of our significant others makes them salient and repeated in our experience. Ordinarily we are inside ourselves looking out at the world and its fleeting, ever-changing images, but language verbalizations are thrust upon us over and over by our significant others. In this case, the outside world is not merely observed; rather, it vigorously and relentlessly forces itself on us. Therefore, our internal representations inadvertently and associatively become linked to the language of the others, because they literally and repeatedly thrust their verbalizations in our faces.

3. Over time then, our internal representations become associatively linked with language.

4. The representations in our head begin to have private speech components; we develop an idiosyncratic self-to-self dialogue.

5. We use this private speech together with the social speech that is thrust upon us in order to refine our GBH searches.

6.   Private and social speech grow together, each enhancing the other.

7.   The overt use of private speech decreases, in part because we use a variant of social conversation as one facet of private speech – conversation always is conversation with ourselves as well as with others.

8.   Social conversation comes to dominate our interpersonal lives and our GBH searches for messages and relationships.

References

Ackerman, J. (2001). *Chance in the House of Fate*. New York: Random House.

Addis, M. E. & Mahalik, J. R. (2003). Men, masculinity, and contexts of help seeking. *American Psychologist*, 58, 1, 5-14.

Alberts, J. K., & Driscoll, G. (1992). Containment versus escalation: The trajectory of couples' conversational complaints. *Western Journal of Communication*, 56, 4, 394-412.

Alexander, F. (1939). Emotional factors in essential hypertension. *Psychosomatic Medicine*, 1, 173-179.

Altmann, G. T. M. (1997). *The Ascent of Babel*. New York: Oxford University Press.

Anderson, C., Keltner, D., & John, O.P. (2003). Emotional convergence of people over time. *Journal of Personality & Social Psychology*, 84, 5, 1054-1068.

Arkes, H. R. & Ayton, P. (1999). The sunk cost and Concorde effects: Are humans less rational than lower animals? *Psychological Bulletin*, 125, 5, 591-600.

Ball, P. (2001). *Stories of the Invisible*. London: Oxford University Press.

Bargh, J. & Ferguson, M. (2000). Beyond behaviorism: On the automaticity of higher mental processes. *Psychological Bulletin*, 126, 6, 925-945.

Bargh, J. & Chartrand, T.L. (1999). The unbearable automaticity of being. *American Psychologist*. 54, 7, 462-479.

Bargh, J. A, Gollwitzer, P. M., Lee-Chai, A., Barndollar, K., & Troetschel, R. (2001). The automated will: Nonconscious activation and pursuit of behavioral goals. *Journal of Personality & Social Psychology*, 81, 6, 1014-1027.

Bartsch, R. (2002). *Consciousness Emerging: The Dynamics of Perception, Imagination, Action, Memory, Thought, and Language*. Amsterdam: John Benjamins.

Baumeister, R. F., Bratslavsky, E., Finkenauer, C., & Vohs, K. D. (2001). Bad is stronger than good. *Review of General Psychology*, 5, 4, 323-370.

Baumeister, R. F., Muraven, M., & Tice, D. M. (2000). Ego depletion: A resource model of volition, self-regulation, and controlled processing. *Social Cognition*, 18, 2, 130-150.

Bavelas, J. B., Coates, L., & Johnson, T. (2000). Listeners as co-narrators. *Journal of Personality & Social Psychology* 79, 6, 941-952.

Beach, S. R. H., Tesser, A., Fincham, F. D., Jones, D. J., Johnson, D., & Whitaker, D. J. (1998). Pleasure and pain in doing well together: An investigation of performance-related affect in close relationships. *Journal of Personality & Social Psychology*, 74, 4, 923-938.

Beilock, S. L. & Carr, T., H. (2002). On the fragility of skilled performance: What governs choking under pressure? *Journal of Experimental Psychology: General*, 130, 4, 701-725.

Berne, E. (1968). *Games People Play: The Psychology of Human Relationships*. New York: Penguin.

Bickerton, D. (1990). *Language and Species*. Chicago: University of Chicago.

Biesanz, J. C., West, S. G., & Graziano, W. G. (1998). Moderators of self-other agreement: Reconsidering temporal stability in personality. *Journal of Personality & Social Psychology*, 75, 2, 467-477.

Big Five Veterinary Pharmaceutical Company. (2003) bigfive.jl.co.za/feeding1.htm

Blackburn, S. (2001). *Being Good*. New York: Oxford University Press.

Blackmore, S. J. (1999). *The Meme Machine*. Oxford, England: Oxford University Press.

Block, J. (1995). A contrarian's view of the five-factor approach to personality description. *Psychological Bulletin*, 117, 187-215.

Bloom, H. (2000). *How to Read and Why*. London: Fourth Estate.

Bodamer, M. D. & Gardner, R. A. (2002). How cross-fostered chimpanzees initiate and maintain conversations. *Journal of Comparative Psychology*, 116, 1, 12-26.

Bongard, S., al' Absi, M., & Lovallo, W., R. (1998) Interactive effects of trait hostility and anger expression on cardiovascular reactivity in young men. *International Journal of Psychophysiology*, 28, 2, 181-191.

Bower, G. H. (1981) Mood and memory. *American Psychologist*, 36, 2, 129-148.

Brennan, S. E. & Clark, H. H. (1996). Conceptual pacts and lexical choice in conversation. *Journal of Experimental Psychology: Learning, Memory, & Cognition*, 22, 6, 1482-1493.

Brickman, P. & Campbell, D. T. (1971). Hedonic relativism and planning the good society. In M. H. Appley (Ed.), *Adaptation Level Theory: A Symposium* (pp. 287—302). New York: Academic Press.

Broadwell, S. D. & Light, K. C. (1999). Family support and cardiovascular responses in married couples during conflict and other interactions. *International Journal of Behavioral Medicine*, 16,1, 40-63.

Bromme, R., Rambow, R., & Nueckles, M. (2001). Expertise and estimating what other people know: The influence of professional experience and type of knowledge. *Journal of Experimental Psychology: Applied*, 7, 4, 317-330.

Bruch, M. A. (2002). Shyness and toughness: Unique and moderated relations with men's emotional inexpression. *Journal of Counseling Psychology*, 49, 1, 28-34.

Buck, R. (1999). The biological affects: A typology. *Psychological Review*, 106, 2, 301-336.

Bugental, D. B. (2000). Acquisition of the algorithms of social life: A domain-based approach. *Psychological Bulletin*, 126, 2, 187-219.

Carmena, J.M., Lebedev, M. A., Crist, R.E., O'Doherty, J. E., Santucci, D. M., Dimitrov, D. F., Patil, P. G., Henriquez, C.S., & Nicolelis, M. A. L. (2003). Learning to control a brain-machine interface for reaching and grasping by primates. *Public Library of Science*, 1, 2, 1-16.

Cartwright, R., Newell, P., & Mercer, P. (2001). Dream incorporation of a sentinel life event and its relation to waking adaptation. *Sleep & Hypnosis*, 3, 1, 25-32

Chafe, W. (1987). Cognitive constraints on information flow. In R. S. Tomlin (Ed.), *Coherence and Grounding in Discourse* (Symposium, Eugene, Oregon, June). Philadelphia: John Benjamins.

Chafe, W. & Danielewicz, J. M. (1987). Properties of spoken and written language. In R. Horowitz & S. J. Samuels (Eds.), *Comprehending Oral and Written Language*. San Diego: Academic Press.

Chartrand, T. L. & Bargh, J. A. (1999). The chameleon effect: The perception-behavior link and social interaction. *Journal of Personality and Social Psychology*, 76, 6, 893-910.

Chen, E., Matthews, K. A., Salomon, K., & Ewart, C. K. (2002). Cardiovascular reactivity during social and nonsocial stressors: Do children's personal goals and expressive skills matter? *Health Psychology*, 21,1, 16-24

Chess, S. & Thomas, A. (1996). *Temperament: Theory and Practice*. New York: Brunner-Routledge.

Crenson, M. Bacterial babble. Associated Press, January 13, 2003.

Crocker, J. & Wolfe, C. T. (2001). Contingencies of self-worth. *Psychological Review*, 108, 3, 593-623.

Damasio, A. R. (1999). *The Feeling of What Happens*. New York: Harcourt Brace.

Damasio, A. R. (1995). *Descartes' Error: Emotion, Reason, and the Human Brain*. New York: Avon.

Davis, J. L. & Rusbult, C. E. (2001). Attitude alignment in close relationships. *Journal of Personality & Social Psychology*, 81,1, 65-84

Davis, M. C. & Matthews, K. A. (1996). Do gender-relevant characteristics determine cardiovascular reactivity? Match versus mismatch of traits and situation. *Journal of Personality and Social Psychology*, 71, 527-535

Dawkins, R. (1976). *The Selfish Gene*. Oxford, England: Oxford Paperbacks.

Deacon, T. W. (1998). *The Symbolic Species: The Co-Evolution of Language and the Brain*. New York: W.W. Norton.

Deese, J. (1996). Contextualism: Truth in advertising. *The General Psychologist*, 32, 2, 56-61.

Dennett, D. (1978). *Brainstorms: Philosophical Essays on Mind and Psychology*. Montgomery, VT: Bradford Books.

Depue, R. A. (1995). Neurobiological factors in personality and depression. *European Journal of Personality*, 9, 413-439.

De Rivera, J. (1977). A structural theory of the emotions. *Psychological Issues*, 10, 4.

De Waal, F. B. M., Aureli, F., & Judge, P. G. (2000). Coping with crowding. *Scientific American*, 282, 5, 76-81.

Dolinski, D. (2001). Emotional seesaw, compliance, and mindlessness. *European Psychologist*, 6, 3, 194-203.

Dragoi, V. & Staddon, J. E. R. (1999). The dynamics of operant conditioning. *Psychological Review*, 106, 1, 20-61.

Drew, M. L., Dobson, K, S., & Stam, H. J. (1999). The negative self-concept in clinical depression: A discourse analysis. *Canadian Psychology*, 40, 2, 192-204.

Dribben, M. (2002). In your face. (In *Inquirer Magazine*, Philadelphia, October 20, pp 12, 14.)

Dugatkin, L. A. (2001). *The Imitation Factor: Evolution Beyond the Gene*. New York: Simon & Schuster.

Dunbar, R. (1996). *Grooming, Gossip, and the Evolution of Language*. Cambridge, MA: Harvard University.

Duncan, R. M. & Cheyne, J. A. (1999). Incidence and functions of self-reported private speech in young adults: A self-verbalization questionnaire. *Canadian Journal of Behavioural Science*, 31,2,133-136.

Egloff, B., Wilhelm, F. H., Neubauer, D. H., Mauss, I. B., & Gross, J. J. (2002). Implicit anxiety measure predicts cardiovascular reactivity to an evaluated speaking task. *Emotion*, 2, 1, 3-11.

Ehret, G & Riecke, S. (2002). Mice and humans perceive multiharmonic communications in the same way. *Proceedings of the National Academy of Sciences*, 99, 479-482.

Elsner, B. & Hommel, B. (2001). Effect anticipation and action control. *Journal of Experimental Psychology: Human Perception & Performance*, 27, 1, 229-240.

Encyclopedia.com (2001). Spontaneous Abortion.

Epstein, S. (1994). An integration of the cognitive and psychodynamic unconscious. *American Psychologist*, 49, 709-724.

Evans, G.W., Lepore, S. J., & Allen, K. M. (2000). Cross-cultural differences in tolerance for crowding: Fact or fiction? *Journal of Personality & Social Psychology*, 79, 2, 204-210.

Everhart, D. E., Shucard, J. L., Quatrin, T., & Shucard, D. W. (2001). Sex-related differences in event-related potentials, face recognition, and facial affect processing in prepubertal children. *Neuropsychology*, 15, 3, 329-341.

Fenichel, O. (1945). *Psychoanalytic Theory of Neurosis*. New York: Norton.

Fichera, V. L. & Andreassi, J.L. (2000). Cardiovascular reactivity during public speaking as a function of personality variables. *International Journal of Psychophysiology*, 37, 3, 267-273.

Forgas, J. P. (1999). On feeling good and being rude: Affective influences on language use and request formulations. *Journal of Personality & Social Psychology*, 76, 6, 928-939.

Frankenberger, K. D. (2000). Adolescent egocentrism: A comparison among adolescents and adults. *Journal of Adolescence*, 23, 3, 343-354.

Freud, S. (1925). Negation. In J. Strachey (Ed.) *The Standard Edition of the Complete Works of Sigmund Freud* (Vol. 23). London: Hogarth, 1964.

Freud, S. (1938). An outline of psychoanalysis. In J. Strachey (Ed.) *The Standard Edition of the Complete Works of Sigmund Freud* (Vol. 23). London: Hogarth, 1964.

Frijda, N. H. (1988). The laws of emotion. *American Psychologist*, 43, 5, 349-358.

Furr, R. M. & Funder, D. C. (1998). A multimodal analysis of personal negativity. *Journal of Personality & Social Psychology*, 74, 1580-1591.

Gabriel, S. & Gardner, W. L. (1999). Are there "his" and "hers" types of interdependence? The implications of gender differences in collective versus relational interdependence for affect, behavior, and cognition. *Journal of Personality & Social Psychology*, 77, 3, 642-655.

Garcia, S., Stinson, L., Ickes, W., & Bissonnette, V. (1991). Shyness and physical attractiveness in mixed-sex dyads. *Journal of Personality & Social Psychology*, 61, 1, 35-49.

Gardenfors, P. (1998). Human and machine perception: Emergence, attention, and creativity. *Pavia*, September 14-17.

Gehring, W. J. (2002). The genetic control of eye development and its implications for the evolution of the various eye-types. *International Journal of Developmental Biology*, 46, 65-73.

Geyman, J.P. & Sullivan, S.D. (1999). *Journal of the American Board of Family Practice*, 12, 55-64.

Giancola, P. R. (2000). Executive functioning: A conceptual framework for alcohol-related aggression. *Experimental & Clinical Psychopharmacology*, 8, 4, 576-597.

Gibbs, W. W. (2001). Cybernetic cells. *Scientific American*, 265, 2, 53-57.

Glass, D. C. & Singer, J. E. (1972). *Urban stress: Experiments on noise and social stressors*. New York: Academic Press.

Goldsmith, D. J. & Baxter, L. A. (1996). Constituting relationships in talk: A taxonomy of speech events in social and personal relationships. *Human Communication Research*, 23, 1, 87-114.

Gosling, S. D. (2001). From mice to men: What can we learn about personality from animal research? *Psychological Bulletin*, 127, 1, 45-86.

Gratch, A. (2002). *If Men Could Talk: Unlocking the Secret Language of Men*. Little New York: Brown.

Gray, J. A. (1982). *The Neuropsychology of Anxiety: An Inquiry into the Functions of the Septohippocampal System*. New York: Oxford University Press.

Greenberg, G., Partridge, T., Weiss, E., & Haraway, M. (1999). Integrative levels, the brain, and the emergence of complex behavior. *Review of General Psychology*, 3, 3, 168-187.

Grice, H. P. (1975). Logic and conversation. In P. Cole and J. Morgan, Eds., *Syntax and Semantics*, Vol. 3, Academic Press, pp. 41-58.

Groopman, J. (2000). The doubting disease. *New Yorker*, April, 10.

Gupta, S. (2003). Why men die young. *Time*, May, 12.

Haines, M.P. (1998). Social norms: A wellness model for health promotion in higher education. *Wellness Management: Newsletter of the National Wellness Association*, 14,4.

Hamilton, M. A. (1991) Schematizing as a measure of leveling-sharpening. *Perceptual & Motor Skills*, 73,1, 95-102.

Harley, K. & Reese, E. (1999). Origins of autobiographical memory. *Developmental Psychology*, 35, 5, 1338-1348.

Heine, S. H., Lehman, D. R., Markus, H. R., & Kitayama, S. (1999). Is there a universal need for positive self-regard? *Psychological Review*, 106, 4, 766-794.

Held, S., Mendl, M., Devereux, C., & Byrne, R. W. (2002). Foraging pigs alter their behaviour in response to exploitation. *Animal Behaviour*, 64, 2, 157-165.

Heyman, R. E. (2001). Observation of couple conflicts: Clinical assessment applications, stubborn truths, and shaky foundations. *Psychological Assessment*, 13, 1, 5-35.

Higgins, E. T. (2000). Making a good decision: Value from fit. *American Psychologist*, 55,11, 1217-1230.

Hobson, J. A. & Leonard, J. A. (2001). *Out of Its Mind: Psychiatry in Crisis.* Cambridge, Massachusetts: Perseus.

Holtgraves, T. (1997). Styles of language use: Individual and cultural variability in conversational indirectness. *Journal of Personality and Social Psychology*, 73, 3, 624-637.

Hughes, C. & Dunn, J. (1998). Understanding mind and emotion: Longitudinal associations with mental-state talk between young friends. *Developmental Psychology*, 34, 5, 1026-1037.

Hupet, M., Chantraine, Y., & Nef, F. (1993). References in conversation between young and old normal adults. *Psychology & Aging*, 1 8, 3, 339-346.

Ickes, W, Stinson, L, Bissonnette, V., & Garcia, S. (1990). Naturalistic social cognition: Empathic accuracy in mixed-sex dyads. *Journal of Personality & Social Psychology*, 59, 4, 730-742.

Iyengar, S. S. & Lepper, M. R. (2000). When choice is demotivating: Can one desire too much of a good thing? *Journal of Personality and Social Psychology*, 79, 6, 995-1006.

Jacob, T, & Johnson, S. L. (2001). Sequential interactions in the parent-child communications of depressed fathers and depressed mothers. *Journal of Family Psychology*, 15,1, 38-52.

James, S. A., Strogatz, D. S., Wing, S. B., & Ramsey, D. L. (1987). Socioeconomic status, John Henryism, and hypertension in Blacks and Whites. *American Journal of Epidemiology*, 126, 664-673.

Johnson, S. (2001). *Emergence.* New York: Scribner.

John-Steiner, V. (1985). *Notebooks of the Mind.* New York: Harper & Row.

Juslin, P. N. & Laukka, P. (2001). Impact of intended emotion intensity on cue utilization and decoding accuracy in vocal expression of emotion. *Emotion*, 1, 4, 381-412.

Just, M. (2002). Carnegie Mellon University speaking on National Public Radio.

Karney, B. R. & Frye, N. E. (2002). "But we've been getting better lately" : Comparing prospective and retrospective views of relationship development. *Journal of Personality & Social Psychology*, 82, 2, 222-238.

Katz, J. (1999). *How Emotions Work*. Chicago: University of Chicago Press.

Kelley, E. L. (1927). *Interpretation of Educational Measurement*. Yonkers, NY: World.

Kelly, A. & McKillop, K. J. (1996). Consequences of revealing personal secrets. *Psychological Bulletin*, 120, 3, 450-465.

Kelly, G. A. (1955). *The Psychology of Personal Constructs*. New York: Norton.

Kendrick, K. M., Da Costa, A. P., Leigh, A. E., Hinton, M. R., & Peirce, J. W. (2001). Sheep don't forget a face. *Nature*, 414, 165-166.

Kitayama, S., & Burnstein, E. (1988). Automaticity in conversations: A reexamination of the mindlessness hypothesis. *Journal of Personality & Social Psychology*, 54, 2, 219-224.

Kitayama, S. & Karasawa, M. (1997). Implicit self-esteem in Japan: Name letters and birthday numbers. *Personality and Social Psychology Bulletin*, 23, 736-742.

Klug, W. & Cummings, M. (2000). *Concepts of Genetics* (6th Edition). Upper Saddle River, NJ: Prentice Hall.

Koole, S. L., Dijksterhuis, A., & van Knippenberg, A. (2001). What's in a name: Implicit self-esteem and the automatic self. *Journal of Personality & Social Psychology*, 80, 4, 669-685.

Kosslyn, S. M. (1994). *Image and Brain: The Resolution of the Imagery Debate*. Cambridge, MA: MIT Press.

Kosslyn, S. M., Cacioppo, J.T., Davidson, R.J., Hugdahl, K., Lovallo, W.R.,

Spiegel, D., & Rose, R. (2002). Bridging psychology and biology: The analysis of individuals in groups. *American Psychologist*, 57,5, 341-351.

Krauss, R. M., Freyberg, R., & Morsella, E. (2002). Inferring speakers' physical attributes from their voices. *Journal of Experimental Social Psychology*, 38, 6, 618-625.

Labouvie-Vief, G., Medler, M. (2002). Affect optimization and affect complexity: Modes and styles of regulation in adulthood. *Psychology & Aging*, 17, 4, 571-587.

Lague, L. (2001). How honest are couples, really? *Reader's Digest*, August, 88-99.

Lakoff, G., & Johnson, M. (1999). *Philosophy in the Flesh : The Embodied Mind and Its Challenge to Western Thought.* New York: Basic Books.

Lakoff, R. (1975). *Language and Women's Place.* New York: Harper Row.

Lang, P. J., Bradley, M., M., & Cuthbert, B., N. (1998). Emotion and attention: Stop, look, and listen. *Cahiers de Psychologie Cognitive/Current Psychology of Cognition*, 17, 4-5, 997-1020.

Langer, E. J. (1997). *The Power of Mindful Learning.* New York: Addison-Wesley.

Langer, E. J., Blank, A., & Chanowitz, B. (1978). The mindlessness of ostensibly thoughtful action: The role of "placebic" information in inter-personal interaction. *Journal of Personality and Social Psychology*, 36, 635-642.

Lapham, L. (2001). Harper Magazine editor and commentator, on C-Span (Media Issues: Close Up Foundation C-Span 3/14/01. John Milewski moderator).

Leaper, C. & Holliday, H. (1995). Gossip in same-gender and cross-gender friends' conversations. *Personal Relationships*, 2, 3, 237-246.

Lefebvre, V. A. (1992). *A Psychological Theory of Bipolarity and Reflexivity.* Lewiston: Edwin Mellen Press.

Legerstee, M, Barna, J., & DiAdamo, C. (2000). Precursors to the development of intention at 6 months: Understanding people and their actions. *Developmental Psychology*, 36, 5, 627-634.

Lepore, S. J., Ragan J.D., & Jones, S. (2000). Talking facilitates cognitive—emotional processes of adaptation to an acute stressor. *Journal of Personality and Social Psychology*, 78, 3, 499-508.

Levy, B. R., Hausdorff, J. M., Hencke, R., & Wei, J. Y. (2000). Reducing cardiovascular stress with positive self-stereotypes of aging. *Journal of Gerontology*, 55B, 205-213.

Levy, M. (2000). *Accidental Genius: Revolutionize Your Thinking Through Private Writing*. San Francisco, CA.: Berrett-Koehler.

Li, S. (2003). Biocultural orchestration of developmental plasticity across levels: The interplay of biology and culture in shaping the mind and behavior across the life span. *Psychological Bulletin*, 129, 2, 171-194.

Locke, J. (2000). Movement patterns in spoken language. *Science*, April.

Lucas, R. E. & Fujita, F. (2000). Factors influencing the relation between extraversion and pleasant affect. *Journal of Personality & Social Psychology*, 79, 6, 1039-1056.

Ludman B.G. (1999). Human seminal plasma protein allergy: A diagnosis rarely considered. *Journal of Obstetric and Gynecologic Neonatal Nursing*, 28, 4, 359-63.

Lyons, A. C., Spicer, J., Tuffin, K., & Chamberlain, K. (2000). Does cardiovascular reactivity during speech reflect self-construction processes? *Psychology & Health*, 14, 6, 1123-1140.

Macrae, C. N., Bodenhausen, G. V., Schloerscheidt, A. M., & Milne, A. B. (1999). Tales of the unexpected: Executive function and person perception. *Journal of Personality & Social Psychology*, 76, 2, 200-213.

Marchand, P. (Life in the Cold, 1996) speaking on National Public Radio (January 3, 2002 at 11:00 A.M. with Marty Moss-Coane)

Massimini, F. & Delle Fave, A. (2000) Individual development in a bio-cultural perspective. *American Psychologist*, 55, 1, 24-33

Mazoyer, B., Mellet, E., Bricogne, S., Etard, O., Crivello, F., Joliot, M., Petit, L., & Tzourio-Mazoyer, N. (2001). Cortical networks for working memory and executive functions sustain the conscious resting state in man. *Brain Research Bulletin*, 54, 93, 287-298.

McAdams, D. P. (2001). The Psychology of Life Stories. *Review of General Psychology*, 5, 2, 100-122.

McAdams, D. P. (1993). *The Stories We Live By: Personal Myths and the Making of the Self.* New York: Morrow.

McCusker, M. (2002) Personal communication.

McKhann G. & Albert M. (2002). *Keep Your Brain Young.* New York: John Wiley & Sons.

McLaughlin, S. (1998). *Introduction to Language Development.* San Diego, CA: Singular.

Miceli, M. & Castelfranchi, C. (2000) Nature and mechanisms of loss of motivation. *Review of General Psychology*, 4, 3, 238-263

Miller, G. F. (2000). *The Mating Mind: How Sexual Choice Shaped the Evolution of Human Nature.* New York: Doubleday.

Montepare, J. M., & Vega, C. (1988). Women's vocal reactions to intimate and casual male friends. *Personality & Social Psychology Bulletin*, 14, 1, 103-113.

Moon, H. & Conlon, D. E. (2002). From acclaim to blame: Evidence of a person sensitivity decision bias. *Journal of Applied Psychology*, 87, 1, 33-42.

Moore, C. C. (2001). *Solitude: A Neglected Path to God.* Cambridge, MA: Cowley.

Muraven, M. & Baumeister, R. F. (2000). Self-regulation and depletion of limited resources: Does self-control resemble a muscle? *Psychological Bulletin*, 126, 2, 247-259

Muraven, M., Tice, D. M., & Baumeister, R. F. (1998). Self-control as a limited resource: Regulatory depletion patterns. *Journal of Personality and Social Psychology*, 74, 774-789.

Natsoulas, T. (1998). On the nature of states of consciousness: James' ubiquitous feeling aspect. *Review of General Psychology*, 2, 2, 123-152.

Neumann, R. & Strack, F. (2000). Mood contagion: The automatic transfer of mood between persons. *Journal of Personality & Social Psychology*, 79, 2, 211-223.

Neumann, R. & Strack, F. (2000). Approach and avoidance: The influence of proprioceptive and exteroceptive cues on encoding of affective information. *Journal of Personality & Social Psychology*, 79, 1, 39-48.

Neuringer, A., Kornell, N., & Olufs, M. (2001). Stability and variability in extinction. *Journal of Experimental Psychology: Animal Behavior Processes*, 27, 1, 79-94.

Nevo, O., Nevo, B., & Derech-Zehavi, A. (1993). The development of the Tendency to Gossip Questionnaire (TGQ): Construct and concurrent validation for a sample of Israeli college students. *Educational and Psychological Measurement*, 53, 4, 973-981.

Newberg, A., d'Aquili, E., & Rause, V. (2001). *Why God Won't Go Away: Brain Science and the Biology of Belief.* New York: Ballantine Books.

Nicholson, N. (2001). The new word on gossip. *Psychology Today*, May/June, 41-45.

Nickerson, R. S. (1999). How we know—and sometimes misjudge—what others know: Imputing one's own knowledge to others. *Psychological Bulletin*, 125, 6, 737-759.

Nickerson, R. S. (1998). Confirmation bias: A ubiquitous phenomenon in many guises. *Review of General Psychology*, 2, 2, 175-220.

Niederhoffer, K. G. & Pennebaker, J. W. (2002). Linguistic style matching in social interaction. *Journal of Language & Social Psychology*, 21, 4, 337-360.

Nikles II, C. D., Brecht, D. L., Klinger, E., & Bursell, A. L. (1998). The effects of current-concern- and nonconcern-related waking suggestions on nocturnal dream content. *Journal of Personality & Social Psychology*, 75, 1, 242-255.

Norman, W. T. (1963). Toward an adequate taxonomy of personality attributes: Replicated factor structure in peer nomination personality ratings. *Journal of Abnormal Psychology*, 66, 574-583

Nowak, A., Vallacher, R. R., Tesser, A., & Borkowski, W. (2000). Society of self. The emergence of collective properties of the self-structure. *Psychological Review*, 107, 1, 39-61.

Oates, K. & Wilson, M. (2002). Nominal kinship cues facilitate altruism. *Proceedings of the Royal Society,* B, DOI: 10.1098.

Orne, M. (1962). On the social psychology of the psychological experiment: With particular reference to demand characteristics and their implications. *American Psychologist*, 17, 11, 776-783.

Osgood, C. E. (1974). Probing subjective culture. Journal of Communication, 24, 1, 21-35 and 82-100. Reprinted in Charles E. Osgood and Oliver C.S. Tzeng. 1990. "Language, Meaning, and Culture." In *The Selected Papers of C.E. Osgood.* Charles E.

Osgood and Oliver C.S. Tzeng (Eds.). New York: Centennial Psychology Series.

Ouellette, J. & Wood, W. (1998). Habit and intention in everyday life: The multiple processes by which past behavior predicts future behavior. *Psychological Bulletin*, 124, 54-74.

Overskeid, G. (2000). Why do we think? Consequences of regarding thinking as behavior. *Journal of Psychology*, 134, 4, 357-374.

Overskeid, G. (2000). The slave of the passions: Experiencing problems and selecting solutions. *Review of General Psychology*, 4, 3, 284-309.

Panskepp, J. (1998). *Affective Neuroscience: The Foundations of Human and Animal Emotions* (Series in Affective Science). New York: Oxford University Press.

Pasupathi, M. (2001). The social construction of the personal past and its implications for adult development. *Psychological Bulletin*, 127, 5, 651-672.

Pavlidis, J., Eberhardt, N. L., & Levine, J. A. (2002). Seeing through the face of deception. *Nature*, 415, 35.

Pearce, J., M, Ward-Robinson, J., Good, M., Fussell, C., & Aydin, A. (2001). Influence of a beacon on spatial learning based on the shape of the test environment. *Journal of Experimental Psychology: Animal Behavior Processes*, 27,4, 329-344.

Pelham, B.W., Mirenberg, M. C., & Jones, J. T. (2002). Why Susie sells seashells by the seashore: Implicit egotism and major life decisions. *Journal of Personality & Social Psychology*, 82, 4, 469-487.

Pennebaker, J. W. & King, L. A. (1999). Linguistic styles: Language use as an individual difference. *Journal of Personality & Social Psychology*, 77, 6, 1296-1312.

Pennebaker, J. W. & Stone, L. D. (2003). Words of wisdom: Language use over the lifespan. *Journal of Personality & Social Psychology*, 85, 2, 291-301.

Peterson, C. (2000). The future of optimism. *American Psychologist*, 55,1 44-55.

Petrie, K. J., Booth, R. J., & Pennebaker, J. W. (1998). The immunological effects of thought suppression. *Journal of Personality & Social Psychology*, 75, 5, 1264-1272.

Piaget, J. (1981). *Intelligence and Affectivity*. New York : Basic Books.

Piattelli-Palmarini, M. (1994). *Inevitable Illusions: How Mistakes of Reason Rule Our Minds*. New York: Wiley.

Pinker, S. (1999). *How the Mind Works*. New York: W. W. Norton.

Plutchik, R. (1997). The circumplex as a general model of the structure of emotions and personality. In R. Plutchik & H. R. Conte (Eds.), *Circumplex Models of Personality and Emotions* (pp. 57-80). Washington, DC: American Psychological Association.

Prose, F. (1999). Why gossip is good for you. *McCall's*, August, 80-81.

Provine, R. R. (2000) *Laughter: A Scientific Investigation*. New York: Viking.

Queenan, E. (2003). *True Believers: The Tragic Inner Life of Sports Fans*. New York: Henry Holt.

Quine, W. V. (1977). *Ontological Relativity*. New York: Columbia University Press.

Rall, J. & Harris, P. L. (2000). Cinderella's slippers? Story comprehension from the protagonist's point of view. *Developmental Psychology*, 36, 2, 202-208.

Raynor, H., A., & Epstein, L. H. (2001). Dietary variety, energy regulation, and obesity. *Psychological Bulletin*, 127, 3, 325-341.

Reber, A. (1996). *Implicit Learning and Tacit Knowledge–An Essay on the Cognitive Unconscious*. New York: Oxford University Press.

Reiss, S. (2000). *Who am I? The 16 Basic Desires that Motivate Our Behavior and Define Our Personality*. New York: Tarcher.

Remland, M. S., Jones, T. S., & Brinkman, H. (1991). Proxemic and haptic behavior in three European countries. *Journal of Nonverbal Behavior*, 15, 4, 215-232.

Rendell, L. & Whitehead, H. (2001). Culture in whales and dolphins. *Behavioral and Brain Sciences*, 24, 2.

Roter, D. L., Hall, J. A., & Aoki, Y. (2002). Physician gender effects in medical communication: A meta-analytic review. *Journal of the American Medical Association*, 288, 6, 756-764.

Rubinstein, J. S., Meyer, D. E., & Evans, J. E. (2001). Executive control of cognitive processes in task switching. *Journal of Experimental Psychology: Human Perception and Performance*, 27, 4, 763-797.

Rusbult, C. E., Van Lange, P. A. M., Wildschut, T, Yovetich, N. A., & Verette, J. (2000). Perceived superiority in close relationships: Why it exists and persists. *Journal of Personality & Social Psychology*, 79, 4, 521-545.

Ruscher, J. B. & Hammer, E. D. (1994). Revising disrupted impressions through conversation. *Journal of Personality & Social Psychology*, 66, 3, 530-541.

Rustad, R. A., Small, J. E., Jobes, D, A., Safer, M. A, & Peterson, R. J. (2003). The impact of rock videos and music with suicidal content on thoughts and attitudes about suicide. *Suicide & Life-Threatening Behavior*, 33, 2, 120-131.

Ruys, J. D. & Schilling, A. J. (2002) Expanding an animal's self-world to include conspecifics. *Journal of Comparative Psychology*, 116, 2, 164-165.

Sankis, L M., Corbitt, E. M., & Widiger, T.A. (1999). Gender bias in the English language? *Journal of Personality & Social Psychology*, 77, 6, 1289-1295.

Saucier, G. & Goldberg, L. R. (1996). The language of personality: Lexical perspectives on the Five-Factor Model. In J. S. Wiggins (Ed.), *The Five-Factor Model of Personality* (pp. 21—50). New York: Guilford.

Saucier, G. & Goldberg, L. R. (1996). Evidence for the Big Five in analyses of familiar English personality adjectives. *European Journal of Personality*, 10, 1, 61-77.

Schacter, D. (2001). *The Seven Sins of Memory: How the Mind Forgets and Remembers*. New York: Houghton Mifflin.

Schank, R. C. (1990). *Tell Me a Story*. Evanston, Illinois: Northwestern University Press.

Scheier, M. F. & Carver, C. S. (1987). Dispositional optimism and physical well-being: The influence of generalized outcome expectancies on health. *Journal of Personality*, 55, 169-210.

Scherer, K. (1984). On the nature and function of emotion: A component process approach. In K. Scherer & P. Ekman (Eds.), *Approaches to Emotion* (pp. 293—318). Hillsdale, NJ: Erlbaum.

Schiffrin, D. (1984). Jewish argument as sociability. *Language in Society*, 13, 3, 311-335.

Schilling, E. A., Baucom, D. H., Burnett, C. K., Allen, E. S., & Ragland, L. (2003). Altering the course of marriage: The effect of PREP communication skills acquisition on couples' risk of becoming martially distressed. *Journal of Family Psychology*, 17, 1, 41-53.

Schneider, B, A., Daneman, M., & Pichora-Fuller, M. K. (2002). Listening in aging adults: From discourse comprehension to psychoacoustics. *Canadian Journal of Experimental Psychology*, 56, 3, 139-152.

Sheet-Johnstone, M. (1999). Emotion and movement. *Journal of Consciousness Studies*, 6, 11-12, 259-277.

Sheldon, K. M., Elliot, A, J., Kim, Y., & Kasser, T. (2001). What is satisfying about satisfying events? Testing 10 candidate psychological needs. *Journal of Personality & Social Psychology*, 80, 2, 325-339.

Shidara, M. & Richmond, B. (2002). Brain signal boosts as monkey nears reward. sciencedaily.com, May, 5, 2002.

Simonet, O., Murphy, M., & Lance, A. (2001). Laughing dog: Vocalizations of domestic dogs during play encounters. Animal Behavior Society conference, July 14-18. Corvallis, Oregon.

Small, M. F. (2001). Sigma chi chimpy. *Scientific American*, July.

Smith, T. W., Gallo, L. C., Goble, L., Ngu, L. Q., & Stark, K. A. (1998). Agency, communion, and cardiovascular reactivity during marital interaction. *Health Psychology*, 17, 537-545.

Solomon, R. L. (1980). The opponent-process theory of acquired motivation· The costs of pleasure and the benefits of pain. *American Psychologist*, 35, 8, 691-712.

Spelke, E. S. (2000). Core knowledge. American Psychologist, 55, 11, 1233-1243.

Spitz, R., & Cobliner, W. G. (1965). *The First Year of Life: A Psychoanalytic Study of Normal and Deviant Object Relations*. New York: International Universities Press.

Stapel, D. A. & Tesser, A. (2001). Self-activation increases social comparison. *Journal of Personality & Social Psychology*, 81, 4, 742-750.

Sternberg, R. J. & Grigorenko, E. L. (2001). Unified psychology. *American Psychologist*, 56, 12, 1069-1079.

Sullivan, H. S. (1953). *The Interpersonal Theory of Psychiatry*. New York: Norton.

Susman, E. (2001). Mind-body interaction and development: Biology, behavior, and context. *European Psychologist*, 6, 3,163-171.

Sutton, J. (1998). *Philosophy and Memory Traces*. Cambridge, England: Cambridge University Press.

Swann, W. B. (1992). Seeking truth, finding despair: Some unhappy consequences of a negative self-concept. *Current Directions in Psychological Science*, 1, 15-18.

Tannen, D. (2001). *I Only Say This Because I Love You: How the Way We Talk Can Make or Break Family Relationships Throughout Our Lives*. New York: Random House.

Tannen, D. (1998). *The Argument Culture*. New York: Random House.

Tannen, D. (1994). *Talking from 9 to 5: Women and Men in the Workplace: Language, Sex, and Power*. New York: Quill.

Tannen, D. (1990). *You Just Don't Understand: Women and Men in Conversation*. New York: Quill.

Tannen, D. (1986). *That's Not What I Meant: How Conversational Style Makes or Breaks Relationships*. New York: Ballantine.

Tannen, D. (1984). *Conversational Style: Analyzing Talk Among Friends*. Norwood, NJ: Ablex.

Tardy, C. H. & Allen, M.T. (1998). Moderators of cardiovascular reactivity to speech: Discourse production and group variation in blood pressure and pulse rate. *International Journal of Psychophysiology*, 29, 3, 247-254.

Taylor, S. E., Kemeny, M. E., Reed, G. M., Bower, J. E., & Gruenewald, T. L. (2000). Psychological resources, positive illusions, and health. *American Psychologist*, 55, 1, 99-109.

Taylor, S. E., Klein, L. C., Lewis, B. P., Gruenewald, T. L, Gurung, R. A. R., &

Updegraff, J. A. (2000). Biobehavioral responses to stress in females: Tend-and-befriend, not fight-or-flight. *Psychological Review*, 107, 3, 411-429.

Technology Review (March, 2001). Wires of Wonder. Interview with Dr. Richard Smalley.

Thelen, E. (1995) Motor development: A new synthesis. *American Psychologist*, 50, 2, 79-95.

Tietze, T. (1949). A study of mothers of schizophrenic patients. *Psychiatry: Journal for the Study of Inter-personal Processes*, 12, 55-65.

Tomasello, M. (2000). *The Cultural Origins of Human Cognition*. Boston: Harvard University Press.

Turhan C., Desmond, J.E., Zhao, Z., & Gabrieli, J.D.E. (2002). Sex differences in the neural basis of emotional memories. *Proceedings of the National Academy of Sciences*, 99, 16, 10789-10794.

Ushakova, T. (2000). Language emergence in infants. *European Psychologist*, 5, 4, 285-292.

van Schaik, C. P., Ancrenaz, M., Borgen, G., Galdikas, B., Knott, C. D., Singleton, I., Suzuki, A., Utami, S. S., & Merrill, M. (2003). Orangutan cultures and the evolution of material culture. *Science*, 299, 102-105.

Watzlawick, P., Beavin J.H., & Jackson D.D. (1967). *Pragmatics of Human Communication*. New York: W.W. Norton.

Weaver, J.B., Watson, K.W., & Barker, L. L. (1996). Individual differences in listening styles: Do you hear what I hear? *Personality & Individual Differences*, 20,3, 381-387.

Wegner, D. M. (1989). *White Bears and Other Unwanted Thoughts*. New York: Guilford.

Wegner, D. M., Erber, R., & Raymond, P. (1991). Transactive memory in close relationships. *Journal of Personality & Social Psychology*, 61, 6, 923-929.

Welkowitz, J., Feldstein, S., Finklestein, M., & Aylesworth, L. (1972). Changes in vocal intensity as a function of interspeaker influence. *Perceptual & Motor Skills*, 35, 3, 715-718.

Wentura, D., Rothermund, K., & Bak, P. (2000). Automatic vigilance: The attention-grabbing power of approach- and avoidance-related social information. *Journal of Personality & Social Psychology*, 78, 6, 1024-1037.

Whiten, A. & Boesch, C. (2001) The culture of chimpanzees. *Scientific American*, January.

Whitlock, K. (1998). The mind's eye. *Perspectives: Research, Scholarship, and Creative Activity at Ohio University*, Spring/Summer.

Wiener, M. & Mehrabian, A. (1968). *Language Within Language: Immediacy, a Channel of Verbal Communication.* New York: Appleton-Century Crofts.

Wiggins, J. S. (1979). A psychological taxonomy of trait-descriptive terms: The interpersonal domain. *Journal of Personality and Social Psychology*, 37, 395-412.

Wiggins, J. S. & Trobst, K. K. (1997). When is a circumplex an "inter-personal circumplex?" The case of supportive actions. In R. Plutchik & H. R. Conte (Eds.), *Circumplex Models of Personality and Emotions* (pp. 57-80). Washington, DC: American Psychological Association.

Willingham, D. B. (1998). A neuropsychological theory of motor skill learning. *Psychological Review*, 105,3, 558-584.

Wilson, A. & Ross, M. (2001) From chump to champ: People's appraisals of their earlier and present selves. *Journal of Personality & Social Psychology*, 80, 4, 572-584.

Winkielman, P., Knaeuper, B., & Schwarz, N. (1998). Looking back at anger: Reference periods change the interpretation of emotion frequency questions. *Journal of Personality & Social Psychology*, 75, 3, 719-728.

Wolfinger, N. & Rabow, J. (1997). The different voices of gender: Social recognition. *Current Research in Social Psychology*, 2, 6.

Zeddies, T. J. (2000). Within, outside, and in between: The relational unconscious. *Psychoanalytic Psychology*, 17, 3, 467-487.

Zeldin, T. (2000). *Conversation: How Talk Can Change Our Lives.* New York: Hiddenspring.

Zorzi, M., Konstantinos, P., & Carlo, U. (2002). Brain damage: Neglect disrupts the mental number line. *Nature*, 417, 138-139.